Two-Brain Business

GROW YOUR GYM

Chris Cooper

copyright 2012 by Catalyst Fitness Inc.

ISBN-13: 9781479277919

ISBN-10: 1479277916

Introduction – the Catalyst Story

LUCK AND KNUCKLES

We come from different areas of the world, you and I, but there's a path we both know.

Most of us started down this path because we were dissatisfied. Working at something we disliked, pouring our sweat into another's business, we thought about striking out on our own. Especially in the fitness industry, where I've spent nearly twenty years, there's a well-worn progression from exerciser to coach to gym owner.

In other industries, that path is straight, and if a bit hilly, at least it's paved. Most business owners, outside the fitness world, have been educated and groomed in the image of the entrepreneur. Not us.

We've been brought up to understand the interaction of muscle and vegetable. We know math – we understand rotational torque, percentages, and incremental increase – but don't use it as a crystal ball. We haven't been told about management theories, or sales, or cash flow.

The seemingly logical progression from coach to business owner is really a big leap over a bottomless gap. Entrepreneurship requires a change in mindset – and education, and effort – that bewilders many Coaches.

"If I build a bigger gym, they'll all come...."
"If I get better at Coaching, I'll be better at business...."
"If I produce a high-level athlete, I'll get more clients..."
"If I get more clients, I'll make a better living..."

None of these are true. At least, not in a cause-and-effect way. While a brighter, bigger gym may service your existing clients better, it won't automatically attract the NEXT client. There's a gap; a missing step.

A Coach who's more proficient at handstand pushups isn't automatically better at making payroll. While skill may thrill your clients, it won't attract the NEXT client. There's a gap here, too.

How do we cross those gaps? That's the question this book will answer, case by case.

WHO THE HECK AM I?

My name is Chris Cooper – Coop, to everyone – and I own a CrossFit gym in Northern Ontario.

Twenty years ago, I was prone to giving up on things. I'd never been seriously challenged - scared - before; my home life, growing up, revolved around school and farm work, but I'd never had real responsibility. Sure, my parents talked a lot about taking responsibility, gave me an allowance, put me on teams - things that are supposed to magically create a sense of steadfastness. They didn't. We had more than enough money. I wasn't good at sports, and didn't care enough to get better. I didn't HAVE to. I drifted through high school and college. Looking back, I may have been able to earn an ADD diagnosis...but I may have just been lazy, too. I could say that I wasn't challenged, but that's just an admission that I didn't push myself to find anything that I liked. I avoided challenge. At the same time, I sought confrontation, imagining myself a zealous rebel who would eventually "take down the man," whoever that was. I wasn't misguided, and I didn't get into trouble; I was *unguided*, and that's my fault. I started down the same trail in college. I skated, showing up when required, and putting in minimal work at the last minute. Teachers didn't care because I didn't care. I started turning out to the weight room, and reading things about training, but couldn't stay awake in Psychology class. When I got home, I'd avoid barnyard work as long as possible. I didn't notice that ONLY after the outside work, I'd feel awake and refreshed; satisfied in something I'd done; hungry and physically tired and of a peaceful mind. I didn't notice that, when placed under extreme pressure - long days, high stress, overwhelming workload - I'd thrive. I just thought that I liked lifting weights.

I moved to Illinois as a sophomore; just packed up my truck and left. I spent a few months there, and again the following year, and then did the same in Wisconsin.

Finishing college, I dropped into a leadership role that was far beyond my experience level. I hadn't earned the job, but was thrown in upside down, and learned while trying not to land on my head. I worked 12-hour days for a ridiculously low wage. I cared about paying my rent, and fretted about the money, but just kept showing up, putting my head down, and ploughing forward. I was challenged every day. I cut department staff from 13 to six, and worked them all to the bone. Eventually, I left for something 'easier.' I didn't realize that what I needed was a break, not a change; I just needed a little rest. Three months into the 'easy' job, I was stir crazy. I analyzed the business down to its grassroots, and when I couldn't sit behind a till any longer, I advised the owner that they were practically bankrupt, tied up my satchel, and left. Greener pastures, full of weeds, called me on.

I took a job selling fitness equipment that, in hindsight, it's likely no one else wanted. I spent years there, building and fixing, learning by doing instead of by example. The owners of the store were four hours away. I learned to use a multimeter over the internet. I put stuff together, and took it apart. I took courses on the sales process. I learned about fitness, and got my first two Personal Training Certifications. But I was still bored. Tired of missing my sales goals every month, I looked to build up my Personal Training repertoire. I had a few clients, but nothing close to enough to make a living.

Still, in 2002, I jumped: I quit my job, and started looking to build a personal training business. I had four clients. Two weeks later, in the middle of the night, the bank padlocked the doors of the gym where I was working. I moved my clients to a 'personal training' facility owned by another trainer.

Over the next two years, the facility tripled in size as my client base exploded. Hemmed in by a tiny room, I'd take my clients into stairwells, halls, parking lots and vacant office space within the building. We got a lot of noise complaints. Some days, I'd train more than ten people. My record was fourteen consecutive training appointments, from 6am until 8pm, without a break. The physical test of endurance – lasting, with a smile, for 12 hours per day – was wearing me down into a joyless robot. Worse, my brain was unchallenged; a large part of our clientele required a caretaker more than a coach. I'd kill an hour at a time, and then get a coffee and do it all over again.

By that time, I was married. We were building a house. I had a new daughter. I was working massive shifts, and making less than twenty thousand per year. My fitness was put on the back burner. I was unmotivated.

One day, a short Frenchman was signed up by his wife. She knew he'd never attend on his own, so she paid for 20 sessions in advance. His frugality finally edged out his pride, and he came in. Within five sessions, he'd made me an offer to partner in a new business. We went out looking for rental space the next day, before I'd even met our third partner. The first space we tried was an office building across the street from my job. The same landlord owned both buildings. By the time I returned to work, my boss already knew what was happening. He was furious, but didn't make me a better offer. He generously allowed me to stick around for two weeks, and instructed me to place a letter around the little facility describing why I'd chosen to leave. It was like letting me print posters for my new business.

We opened in 400 square feet (including a walk-in safe) above a greeting card store. Two weeks later, another trainer from the old 'personal training studio' walked over for lunch. He stayed for six years. We put a Massage Therapist's bed in the walk-in safe, and the three of us jammed the place for twelve months.

What's been the real secret? WORK. Raised a farmer, trained in the humidity of an Illinois cornfield, and honed by responsibility far beyond my pay scale, I've learned to shoulder my fatigue and soldier on. Head down or up, I'm most proud of the way I've drug that mule to water and held its head down until it learned to drink on its own.

Years ago, three years into owning my own company, with cash flow still very variable and everyone's paycheck always at risk, I'd stand in the second-storey window of our gym at 5am and look out. I'd check the competition – another Personal Training Studio – to make sure its lights were still off. Then I'd flick on all of mine, the first on the block, and take a perverse joy from being the sole source of light on the dark street. At 9pm, I'd make the same rounds in reverse, and ride that self-satisfaction home. I missed my wife and kids, to be sure, but I slept with the knowledge that I was doing EVERYTHING I could to provide them with the life they deserved. It's hard to exhaust a mind that's addicted to stimulation, but I did it. I've done it every day for seven years.

Since October 25, 2005, I've been happy; sad; angry; VERY angry; scared, exultant, cocky, depressed...and thankful. But NEVER bored. Every client we've ever had the pleasure of greeting at the door of Catalyst has taught me something – even if it's patience. For a ginger-headed powerlifter with a taste for books, this is the life of a Billionaire.

DONTBUYADS.COM

By 2008, I had made a startling discovery: a great coach didn't make a great business owner. They're not the same. The roles parallel one another, yes. Experience on both sides is invaluable, yes. The skills needed to be successful at either frequently overlap. No argument. That said, a business owner spends his day differently than a coach does.

A good coach centres his waking hours around client development: they read, they think, and they make connections. When they see swimmers on television, they think, "how can I incorporate their postural drills into my gymnast's workouts?" They recommend treatments and programs that will increase client progress as rapidly as possible. They devote time beyond the training session to discussing clients; speaking with clients and other coaches; and thinking about their clients.

The business owner has to spend her brain-time differently. Between clients, she's responsible for checking email and social media. Someone has to balance last week's receipts; someone has to have cheques ready by Friday; someone has to make sure there's enough in the account to make those cheques go through.

If she has an hour between clients, that time is typically spent updating records, changing her website, and returning phone calls. While she does make time for her client's programming – of course – she does so early in the morning, when her mind is fresh. While she's thinking about a staff member's lack of uniform, it's hard to watch the swimmers on television and think about midline stability.

These seem obvious, but they weren't at Catalyst in 2007. Now desperate for success, we trained more people every day. We billed them at the end of the month....meaning there was NO money in our account the day before the rent was due. Ever. We didn't sell packages. Cash flow was very lumpy gravy: a big spike up, surrounded in a weak, watery soup. Not attractive.

In the spring of 2008, we ran into trouble. While we had large accounts receivable (money owed to us, but not yet paid) we had nothing in the bank. Most of the problem came from the way our payroll worked: we paid weekly, and collected monthly, leaving a very thin film of money in the middle. In a weak month, we got very threadbare in the middle. I missed a few of my own paychecks, and started thinking about how to sell the company.....and our debt along with it.

My shareholders encouraged me to stay the course, and we pulled through...but I still realized that I needed to make big changes in the way the company was run. I'd been reading business books, and started purchasing audiobooks so that I could spend my daily hour-long commute more efficiently.

I also knew that I learned best when I rewrote the concepts of others to make connections that were relevant to myself. Einstein's old mantra: "You don't understand physics until you can explain it to a ten-year-old" has always stuck with me. I started to write down the basic concepts of the texts, and apply them to my own business.

An early influence, Seth Godin, changed the way I thought about 'marketing' and 'sales.' I KNEW that advertisements didn't work, through my own diverse and deep experience. I searched for DontBuyAds.com, bought it, and started writing my stuff there. No one read it; I didn't expect anyone to read it.

And then, one day, they did. After writing a post on sharing the best of the community around your business, I contacted five CrossFit writers I admired and asked permission to highlight each for a week. Every single one agreed. One was Lisbeth Darsh, one was Jon Gilson. Both have had profound influence on my approach to business, and I hope that this book continues their tradition of help.

I've had a give-and-take relationship with DontBuyAds.com over the last 4 years (and over 350 posts.) Owning a business blog, and tracking its readership, pushes me to study when I don't feel like studying. With a successful Box, and our bills covered, it would be very easy to settle for complacency as a business owner. In other words, we could 'coast' for a year or two before things became dire; just ride out the wave to the shore, and then turn around and swim back out. Against the current. Again.

DBA has also given me a connection and discussion point with many of the best minds in the industry. I've had long conversations with owners on the other side of the planet over best practices, funny clients, and keeping staff happy. It's been almost exclusively positive; how many relationships in your life share that tradition? Even when a point is argued – far less often than you'd think – it's typically done in a very tasteful, mutually-educating fashion.

At the end of 2011, one particular reader stumbled onto DontBuyAds. Clay Weldon, brother-in-law to Chris Spealler, liked what he saw, and sent me an email. I'm so glad he did. Clay also initiated the idea of providing a one-on-one opportunity for his clients at 321GoProject.com; I was hesitant, but reached deep to find the lessons learned from the all-time greats, Ziglar and Godin, and my new heroes, Darsh and Gilson: you can have anything you want in life, if you help enough other people get what THEY want in life. I agreed to help almost immediately, and now work with a rapidly-growing group of gym owners who want to try things another way.

Many of these folks are about to open new CrossFit gyms; their approaches aren't the same as most existing CrossFit Affiliates. Some, though, have been around for years – including some of the original Affiliates – and have come around to the same realization that I had several years ago. They, like me, finally realized that they don't KNOW what they don't know, and don't know where to start. They'll benefit from my trial and error, the knowledge of the business community, AND new research in the fields of psychology and behaviourism.

Every week, I have conversations with up to twenty Affiliate owners who are struggling. I try my best to help. Sometimes, a quick tip is enough to get them back on track. Usually, they need a step-by-step process, and we provide that service through 321GoProject.com. It's always cheaper than they think, and the payoff is always exponentially higher than the cost of 10 sessions. It's my distinct pleasure to speak with them, and I learn something new every time that I can take back to 321Go clients or write about on DontBuyAds.com. In this way, we're all enriched.

I usually start the conversation with a discussion on their High-Level Goals (we'll get to that,) but within that first hour of discussion, I always like to ask: What's CrossFit? The answer is different every time, and none are ever wrong. For the purposes of this book, though, I hope that we can agree on what it is we're trying to build here.

THE GYM TECHNOLOGY AND THE ART OF COACHING

Once upon a time, there was an innovator.

He built a great company based on his ideas; was fired; and returned to lead the company to glory years later.

He famously claimed that technology was "the intersection of art and science," and repeated that message to anyone who would listen.

He wasn't Steve Jobs.

He WAS Jobs' hero. Edwin Land was the inventor who brought us the Polaroid camera. He snuck into labs at Columbia University late at night to use their equipment, having none of his own. He was so brilliant that he almost flunked out of Harvard: he solved problems so quickly in his head that he was unmotivated to write down his methodology, and so lacked proof to many of his solutions.

Land was a dreamer, and cared little for organization or project management. His wife would have to coax his chemical equations from him so that others could understand, because they existed only in his head. He once wore the same clothes for 18 straight days while working on a project, and his wife would frequently have to bring him food - and force him to eat - while working. Even his short Wikipedia biography is an entertaining read. His success, though, can largely be attributed to his wife, without whom none of Land's work would have been noticed by anyone.

His advice to us is simple: "Managers are around to protect dreamers." In other words, systems have to be built to keep the creative people - your coaches, your programmers, and your members - doing what they do best: creating communities. Planning exciting and progressive workouts. Finding solutions.

People are your Art. Business practices, like billing and tracking, are your science. Your technology is where they meet.

OUR 'OTHER' PROJECT: IGNITE

The word, "enrichment" can mean different things. To me, it's fulfilment. It's the rounding-out of an experience. This can mean financial compensation, yes; it can also mean greater insight, a new connection, or better understanding of a previously-held concept.

We've been studying the effects of motivation on exercise since the beginning. After all, the best fitness program in the world has little effect if the client won't fulfil their duties and do their 'homework'...right? With the notion that all motivation was intrinsic, but that everyone had 'buttons' that could be pushed, we started reading psychology textbooks in 2006. Later, you'll read about our own endeavours to understand the motivation to desire exercise, and how those epiphanies led us to CrossFit.

For now, though, suffice to say that motivation doesn't work the way we first believed. It's both complex and simple, and it's powerful enough to change the physical layout of the brain. You're not predisposed to be more or less motivated. You can change.

In 2010, with our feet on slightly firmer ground, we were plowing ahead with CrossFit and personal training in our new gym: a second facility, built with our new-found knowledge on motivation, Community-building, and commonality. We were exposed to greater risk with a second lease, and my days were longer. Cash flow still hadn't completely caught up to the profit initiative, but I wasn't missing my own paychecks anymore, either.

One of our top Trainers, Tyler Belanger, brought an idea to me out of the blue. "Coop," he said, over the phone, "I can't do this anymore." He was calling from a school office, where he'd been working on a 'long-term' (read: short-term) contract as a phys. ed. Teacher. He'd become interested in the application of our research on exercise and motivation, and spurred by John Ratey's research into exercise and learning. He wanted to leave the bureaucratic teaching system, and develop a method for delivering education through exercise. He wanted to enrich kids. I liked the idea. He quit his job, I committed to paying a second salary at the gym, and we began the Ignite journey.

Our initial efforts to penetrate the school system were largely unnoticed. While we received some token single-day contracts to teach "fitness," we sound realized that we'd need more revenue to support Tyler in the long term. In what seemed like an innocuous conversation at the time, a local Speech Pathologist mentioned that one of her clients might benefit from the Ignite training. The client was attempting to return to college after a severe brain injury, but couldn't recall anything a few seconds after reading it. We agreed to try Ignite.

It worked.

In short order, other clients volunteered other connections: a teacher asked if we'd do research using her class of at-risk high school students. Another teacher offered to write a proposal to run research – paid this time – on her class of 10th-grade math students. We seized every opportunity. We started IgniteGym.com to differentiate the service from our regular broad offerings. We started formalizing our methods, which had been pulled from every direction to build programs on a case-by-case basis. We found the common threads and wrote them down into a coherent procedure (which has evolved to become the Ignite 7 Steps.)

Our renown grew within the insurance company world. We gained a second client, and then a third. In the past, victims of Motor Vehicle Accident (MVA) were often placed into various therapies for years, managed as well as possible. Some successfully returned to work, or a new type of 'normal.' Some settled their claim and tried to minimize the burden on their families.

With Ignite, though, we had something different: clients liked coming to therapy. We could apply physical tasks in a new way that the clients enjoyed. We could make up 'challenges' combining cognitive tasks and physical ones, and show them success in both. Clients who had been virtually given up by others showed remarkable improvement, and insurance companies are eager to try Ignite on an increasing basis.

At around the same time, a parent desperate to help her autistic son contacted us. Using the money left in his grandfather's will, he began a long journey (chronicled in our book, Enrichment Through Exercise) toward the mainstream educational experience. He started with a 'violent' label, and had been out of school for three years when we met him. Last September, he restarted school in tenth grade – the same level as his peers – and was reassessed as 'borderline autistic.' We don't claim to have 'cured' him...but the symptoms that earned him the initial diagnosis of 'autistic' are no longer prevalent enough to warrant the same diagnosis. How many other kids whose diagnoses could fall on either side of the 'autism' label are tripped up for YEARS – or forever – because they aren't given the proper help?

Our scope has expanded to include those with anxiety and depression; those who have been through ChemoTherapy; those who suffer from all different manifestations of learning disabilities, autism, ADHD....and, of course, students. Our school program taken on new life with Melanie Rose. After an appeal for help from another gym owner in 2010, we wrote our first book; its second edition is in print, as well as hundreds of pages of additional knowledge we've been writing as we learn new methods. We have Ignite Academies (our Affiliate program) all over North America, with small islands of growth in both Australia and Africa. In July 2012, we won Innovation Company of the Year for Northern Ontario.

How does this relate to YOUR business? The insight gained into motivation, rationale, and Community doesn't just help our clients. It doesn't just help us expand care through Ignite. It helps us build a better business. In-depth knowledge of the way people think trumps any research on business/marketing theory. It addresses the root of human behaviour. It speaks to the 'why?" of purchasing and sales theory. It HELPS people.

WHY BRAINS? THE CREATIVITY PARADOX OF THE COACH/OWNER

The right hemisphere of your brain is most commonly associated with creative tasks. It also handles most of the stuff we identify as desirable character traits: spirituality, empathy, a sense of shared identity. It's where the intent to speak is formed -where ideas are put together. When your client asks, "How do you dream this stuff up?!? Do you lie awake at night thinking of new ways to torture us?" You can just tap your cranium and say, "Nah, it's just my right hemisphere."

When we're describing ourselves in a personal ad, or online, or in a resume, we boast about skills borne of the right hemisphere. "I'm very creative," you'll say. "I'm spiritual," or, "I work well in a group." It's these tendencies that we prize, and for that reason, we tend to value the right side of our brains as more important.

New gym owners think about the white canvas: what will my gym be? How will we behave? What will it look like? How will I program? They see themselves, the Great Artist, painting a landscape that turns itself, layer by layer, into a masterpiece. It's a beautiful process, and perhaps the triumph of entrepreneurialism: your practice is your art, and your gym is your medium.

But. No one thinks about the easel. No one thinks about where the next brush is coming from, how tightly to stretch the fabric. No one thinks about building the frame. This is the world of the left hemisphere: the organizer, sorter, translator. A beautiful idea, left untold, is just a dream. Your empathy, unshared, is just a prayer.

The left hemisphere organizes thoughts into language, objects into numbers, randomness into programming. Without the left hemisphere to form concrete ideas and actions, the right would be left to its own mute conceptualization.

In a franchise model, you get a shrink-wrapped, "just-add-water" color by numbers kit. Not so with a garage gym, martial arts studio, or CrossFit box. What you get are instructions on plucking the hair of the horse to make the brush, perhaps, or how to fold black into red to make bloodtone. This is the way we want it, right? We want to be right-side Creative; free to experiment and make mistakes; to build our wings on the way down. Or, maybe, just a little help with building a frame....

Both sides of our brain require energy. Just like a muscle, the brain has to be fuelled; it can become stronger through testing its limits. When a muscle becomes more efficient in its movement patterns - what some still call 'muscle memory' - other muscles can work harder, because the surplus energy is available for use. If we can create smooth, nearly-automated process that make our business run more smoothly, we'll have more time for creative tasks. "Fighting fires"- answering the same policy questions again and again, urging people to put their bars away every day, trying to remember who's paid their dues - these are the left-hemisphere tasks that drain our energy. They sap our potential. They occupy time that could be better spent thinking of new, creative workouts; rewarding our clients; teaching our staff.

This is the ultimate irony of business - or is it logic? The more well-honed our left hemisphere, the more practised our business practices, the more free we can be to explore our creative side. Within all of us lies the desire to do the best thing for our clients: to give them fun, exciting workouts. To deliver the BEST programming to get them the BEST results. To learn new techniques; to constantly strive to be the best possible trainers and coaches. We start our businesses with the best possible intentions. Many of us, while working for others, can't see how they can become so wrapped up in "the business side" that they don't spend hours each day on creative tasks. The answer isn't that they LIKE the 'back-end' better. It isn't that they're bored with coaching, as I once believed.

 The reason they have to spend all their time poring over the books, fighting with staff, and calling people for payment is because they haven't become efficient. They haven't trained the left hemisphere of their business to produce on its own. Let's compare a simple movement, like a front squat, to a simple business task like charging memberships. Both are incredibly important to your success - one to an athlete, one to a business owner. If you don't perform front squats, it's tough to get better at them. Your best front squat won't improve much, unless you're a complete beginner, by doing back squats and lunges. Worse, the carryover effects from a weak front squat - a lower clean, a slower thruster - can affect your performance in other peripheral tasks.

CrossFit has a fantastic workout called, "Fran." In Fran. you do 21 reps of Thrusters - a front squat that transitions into a press - and then 21 pullups. You return to the bar and do 15 thrusters, and then 15 pullups; finally, you do 9 thrusters, and 9 pullups. On the clock. This simple-but-deadly couplet is revered the world over as a 'benchmark' - if you're travelling to Germany, and visit a CrossFit box, they'll want to know your Fran time before they ask the name of your gym. It's a universal measurement. If you don't practice front squats, the thruster movement won't become more ingrained. Its efficiency won't increase, and you'll continue to use more energy than necessary as you fight your joints into position on every rep. The weight will feel heavier because your maximum front squat weight hasn't increased. Your shoulders, even, will fatigue if you haven't practised the front squat 'rack' position, which allows them to rest while you're doing the squat portion of the Thruster. You can work on pullups all you like, but if your front squat hasn't improved, your Fran time can only improve so much.

On the business side, you may not charge members on a pre-authorized debit arrangement, preferring to sell them 3-month or 6-month packages. Worse, you may try to collect cheques and payment from them EVERY MONTH individually, placing your cash flow cycle on a vicious, unpredictable roller coaster. Starting a pre-authorized payment system is a bit challenging. It requires some study; some patience; some practice. It requires training, and then it gets easier as you become more adept.

If you DON'T push through that challenge, you'll never become more efficient, and your cash flow won't improve. The time and effort required to collect money from members will never decrease. You'll become tied to the front desk, constantly 'reminding' people - also called 'pleading' - to bring in a cheque on their next visit.

Front squatting, like PAD, seems like the obvious solution. It will take some effort, but you'll improve. This point can be illustrated through endless examples, and many will be discussed case-by-case throughout this book. Staffing procedures alone could fill an entire volume (and may, at a later date.) Each new coach or trainer or desk person you hire brings not only their biases, quirks, preferences and nuances, but carries the weight of their life experiences into every decision they make. We'll discuss the value and methodology of removing those decisions from their hands, leaving them free to do what they love: coach.

WHY THIS BOOK, AND WHY NOW? THE 'Ps'

Back in the 1970s, marketers built something called a "marketing plan" around basic market considerations. They called this stuttering notion "The Five P's," and were excited to announce that THE ANSWER to attracting new sales lay in addressing each of:

- ⋏ Product
- ⋏ Price
- ⋏ Place
- ⋏ Promotion
- ⋏ People.

At first, the last one - the fifth 'P' - was left out, but as one current 'marketing' site proudly proclaims, *"The focus of marketing has shifted from being product-centric to relationship-centric, particularly in the last 15 to 20 years. Businesses and entrepreneurs have realized the power of relationships."* In the world of 'marketing,' trends that have occurred in the 'last 15 to 20 years' are still considered 'new.'

When each of these criteria, phrased in one-word questions, were satisfied, the marketing department closed the books and headed to social hour (three-drink minimum, please.) The system was so easy that an account could be meticulously considered; passionately debated; cautiously plotted; put into colourful graphs; and sold to the client within...about 47 minutes. Drop the new toothpaste brand into the machine, pull this lever...wait...and out pops the answer: buy more television ads! High five. The description of each of the five "Ps" - still being taught in the late 1990s, and likely today - went something like this:

- Product - what are you selling? Consider the differences from other products (the 'features.')

- Price - how can you deliver it for less than the competition?

- Place - where will it receive the most attention, particularly from people who aren't seeking it?

- Promotion - what can we do to get people to take action NOW? How can we make it seem as if something this good can't last forever?

- People - who will use this service/product?

If a marketer (or, more likely, a team of 12-15 in a 'department') could answer those questions with enough time left to chase their secretaries around the desk, it was a productive day. Finally, the art of sales, practised as long as the art of cell division, could be boiled down to a checklist.

Small problem: it doesn't work. At least, it doesn't work anymore. Everyone's aware of the process. We KNOW we're being sold to, and we know what comes next. We're hyper-aware and defensive. The cycle is so predictable, now, that we can recognize it before it starts: when you answer your phone and there's a pause before someone speaks, you immediately hang up, assuming a telemarketer's on the other end of the line. When you're watching television and you think of something that needs doing, you wait until the next commercial, and then go do it. Commercials have gone from interesting and informational to the margins between programming. We blank them out. Our brains don't store their information.

The 5 Ps - we're probably due for a sixth any day now - were convenient for marketers and marketing teachers. Their failure lies in their lack of ability to address the way the brain works. Television commercials can't control desire; they can merely appeal to the side of the brain that controls 'want.' As consumers (shudder,) we've grown calluses over that spot. No one is 'loyal' to a brand anymore, because a brand can't fulfil its end of a social contract; it can't be loyal in return.

If you're sick, and washing bedsheets to kill germs, Tide won't call or send flowers. Ben and Jerry won't notice that you're eating more Double-Chocolate Chip lately and call to ask if things are OK. There's no relationship. Though they can now target their advertising - Target knows when you're pregnant! - they can't make you care.

By studying the way the brain works to form relationships, desires, and empathy, we can structure a business that actually benefits people. We can satisfy basic human needs. We can use science and research to build a sustainable business without creating a 'returns policy.' Best of all, we can do it while keeping our members happy, and helping them lead better lives.

OUR SPECIALTY: RETENTION AND ADHERENCE

In 2005, as I was preparing to launch my own business, I started worrying about retention. I was fortunate enough to have clients who would follow me into the cramped, overheated rental space above a greeting card store...but I wondered how long I could keep them there. With carpeted floors, large windows, and unpredictable climate control, even the best coaching couldn't keep them engaged forever...could it?

I decided to put my theories to the test, and in a flash of insight, started searching for data on what made people stick to their exercise routines. There wasn't much. Despite my best search queries, I couldn't locate any study that shed light on the question, "Why do you show up to train? Why do you do your exercises every day? Why DON'T you?" There was some weak data showing that clients for physiotherapy services stopped doing their routines after about a month..but that was it.

Years later, I'd be privy to the REAL stuff: the data collected by big-chain gyms on dropout rates, adherence, and billing policies designed to encourage long-term retention, but discourage attendance.

We launched our own study. We put out a call for volunteers; 14 people signed up. Meeting on a Saturday afternoon, they had the program outlined by another coach, and were randomly divided into two groups. One group would receive a package listing all of the workouts for the month, with a checklist and a picture tutorial of the exercises. Each time they did one of the workouts, they'd just check it off the list. If they missed a day, they couldn't do it later.

The second group was the interesting one. Instead of getting a list of workouts up front, they had a daily 'challenge' emailed to them each day, with relevant pictures included. The pictures were the same; the workouts were identical. But there was a big difference. Group #1 stuck to the program at a predictable rate: about 47% of the workouts were reported as complete. We didn't ask for scores or weight used, just whether they'd done them or not. Group #2, though, finished over 70% of the workouts.

This was early 2006. CrossFit.com had just been launched, but we had no knowledge of the system. It was February in Northern Ontario, and we couldn't program many workouts outdoors, with the exception of a rare 2k run. Hardly believing the results, we continued the test for three more months. After the first 30 days, though, many members of Group #1 requested that they receive their workouts on a daily basis through email also. We added everyone to the 'daily email' group, started posted on a site called "MorningCatalyst.com," and then tracked their scores.

We didn't prescribe weights, but we did ask for times or rounds or some other measurable criteria. We didn't name workouts, and we never repeated them. Our roster grew; we started sending our Personal Training clients to MorningCatalyst to receive their homework.

Many months later, while volunteering at a local Triathlon, I heard my first mention of "CrossFit" from the member of a team who was waiting his turn on the bike. I didn't even understand what he was saying, at first: he had to draw a cross in the air with his finger. "Cross -Fit." he said. "Check it out. It's crazy." He was a military brat (still is) and described running with a loaded pack, tying ropes to trees, and throwing rocks around. "It sounds like bullshit," I clearly remember saying, but promised to check it out.

I didn't go to the site.

As time went on, we manipulated different variables in our little study. We charged for the service. We moved tougher workouts to earlier in the week. We sent back feedback on how often they completed their workouts. We ranked them ("You got 90% this month! You're the top score! Winner!") After two years, we were narrowing things down to the 'best practices' - a phrase you'll see often in this book. We were sticking with the things that worked best:

- ⅄ Novelty
- ⅄ Surprise
- ⅄ Fear
- ⅄ Simplicity in exercise and description
- ⅄ Feedback.

By 2008, we were doing CrossFit. As soon as we realized what had happened, we faced a crisis point: the realization that something we'd discarded could make a huge difference. With this new knowledge, we couldn't continue on the way we were headed: we had to 'pick a side.' We were with CrossFit, or we were traditionalists.

One member of our Team volunteered to do CrossFit.com workouts verbatim for 30 days. On Day 1, he drew a 10k run - his first ever, and something I've seen repeated on CrossFit.com only two other times in four years. He hated it.

After 30 days, though, he mentioned that he'd like to go for another 30 "to see what else they do." Another Coach jumped in with him. By May, we had invited members of our original test group to take part in "Morning Catalyst Live" - a group that, without knowing, would do CrossFit in our PT facility for 30 days. They loved it.

We revealed that they'd been doing CrossFit; they asked how to sign up. We didn't know the answer.

By July, we were CrossFit Affiliates. We hadn't set out to prove that the system worked - not by any stretch - but were left with the unavoidable conclusion that CrossFit brought all the things we needed to address to the table.

WHY THE Ps ARE NO LONGER THE Qs

You were brought up in the Advertising Age. Like the former rules of life taught to our parents - brush your teeth, don't go out at night, don't take candy from strangers - we've been taught to ignore advertising. In so many words, our parents have taught us that the *New! Improved!* label is just a big empty van with *"free candy!"* painted on the side. Framing your gym's services using the limitations of the 5 Ps will now go unnoticed. Having a 'price special' is so ho-hum that it no longer warrants attention; promotions, we all know, are a recurring flywheel from which retail businesses never escape.

Let's break them down: Promotion - we'll be positioning ourselves as a quality, high-level, high-service product. When your quality is beyond negotiation, so is your price.

Place - I learned this lesson at the hand of a retail pro. As the potential market expands, commodities are purchased from home. However, for speciality services and perishables, people are willing to drive farther than ever. This seems paradoxical, until you factor in the time commitment: time saved by purchasing things (like clothing) online can be 'spent' or 'invested' into things which are out of the way. For example, nonspecialized stores like Sears, the Bay, and K-Mart are suffering, because they're selling commodities. Their everyday goods, like soap and towels, can be purchased cheaper from Wal-Mart, along with everything else you'll need at home. Semi-Special goods can be purchased more cheaply online. When there's a small price difference between online and in-store, and you need to purchase multiple items, it makes sense to go to Target. However, if you're seeking one bottle of perfume, which has a high markup, it's very easy to find a better price online. These high-margin items were the main revenue source of most large 'department stores.' To that end, we're seeing their death. Oppositely, true speciality services are enjoying an upswing in local visits. The differentiator? Knowledge. You can purchase a workout online, for example, but can't form a relationship with the seller. You can't gauge their expertise, or their personality, or their experience, no matter how good their LinkedIn profile. If you can demonstrate speciality knowledge - expertise - you can draw a crowd from across town.

Well over a decade ago, I was spending my days and nights selling fitness equipment for a local retail shop. Frustrated by the lack of walk-in traffic in the first week, I asked the owner why she wouldn't consider opening her shop in a mall. After all, the rent we were paying was almost equivalent, and the walking traffic would be increased exponentially. "Because we don't want everyone," she said. She went on to explain that the short drive - a few minutes for most of the population of our City - was an important filter. Those who were willing to invest the time in the drive were more willing to hear about high-quality treadmills. Those who purchased a treadmill from a store in the mall were looking for a convenient purchase, and were less likely to spend the extra money. Optimal location doesn't mean 'most traffic.' If they seek you out, they've already prequalified themselves as someone who wants to believe in you.

Price - There's a strategy to setting your price that no longer relies on being cheapest. In the late 1980s, Nike dared charge over a hundred dollars for a pair of shoes. Parents thought that was crazy. It was unrealistic, unwarranted, and certainly wouldn't help your kid make the basketball team. It didn't fit within the normal family budget; it didn't even fit the scope of our clothing bills for most of us. We kids desired them even more.

Around that same time, not coincidentally, the psychological study of "Buyer's Remorse" began. When we got the shoes home, put them on and showed our friends, the specialness ended. We weren't faster. We didn't jump higher, we soon realized. As the adoration and envy of our peers wore off, we lost interest. Some looked to the NEXT shoe; some looked to the competition.

When you have the most expensive shoes, though, it's hard to go backward; usually, the investment in being FIRST is a habit that you can't break. As Nike drew in more kids, they knew that we'd never go back to Reebok...despite the Reebok "ERS" offplay, they took a massive beating in the 1980s. Setting your price high sets a high expectation for service. You'll deliver a service to match the price.

Many CrossFit Affiliates and garage gyms try to validate their price to potential clients. They're not confident - they wouldn't pay the same price for the training if the roles were reversed - and so, like a drug dealer, they try to 'educate' people on value. That's fine, if it's done confidently. When someone asks why CrossFit costs five times as much as a normal gym membership, it's fine to say that it's half as much as a personal trainer. Leading the conversation with price, though, shows that you're sensitive and feel you need to defend or validate the cost.

People - this is where the conversation starts to turn. Once upon a time, in a fairytale-like marketplace, marketers imagined that they could identify people who were likely to desire their product. People could be pigeonholed: if they liked swing music, they probably also liked a certain type of dress. Women probably - statistically - worked in the home, and probably relished the controls afforded to them: the family budget; the family clothes; the quality of their dinner. Groups behaved similarly and predictably. This is not the case anymore: exposure to art, culture, work, and a thousand other stimuli has created a renaissance culture, where everyone is interested in everything...but only for a little while. It's a culture of novelty, where things are discarded more frequently but embraced more quickly. Our guards are down, but our garbage chutes are stuck on Open, too. While marketers and businesses struggle to view this new situation through its old lenses, and reconsider motivations for brand loyalty and other levers, we're going in the other direction. Brand loyalty no longer exists - nor should it. Community loyalty is rising from the ashes. Distrust of The Corporation has led not to an aversion to trust in general, but a more careful placing of empathy. We're less likely to trust a chain restaurant, for example, but more likely to believe in a movement. Anyone who witnessed the Kony 2012 wave and undertow in Spring 2012 saw this happen: an overwhelming surge of support for a false charity, followed by regret (by some) and denial by others. Even when faced with evidence that their hero was using child soldiers, and that his clever video on YouTube was drumming up support for his drug trade and military cartel, many stuck to their earlier empathies because they couldn't relegate their emotional beliefs to the hard truth.

The human psyche has never been better understood than it is today. What we believed 30 years ago has either been proven more conclusively true, or undeniably false. New hypotheses, promising for business people, are part of the game. And yet...we're still taught to consider price, promotion, and place. Behaviours change...or do they? Could it possibly be that the consumer is coming of age?

Now more knowledgeable, the buyer DOES beware. Driven by emotion, and rewarded chemically through logical reinforcement, people are now seeking the experience more than the product. In other words, many would rather DO something than HAVE something. This is good news for us. While it's possible for people to wear their fitness brand on their sleeve (or IN their sleeve,) it's now more likely that they'll talk about their fitness experience than simply pose in the mall. Performance, thankfully, will trump mere posture, and only the most narcissistic will still pursue the biceps curl machine with any misplaced notion of glory. There are very few posers in a CrossFit Box or garage gym, because they'll be laughed out. That feeling - of realness, of antiheroes - is part of the chemical and neurological draw that the community-based gym provides.

WHY SHOULD YOU READ THIS BOOK?

"I'm not in this for the money...."

Through travelling, writing, interviews, and my work with the 321GoProject, I'm lucky enough to chat with many different Affiliate owners every week. Some have had their gym for years; some are just starting out. Almost without fail, they repeat something like the above. They're passionate about CrossFit, and it's important to them that I know their motives. Good for them. It's rare to hear a new Box owner say, "I think there's a great chance to capitalize here. What's this CrossFit thing all about?" Money may not be your primary motivation. That doesn't mean it's unimportant, or that you can escape giving it your close attention. "I don't care about money" is the same as saying, "I don't care about barbells."

The supposition, I suppose, is that you care about PEOPLE: delivering the benefits of the joyful, physical life to your clients. You care about CrossFit: the method you've found, finally, and want to share with the world. You care about your Family, and want to bring them up in the best, healthiest environment. You care about The Community, and want to 'give back.' Business, like everything else, is cyclical in nature. You'll have good years; you'll have bad days. Let's imagine what happens to each of those folks above if you're strapped for cash, or worse, you can't afford to Coach any more.

People (your clients, now and future.) You're walking through a crowded mall with your wife. One month ago, you were forced to close your doors because you couldn't pay the rent, and the landlord had reached the limit of his patience. You can't blame him, but now he's suing you for the remainder of your lease. You're still wondering how to get out of that one; still trying to find another job after being "out" of the normal corporate world for two years. You're stressed, to say the least. Your wife's job can't pay the bills for much longer; you'll have to take a job with a lawn care company if you can't find something better FAST. Walking through the crowd, a member of your former gym catches your eye. You consider avoiding her; you don't want to have the "What happened?!?" conversation again. It's too late. She zigzags toward you, and the conversation starts with questions about 'how you're holding up.' Unerringly, she gets to the target: "Why did you close?!? We were all shocked!" Cash, you tell her. You just couldn't afford to do it anymore. "Why didn't you TELL us? We would have all paid another 5 or 10 dollars per month! Oh, if only we'd known! Now we have nowhere to go!" It's not the first time you've heard it since closing...

How about the CrossFit program at large? It's changed your life, and you want to tell the world...right? Cynics are already predicting that "weaker" Affiliates will fold; that we're riding some sort of bubble; that the "hockey stick growth chart" can't continue forever. It's OUR responsibility as Affiliates to make sure that doesn't happen. You want CrossFit to be successful long-term? Keep your Affiliate healthy and your car waxed. Your family deserves to eat. You're going to be away from them, at work. Your busiest times at the Box will be when they're eating breakfast, and when they're going to bed. That's going to get tough. If you're also asking them to sacrifice small niceties AND their time with you...that's not fair. If they're short on groceries because you're "not in it for the money," that's irresponsible. It's your DUTY to know this stuff. How you acquire that knowledge is up to you.

Finally, you care about The Community. You like going to other cities and visiting CrossFit gyms. You like talking to local Affiliates and competing at events. You like knowing that there's an army behind you when you're talking about this stuff in public. You even like it when someone calls us a "cult." The best way to contribute to the health of that Community is to keep yourself well-fed. A martyr makes everyone look bad.

If you were catching a flight and saw the pilot looking tired, unshaven, and stained...how would you feel about the airline? Your intentions are noble. Your sacrifice is impressive. Don't use either as an excuse to abdicate your REAL responsibility as a business owner.

Just 'breaking even' doesn't help anyone involved here. Would you be content to keep your 300lbs deadlift forever?

THE BUSINESS TALENT MYTH

In 2011, while editing a piece on *The Talent Myth* for the Ignite Certification textbook, I was the benefactor of a true moment of serendipity.

I sent an email to a few trusted advisors in the public and private sectors. Faced with a multitude of options, I had recognized my old foe - paralysis by analysis - descending on my brain, and requested a 'meeting of the minds' for advice. This was the email I received :

"However, Chris – I do believe that you just need someone to bounce the ideas off of - & look at it from all sides (risk/reward). Your instincts are truly excellent."

My opinion: I don't have 'instincts.' I have experience. Though the email was meant to be complimentary (and received as such,) the sum of my experiences are what lead me toward better decisions. Those experiences, good AND bad, are also of value to others.

The Talent Myth is the idea that people are born with 'good instincts,' or 'talent.' Malcolm Gladwell's Outliers was the the most popular counter-thesis in the last few years. Gladwell argues that opportunity to practice, make mistakes, receive feedback, and practice again was the critical factor behind the success of any 'genius' or 'prodigy' that one may name.

The Beatles played 10 hours per day for over five years in a tiny bar outside of Great Britain before ever getting a gig in England.

The Rolling Stones lived and slept together for a decade, stealing food and forgoing heat in the winter, before they could actually pay themselves.

Einstein worked at the Patent Registration office for years, reviewing the ideas of the best minds in the country. Beethoven's father wrote symphonies. Mozart had 10,000 hours of quality practice - his father taught music - before the age of 13. Tiger Woods....well, we know that one. Bill Gates attended one of only three schools in the country to have a mainframe computer as a child, and then somehow lucked into unlimited programming practice time at a University when he was in high school.

Practice is specific; must provide feedback; and goes on forever. Tiger Woods is arguably the best golfer in history...but he's not great at social relationships. Bill Gates is a brilliant programmer....but maybe not the best runner in the world. Both still practice their strengths, and largely avoid their weaknesses.

Personally, I've only been a business owner for six years. However, I've been lucky enough to live in a place that requires 30 minutes' driving time to and from work. That means one hour per day, six days a week, of learning about business, coaching, motivation, or all these other topics on which I ramble. I usually work from 6am until 8 or 9 at night, which means I have the opportunity to make all the mistakes I can possibly dream up.

Feedback has, in the past, been swift and critical. These days, people are much more forgiving (they know that I mean well, even if my point seems a bit sharp.) But everything I - and you, and we as a CrossFit community - do is still practice. How do we cope with 70,000 people entering the Games in 2012? We build a huge filter that no one's ever done before. It won't be perfect, but it'll be good, and we'll learn from it. How do we roll out a new program at our Box? We try it. Then we tweak it, and it's better.

I sincerely hope that you get to make a lot of mistakes early; that they're not too expensive; and that you don't make the same mistakes twice (though there's a lesson to be learned, even then.)

THE BRAIN – BUSINESS ANALOGY

Over the past few months, through my work with the 321GoProject, I've been fortunate enough to share many conversations with CrossFit Affiliate owners who are struggling. We try to help them turn things around, and most of the time we can help.

Many of these Affiliates have common complaints: they're working long hours, they're very passionate about CrossFit, they love coaching people...but they're not making ends meet. They're taking secondary jobs to buy their groceries. Staff and members "don't get it" and wander in and out of the program frequently.

While attempting to discover the real mechanisms behind attention, focus, and adherence, we've found that many current business and marketing practices simply don't parallel the ways in which our brain actually stores, recalls, and prioritizes information. We can also draw parallels between the way our brain functions best, and the ways in which our business can run most efficiently.

First, a model of the brain's two hemispheres, the left side and the right:

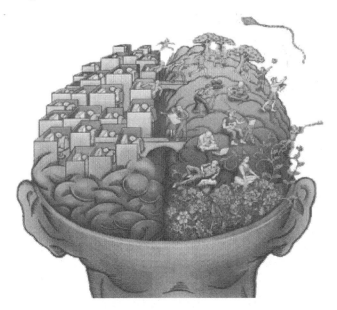

Left Side	**Right Side**
Organizing	Creative
Structured	Flowing
Critical	Empathetic
Translator	Dreamer
Individualizer	Group-builder
Coordinator	Conceptualizer
Worker	Player
Dispassionate	Emotional
Loves predictability	Loves novelty

This is an oversimplification, of course, but you may also

visualize the left hemisphere as a giant spreadsheet, and the right side as an artist's canvas. They can (and must) work well together all the time, but one side can easily begin to dominate the other. For example, many innovators and scientists are right-hemisphere dominant, while technicians and managers are best served through the left hemisphere.

Many CrossFit Affiliate owners are right-hemispheric. They start their own Box out of passion and empathy: they LOVE the community, and want to share it with others. They have great programming ideas, and are open to new ones. They love being part of a movement; they love the sense of 'flow' granted by the tough workouts.

They are NOT structured.

While they may collaborate to plan their Box's programming months in advance, they love the apparent randomness of it all, and don't share that big-picture plan with their members.

When a member quits, the Coach is shocked. They're not sure why the member is leaving; they liken it to a 'breakup'; and they appeal to the member either on an emotional basis (they take it personally) or not at all, because they're scared to have their feelings hurt.

When members chat while she is describing the split jerk, the Coach become upset; why aren't they paying attention? She may not have a system for processing interruptions in her brain, and so the resulting cognitive dissonance causes her to overreact, singling out the member in front of the group and embarrassing them:

> *"When Bill's done talking, we'll continue."*

When Bob doesn't put his bar away, the Coach "loses it!" They comment on facebook, or harbour a grudge until the next time Bob comes in, and then hand them a ridiculous burpee penalty in front of others. When Jane pays her monthly membership at a different time each month, she creates a cash flow problem...but the owner doesn't know how to address the issue; hates asking for money; and starts to act differently toward Jane than the other clients.

Sal is always a bit scared that his Coaches won't show up on time, and finds himself hovering around his Box at all hours, just to "make sure." When a Coach rolls in with his hair matted and teeth unbrushed, Sal "rips into him," because he "should know better." He doesn't....because Sal hasn't told him.

What do these reactions have in common? They're emotional, and they exist ONLY because expectations and systems have not been implemented to take care of the "left-hemisphere" tasks. When clear standards have been set for members and staff, the "left" side of the business runs efficiently and automatically.

The left side of your brain LOVES efficiency and THRIVES on automation. By creating business systems, teaching your staff and clients what the standard for behaviour is at your Box, and removing those emotional triggers, the right hemisphere is free to act. The business can remove the chain of stress that's limiting its power to be creative, and finally do its job: making you feel joy.

Over the past several months, dozens of CrossFit Affiliates have shown me the space behind their curtains. After we've connected through the 321GoProject, they've answered every question I've posed, no matter how blunt; they've withheld nothing. Revenues? No problem. Staff policies? Here they are. Membership? Here you go....

What many of these Affiliates were most missing was the infrastructure that supports the business: the bricks-and-mortar policies and procedures that guide the staff so the owner can worry about the most important stuff. After a few weeks, they're scripting their progress in advance; they're installing fire hydrants; they're acting, instead of REacting. To paraphrase Michael Gerber, author of the E-Myth series, they're now working ON their businesses instead of IN their businesses.

Many of us started along this track without a business background. Driven by fear and hunger, some have studied business as hard as they've pursued their CrossFit Total. Some have worked hard to perfect their coaching skills instead. Both are equally valid: given the same number of hours per day, there's a good chance the second coach can teach me a thing or two about my clean pull.

Most, understandably, want to know how to get people in the door RIGHT. NOW! Some are worried; some are tired; all just want the same things as everyone else: security and time. We're working on it – and also working to ensure that THESE clients stick around.

This organizing behaviour - putting systems and procedures in place to automate the business and free the entrepreneur - takes a lot of spreadsheets. It sometimes means writing 'boring' things like job descriptions and checklists instead of motivational posts about pullups. While getting ready for the next Generation of new clients, they're writing plans instead of painting their walls. In short: a bunch of left-brain activity.

The left hemisphere of the brain is responsible for the organization of language; for math, and columns and rows. It's the automaton. It's the rulemaker, and the enforcer of Chalk Bowl Tidiness. While the right hemisphere is sleeping, the left is plotting; envisioning the worst-case scenario; working on Plan B; judging people's weaknesses.

When you have rules and policies written down, though, and enforced evenly from the start...the left hemisphere of the Entrepreneurial Brain can relax. The crux, perhaps ironically, is that the left hemisphere can organize itself out of a job.

And that, my friend, is when you'll start to love people.

What are the tasks of the right hemisphere? Empathy. Finding similarities. Building partnerships...and then, communities. Nations will follow when the right hemisphere is in charge.

When you're anxious because class hasn't started at 7:06; when you're stressed because you're not sure who will pay on time; when you're distracted by a thousand little irritants, the left hemisphere is in control. Ease your left mind. Satisfy its thirst for rigor. Free the right hemisphere, held hostage by need. Love people. Welcome them. Smile because you're happy to see them. Fist-bump, high-five, mingle. Do the things that come naturally to the right hemisphere of the brain, and community will naturally follow.

Can't get happy about your job? Can't welcome people with genuine enthusiasm? Satisfy the left first. THEN lead with the right.

The Left Brain: Running Your Gym

OWNING A BUSINESS, OR BUYING A JOB?

Every day, I'm lucky enough to get 2 or 3 emails just like this one:

> *"Hi. I fell in love with CrossFit in 2010, after my friend dragged me to a class. It was tough, but I stayed with it, and I've lost 60 pounds! In December, I finally took my Level 1 course. I want to help people be as happy as I've become, and show them anything is possible. If I can do it, anyone can! How many rowers should I buy?"*

My first thought is always, "Congratulations!" because I KNOW exactly how they feel. I remember all of it: the feelings of jumping off a cliff, the confidence and doubt, the fear...and the elation of cutting all ties, running away, joining the Circus. Every week, I live this vicariously through half a dozen new Affiliates. I'm a lucky guy.

My duty is to make sure the parachute opens; to make sure they land on their feet, chests still pumped out, marching forward.

There's s difference between owning a business and buying yourself a job. I didn't know the difference at first, because when you start setting up your business, your first goal is to eat. Not to pay the rent; not to deliver CrossFit to people; to buy groceries. Not to change lives, but to maintain your own lifestyle - or, at least, the minimum. For now. If the rain is off your head, you're happy.

One year later, you're working more...but still taking home the same pay. You're doing the right things for your clients; you're taking more Certification classes; you're bringing in guest speakers and delivering knowledge that is broad and inclusive. You're reading and watching and programming hard. You're reinvesting every dollar you take in. You're working for yourself...and it's not too bad.

After another two years, though, things start to sink in: there's no one to ask for a raise. Your hard work merits more money...but there isn't any. Clients are joining at about the same rate they're leaving; you're paying your bills, but there's nothing in reserve, and worse - there are rumours that one of your clients is leaving to start his own Box. Congratulations: you've bought yourself a job. You haven't created a business. Not yet.

A business is a series of systems that support what YOU want in life. If what you want is to be hands-off, and have more free time; to set your own schedule and spend money the way you want, then that's how we'll set up your business. If you want to coach people and change lives and work every day, then that's how we'll set up your business. Failing to consider these goals and work backward, though, is doing yourself a disservice and potentially harming your clients.

Consider this scenario: you've built a solid base of 100 people. Their lives are forever changed. They can't go back to McGym...no way. Unfortunately, you're not paying the rent - or yourself - and you're starting to resent the 6am to 9pm workday. You have debt, and kids. You are not providing for them in the way you'd like, and so, when a job appears at another company, you're tempted to take it. What happens to your clients if your Box closes?

It is your duty to be profitable. It's your duty to be open and STAY open. Others have taken this risk - social, financial, and time - and they deserve to capitalize on it. YOU deserve to get what you want in life, because the real risk is time spent...not cash invested. Time can be well-invested, or it can be wasted, just like dollars and cents.

Have you ever bought a piece of equipment you don't use? We have. Have you ever poured a lot of energy into a program that no one attends? Us, too. And it's not a sin, if you don't repeat it. Business planning isn't like a crystal ball; it won't tell you when the storms will appear. It IS like a boat. When growth comes, you'll be ready. When the baby comes, you'll be ready. When a client asks for a refund, sends in a referral, wants to sign up, you'll be ready.

During one of my very first visits with my own mentor, we were discussing goals. I said that for me to achieve self-actualization, I'd need prolonged periods of time to myself. *"I need the business to run itself,"* I said.
"No business runs itself." was his answer. I felt a hole open in the floor beneath me, and immediately began to worry anew that I'd never be free of my responsibilities.

"But..." he began, and my heart leaped. The next part of this book is devoted to the *'but....'*

My role with 321GoProject is Business Mentor. While we don't believe in the franchise system for garage gyms or CrossFit Affiliates, we DO know firsthand the value of structure in a business. Without structure – methods, plans, forecasts and instructions – there IS no business beyond the name. Ask for a valuation of your company, and you'll hear, *"Where are your processes?"* What, in short, IS your company?

My job is to build you a business: to make systems that are repeatable and replicable. In a nutshell, if you were hit by a car tonight, could someone else walk in tomorrow and pick up where you left off? Could you sell your business, or is it too reliant on your own personality? If the latter, then it's going to be VERY hard to extricate yourself, even in small doses (like a weekend off, for instance.)

For less than the price of a rowing erg, we spend hours with Affiliates. We give them homework. In this way, they're building solid systems that are unique to their business. Their business model reflects their personality, goals, and dreams...but doesn't create drudgery, either.

Every Affiliate is different. This is as it should be: we're CrossFit licensees, or unique garage gyms. We don't WANT to be franchisees. However, there's a logical process to creating your business, and that's reflected in the template below (which changes slightly every few months.) For instance, until your retention rate is solid, and your intake procedures set people up for long-term success, it doesn't make sense to start blitzing for new clients. Who wants to run a flow-through business? For that reason, we first create systems that keep members around for the long term; THEN we start working to attract new members.

When I start with any new consulting client, I like to approach the long road ahead this way:

Business Coaching 10-Week Template

Week One – Mission – who do you want to be in life?
Vision – how will it look when you're there?
High Level Goals – What do you want for yourself? What must happen in order to accomplish your Mission (ie revenues, family, time...)
Bright Spots – What are you already doing toward that end?

Week Two – Market/Product Chart
Exercise: identifying potential services of great benefit to your members.
Identify every potential market you can. Then identify every product you currently offer. Look for intersections.
At each intersection, identify possible sources of revenue

and prioritize based on total revenue.

Week Three – Strategy.
Exercise: Forecasting based on revenue potentials from
Week Two.
Identify One-, Two-, and Three-year target revenues for
those intersections that bring you closest to your HLGs.
Identify ways to achieve those targets (specific examples.)
Then assign responsibility, using job titles – not names.

Week Four – Staffing
Exercise: what will it take to get us there? Who will do the
work?
Business Operations Chart, Staff Handbook
Paying Staff – Contractors, sales bonuses, motivation and
goal-setting
The Owner's Intent

Week Five – Keeping People
Exercise: Building a foundation of client referral systems
Intake procedures
Telling Stories
Giving them Mangoes
Setting up the 'yearbook committee' and the Mavens
Delivery
Client's "Bill of Rights"

Week Six – Getting People In The Door
Exercise: Recruitment of new members
Sales Boxes
Propagation
Events, fundraisers
Overlapping 'bubbles'
Newsletter

Week Seven – Building Esteem
Exercise: finding your niche

Being "The Expert" in your locale
Publication
social Marketing
Intake and OnRamp

Week Eight – Expansion
Exercise: Average Revenue Per Client
Timelining – how do you replace yourself?
Interning – build a program
Brand consistency
Owning your Time

Week Nine – Money
Exercise: Variable Expenses and Contracts
Keeping more of it – contractors vs employees
Taxation filters
Research and Development
Internships

Week Ten – Perpetuity
Systemization
Duplication
Fulfillment
Summary and final Timelining

Again, this is a generalization, and every case is different. Working 1-on-1 with a business coach allows for personalization and specialization. We'll explore these concepts in detail in the next sections.

THE CONSULTANT STORY
By 2009, our little company had reached an "Inflection Point." That is, five years in, we were faced with a unique choice: get much bigger, or get much more exclusive. In other words, to be sustainable for the next five years, our 'out' has to generate much more 'in.' Decrease the 'out,' or increase the 'in,' or fade away like the rest.

A few months before we started with our first mentor, a local "Personal Trainer" deleted his facebook profile, locked his doors in the dark, and left town. He'd been in business for a year; had sold some very cheap long-term packages; had a hundred 'friends' on facebook. He left with a lot of unfulfilled packages, and a LOT of angry customers. That's dirty, no doubt, but I don't believe that he started out with the intention to deceive anyone. Rather, he simply couldn't survive without new cash flow, and he couldn't attract enough new clientele to keep the lights on while he fulfilled his promise to his startup clients.

At the other end of the spectrum, a local 'gym' (bankrupt three years now,) started with a massive influx of cash - nearly $300,000, by their own reporting. They lasted eleven months; investors simply couldn't realize a return quickly enough, and they fled. They left a note to their members with a dead-end email address.....

"What's your best lift?" said The Consultant, who maybe hadn't seen a deadlift bar in awhile. *"Well, I had a 520 in a Prison PL meet a few years ago...."* I said, anticipating the usual reaction that a 500+ lift gets from "the Public."

I was learning that The Consultant was not the usual:

"Well, get ready for the hard stuff."

He's right. Change is hard. Risk is hard. Math and organization and being a boss is hard. It's much, much easier to show up at 5am, for twenty years, to mop the floor and stress about your checking account.

THE REAL COST OF DOING EVERYTHING

Seven years ago, I was sitting in the heavily-curtained living room of my wife's parents. I'd just told them that I was going to take the summer off from my job - Personal Training at a One-On-One 'Studio'. I loved my job, and my client list was heavy...but I wasn't making as much money as my wife. And we had no house, though we owned the property. We also had a baby.

If I'm confident in anything about myself, it's my capacity to learn ANYTHING, given time and frequent error. The practice mentality was burgeoning then, and I was confident enough to buy a 'How-To-Build-A-House' book somewhere.

My father-in-law was skeptical; he'd seen my carpentry (questionable at best, dangerous at worst) but in one of his greatest moments of diplomacy, suggested that I'd better refigure the actual cost of building a house myself.He asked me this:

"How much do you make an hour?" It wasn't much. But it was more than a general carpenter's labourer, at the time.

If you're doing your bookkeeping; your cleaning; your scheduling; your staffing; your shopping...chances are, there's someone better at it. You're a METCON king...but you're not very efficient at doing month-end, are you?

Your value to your company is, in this order:

1. CEO

2. Spokesperson

3. Trainer.

4. Bookkeeper.

5. Janitor.

Maybe you're going to the Games, but that's not WHY your business is succeeding. It's growing because you're managing it...not because you're winning the WODs. Personally, I was lucky enough to finish a respectable 4th among men on our team for the 2012 Open...and that's good enough, because my true value during the WOD is not 'rabbit.' It's Cheerleader.

My bookkeeper costs about $125 per month. That's less than two hours' personal training time. If I did the books myself, it would take me twice as long. That's a $250 value. Are you telling me that you can't sell TWO more training spots per month?

Trainers, even, are easier to come by than business leaders, who see the whole big picture, goals and warts and all. Trainers don't have to plan; they have to smile. Teaching the snatch pull is easier, sometimes, than balancing your payroll taxes.

When confronted with a time decision, do you cancel a client to finish your mopping? I'd like to put forward the idea that you try prioritizing tasks by the hierarchy above. Each trumps all below itself.

exception: if you're JUST starting, your time ain't worth much, muchacho. But it's the only asset you have, so squeeze it dry.

AUTOMATION

Your members aren't robots. Neither are your staff, and neither are you. Of course not.

You're human, and a large part of the human cognizance is multifocus: the ability to think about several things at once. In other words, distraction.

I advocate for the automation of processes - hiring, staff training, checklists, contracts, leases, agreements, check-ins, email notifications, bookings, reminders, billing - because I know CrossFit coaches. Heck, I am one: I love to coach. It's my joy, my pride, and my passion. But when I'm worried about which group participant owes us money, or which is over her monthly visits limit...I'm less effective as a coach. It's hard to concentrate on Jamina's hip extension when you're dying to tell her that her cheque bounced yesterday.

Our members have been trained, over time, to swipe their cards when they enter; to prepurchase personal training sessions and CrossFit passes and gym memberships. They all bring VOID cheques because...it's what everyone does. It's automatic.

It's also fair: the price is the price, and my members don't have to worry that Sally on the next platform is getting a better rate than they are. They don't have to think about which members of the group are up-to-date on their membership, because it's addressed automatically, fairly, and predictably.

The next time you're considering letting Jill come for free, or for half price, or when her membership is overdue, or during group times to do her own workout, consider this: the ethics in this equation are not between you and Jill, but between you and everyone else who comes to your Box. Your duty is to be equitable: to provide reliable sameness when it comes to rules and policies.

Diversity is great, when you're talking about coaching: a different perspective can make a huge difference. As Gilson once shared with me at a Level 1 Cert, "You can be a muscle-up expert. You can work with a client for months to get a muscle-up. You can get them doing 30 ring dips and 30 chest-to-bar pullups in the rings, but you can't get them a muscle-up. Then, one day, another coach walks through the door and says, 'poke your chin down.' Boom, muscle-up! It's not a better cue, just a different one, that matters.'"

Treating clients in an unpredictable way when it comes to money, though, is like bringing home a new boyfriend every weekend, and introducing them to your kids: you're going to have disfunction. There are going to be fights. And someone's going to end up on The Couch instead of in your nice, warm family.

Don't like it? Use MindBodyOnline, or another service to

make things easier. If you can't be predictable, though, you don't have a business: you have a hobby that others support.

HIGH-LEVEL GOALS

You think the fitness industry is spilling over with buzzwords? Try the business sector.

Drawing a flowchart on the whiteboard, my consultant warned me in advance: *"Chris, this is all going to look like catchphrase. To most people, it IS, because they don't drill down into what the words MEAN."*

He wrote:

MISSION

VISION

HLG

STRATEGY

MARKET - PRODUCT

He was right: it sure DID look like buzzword and hype to me. Turned off to the idea of "mission statements" and "vision mantras" by Tony Robbins years ago, I would normally be quick to dismiss the ideas. On that day, though, I'd resolved to maintain 'beginner's mind' for three solid hours. Just before leaving for the meeting, I'd done five minutes of skipping, and five minutes of Ignite-style focusing exercises. I wanted to give the investment - my time, plus over $5000 in public funds - every opportunity to pan out.

"Most of this stuff just looks like empty rhetoric," he said. *"And to most business people, it is. Ask them to define one term, and they'll use the other terms in the definition. But we're going to use this stuff to get a clear vision of what*

you're about here."

Why are we doing it? Let's try an example: who are your staff, and what are their jobs? Unless you have a clear picture of your business and your services, you can't possibly know your staffing needs. If, like me, you hired great trainers and built programs around their likes...well, that's pretty fun. But not very efficient. It leads to an irregular service offering with huge gaps in business progress.

This is an instance where having a clear line of sight really helps. The first step is to get things down on paper so that you can refer to the highest level when you're having trouble at the lowest. How does this staff person / program contribute to our overall mission? Are we just adding this group because it "sounds good," or does it actually move us closer to our vision? Until that's written down, it's just smoke.

Quick: define "goals." Did you use the word, "objective?" I sure did, the first time. But they're different.

Part of the process for improving your business - after defining your Mission and Vision - is to set High-Level Goals. For instance, if your Mission is to create a certain standard of life for you and your family, and your Vision is a CrossFit box that generates $100,000 per year in net income to you, the next step is to create High-Level Goals to get you there.

Objectives are broad (*"We want to use a CrossFit gym to achieve our dreams!"*) Goals are specific (*"We want to generate $100,000 per year in net income using this CrossFit gym."*)

We're going to choose three High-Level Goals, and use a five-year timeframe for each. We'll work backward from these goals later. But for now, the three High-Level Goals must each be:

1.Objective and measurable

2.Divisible (they can be broken down into a step-by-step process, unlike winning the lottery)

3.They have to move you closer to realizing the Mission.

Look familiar? They should to a CrossFitter.

Most businesses will choose High-Level Goals that are number-centric. The Consultant was surprised when I chose "Keep The Family Culture" as one of my three. *"That's part of your strategy,"* he argued, *"not an end unto itself."*

"It's my goal." I said. *"If my gym can't meet revenue targets without sacrificing the "Catalyst Family" environment, I simply don't want to do it anymore."* He relented.

If it had been necessary to run a gym WITHOUT the 'family culture' of Catalyst, then I simply would have found another way to achieve my Vision.

My other two HLGs were more related to my personal income and Catalyst's gross revenues. I chose very specific numbers; I also realized, during the process to choose those numbers, that I'd have to look into the future and ask, *"Where do I want to be - and where does my family want to be - in five years?"*

I realized I'd have to go through this process personally, as well as for the business, and in that order. I said as much. *"You're right,"* said The Consultant, *"it's impossible to complete this process without involving your wife. You have to make sure you're both moving toward the same end point. If not, you're violating your psychological contract with her."*

In the background, I could hear the creaking sound of a can opener. A whole new can of worms was being opened......

If you're like me, a prioritization exercise may help streamline how you use your time, space, resources and coaches better. You can't PURSUE every possible opportunity in hopes of identifying the best. We'll need to set priorities. To choose our best avenues for the next few months, let's colour some boxes.

EXERCISE: OPPORTUNITIES CHART

Step #1: Write down every potential market segment you can dream up on the 'X' axis.

Step #2: Write down the individual services you currently offer on the 'Y' axis.

Step #3: Locate every intersection possible, where a service you offer meets the demands of a market.

Step #4: Color-code your priorities, based on revenue. For instance, services generating more than $20,000 in revenue annually are coloured green; services generating $10-20,000 annually are coloured yellow, etc.

Step #5: Your 'green' blocks are your 'A' priorities - for staffing, planning in advance, marketing, etc.

Now that you have the chart, you can apply your cash flow forecasts to coordinate staff and promotion in advance. Just do the same chart with colors reflecting what you EXPECT to happen, instead of what's currently happening. We use the 'current' numbers first, because they may surprise you....

MARKET

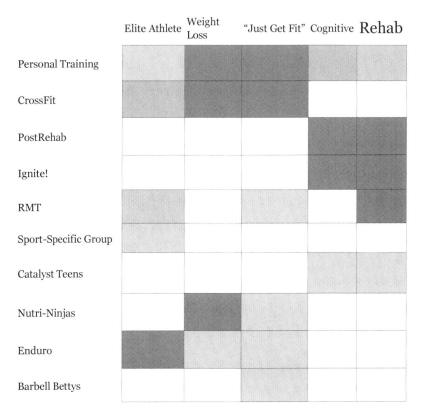

This isn't a hard exercise, but we'll get more technical as we move along. As our mentor told me, *"Your business is five years old. You have six staff, a few hundred members, and two facilities. NOW comes the hard part."* He was right.

Writing down a MISSION and VISION isn't too hard; it just requires some reflection. High-Level Goals are a bit tougher, but it helps to have a clear picture of our Markets and Products, which we outlined in the chart above. From there, prioritizing which services are most important is a snap: those intersections between markets and products which generated the most revenue should stand out clearly. Even if your Box is exclusively CrossFit group classes, this is a worthwhile exercise, since your service can be subdivided into smaller offerings (personal training, small-group coaching, big-group coaching, CFK, etc.) We'll talk more about the stratified model, and earning more PER client, later in this book.

It would appear that the beast is, for the most part, slain. But now comes the dissection.

Strategy is the way you're going to use your best intersections to achieve your High-End Goals. As an example, let's imagine that your High-End Goal #1 is $1,000,000 in gross revenues.

Since we've used GROSS revenues for this example, we'll choose the most expensive services that meet the largest market to create the largest GROSS income (note: this may not be the same 'intersection' if your High-Level Goal is a NET-revenue number, since incremental cost may be higher for these services, like Personal Training.)

Step #1: Choose services which will generate the highest GROSS revenue.

Step #2: Working backward from your High-Level Goal ($1,000,000) identify one-year, two-year, and three-year objective targets. For instance, $250,000 GROSS in Year #1; $500,000 GROSS in year #2; $700,000 GROSS in year #3....

Step #3: Continuing to work backward, you can start to identify activities that will result in achieving these annual objective targets. Again, the act of merely writing this stuff down is incredibly helpful.

Example: book six local soccer teams in Year #1. GROSS Revenue: $4200.

Step #4: When you've got each activity down to its most

basic iteration, assign responsibility. Don't use names yet, use job titles. (Unless you're the only staff member.....in that case, guess whose name goes into the box?)

Step #5: Timeline everything. We'll use a Gantt chart in the next section. For now, here's an example of the timeline we used in 2011 for Ignite:

Sheet1

Activities	Who's Accountable?	Year 1	Year 2
Ignite		██████ in gross receipts	
Therapy			
Package services for other insurance funding providers	Chris / Tyler		
(ie ██████, ██████)			
Initiate a Board of Directors	Tyler/Chris		
Approach service providers (other therapists)	Tyler		
Train Ignite clients	Tyler / Chris		
Invoicing, scheduling, PR	Chris		
Schools			
Visit schools	Tyler / Intern		
Involve schools in research	Tyler / Chris		
Initiate a kids' fitness leadership program	Tyler		
Initiate school visits to our facility	Tyler		
Initiate teacher referrals	Tyler / Board of Dir		
Teacher in-class training (certification)	Tyler		
Academy (facility)			
special gym	Chris		
sport psych	Tyler		
Day-long and week-long camps, summer camps	Tyler / Intern / Assist		
Extra classes – speaking, $, collaboration	Tyler / Intern		
After-school membership program	Tyler / supply		
Certification			
Teacher in-class training (certification)	Tyler		
CrossFit coaches	Tyler		
Therapists / RSWs / care providers, program leaders	Tyler		
Parents	Tyler		
Certification manual	Tyler/Chris	May 31st	
HR / ORG			
Director of Ed	Tyler		
Intern		Jan 15th	
Kids' Coach - 1st coach certified – assistant			

Page 1

Missing: a Facilities section. As we were still in the acquisition process for a new facility, we laid out the space and equipment needs for Ignite, and assigned all the responsibility to me for providing them.

Had we done this work before initiating the huge Ignite program, there would have been an empty box where Tyler's name appears. The responsibilities assigned to that box would then provide a job description for a staff member.

No matter WHERE you stand with staff now, leave the 'name' boxes blank for the time being.

Later, we'll be digging deeper into staffing, responsibilities, and timelines. For now, though, let's stay a few miles above the surface.

SALES BOXES

In the last section, we started with the identification and prioritization of business ideas by revenue. Specifically, choosing a path for the business based on the most likely areas of opportunity. We identified our current services and markets by category.

This is a simple start to a real eye-opening revelation. It's pretty easy, takes about five minutes, and is absolutely critical to identifying how you spend your time; how you hire staff for the next three years; and how to bring tomorrow's potential revenues into your hands NOW.

I give you: sales boxes.

SALES BOXES EXERCISE:	IDENTIFY AND LIST YOUR CURRENT SERVICES BY BOX.
CURRENT CLIENTS, NEW PRODUCTS	CURRENT CLIENTS, CURRENT PRODUCTS
NEW CLIENTS, NEW PRODUCTS	NEW CLIENTS, CURRENT PRODUCTS

Example: everything you're currently doing would go into *'Current Clients, Current Products.'* Opportunities to attract NEW CrossFitters into your program would fall into *'New Clients, Current Products.'* However, the ability to expand your programming to your current members (for instance, adding a CrossFit Kids and/or Ignite program) would go into the *"Current Clients, New Products"* box.

When considering the ways to grow GROSS revenue, many business owners look at what they're currently doing, and then go diagonally down and left. They believe that, to attract more revenue, they have to attract more clients, and that means new services. This is not the simplest approach.

It's much easier to sell a new service to an existing client. They already like you. They trust you, and you KNOW the new service will benefit them....after all, that's why you're offering the new service.

Likewise, it's easier to sell an established service to a new client because you'll have dozens – hundreds – of fans doing the work for you. Imagine a current client raving to his wife about CrossFit: *"It's fun. They can scale the workouts for you. You'll love it! Just come with me on Saturday!"*

Now imagine the same client trying to sell his wife on a new service, with which he isn't familiar: *"Well, it sounds like they're going to make a class for people who just want to lose weight. You might like it. No, I'm not sure about that detail....I don't know the answer to that question....you should just call them, I guess. What's for dinner?"*

The farther you move from the top right, the tougher revenues will be to generate.

Revenues mean selling. You may not want to hear that sentence. "Marketing" and "sales" are words that many of us dislike. They don't have to mean trickery, falsehood, or moustaches, though; they can simply mean readiness to accept money in exchange for services. Better?

We're going to try something. Find a clock. Get out your schedule.

EXERCISE: SALES VS. DELIVERY

Definitions:

Sales - time spent talking to current clients about new products, new clients about current products, or new clients about potential new products. Includes: newsletter writing, phone calls, answering emails with 'Free Trial' in the subject line, faxing quotes. Does not include: inventory/ordering, scheduling, paying bills, designing marketing products. DOES NOT have to mean cold calls, "prospecting," buying radio time, or writing online ad copy.

Delivery - time spent actually coaching. Personal Training,

CrossFit, other groups.

Other - administrative stuff. Everything else. Don't worry about this category for now.

Total the number of hours you spend on Delivery first (just count up PT sessions, groups, etc. on your schedule. Using scheduling software makes this really easy....)

Now, set up your stopwatch next to your computer. Every time you do a Sales-related task from the above list, start the stopwatch. Stop it at the end of the call, when you hit 'send' on the email, or when you fax the quote.

Each day, total your hours. Here's a handy spreadsheet to help:

Hours Spent In Your Box, By Percentage

	Delivery Hours	Sales Hours	Other Hours
	1	0	
% Total	100.00%	0.00%	0.00%

Sales Hours Log

Monday	
Tuesday	
Wednesday	
Thursday	
Friday	
Saturday	
Sunday	

I think you know what's coming, right? Hours spent working IN your business, vs. hours spent working ON your business. I heard about it 3 years ago from Gerber; it took The Consultant to put a clock on it.

If you did the exercise, and you're like me, you were probably pretty shocked, because the 'Sales' side was virtually empty.

In my case, there was nothing proactive listed. There were a few reactive sales (requests for quotes, replies to emails, bookings) but only one where I'd approached a client with a proposition. Only in ONE instance had I done anything proactive to grow my business. Though I was "committed" to expanding our services AND clientele, I wasn't acting; I was waiting.

Your business NEEDS sales. You probably don't like doing proactive sales (I sure don't,) but luckily, there are people who DO.

The answer most commonly accepted in the business world: 30% of your staff should be engaged in selling, and 70% in delivery. Let's say, now, that you tallied up the hours worked by ALL staff in your Box. Divide it by ten. Are you actively engaging in this much time selling each week? And that's only 10% - a THIRD of the recommended dose!

Let's say that you had an athlete competing in the Open. Would you let them show up once per week to compete, with no other training for the next six weeks? Of course not. So where is YOUR practice time - the time that actually makes the difference in the performance of your Box?

Like everything else in CrossFit, start quantifying your time. 30% of the total should be devoted to creating new business, thinking about new business, identifying WHO the 'new clients' will be, and matching new products to existing AND new clients.

It's a tough task. But so is Murph, and you've done that before....

THE READY STATE: PREPARING TO TRANSFORM YOUR BUSINESS

The earliest "fitness" testing - mostly written for military and paramilitary organizations, like police forces - measured the "ready state." The question which the tests were created to answer: Is this candidate ready and able to act at an appropriate level?

'Fitness' is an ephereal concept. It's hard to measure in an objective, replicable way; but that's why we like CrossFit, isn't it? Objective and measurable. Well, "ready" is just as slick; trying to define "readiness" without using the word "prepared" is like trying to nail green Jell-O to the wall.

"So, five years in, here's where you are: six staff, hundreds of members, no partners. Annual revenues are covering expenses. You JUST wrote your first business plan. You have no written objectives; no recorded business - or personal - goals. How did you get this far?" It wasn't a rhetorical question. I was fast learning that, when The Consultant asked, he really wanted to know the answer.

"Well, a lot of luck," I said. *"First off, my original partners - aggressive business-types - started doing Personal Training with me at an old workplace. They pitched the idea of going solo when I was most desperate for more income. Then Mike - with whom I'd been training and studying for nearly a year - decided to come with me. So did Jo Ann, the best RMT for rehab around. We got funding for research early."* I was ticking lucky strikes off my fingers. *"A year and a half in, Tyler approached us for work. Our exercise adherence study had led us right to CrossFit, and we formed a free trial group. In that group was Whitney, who's now our OnRamp coach, and Kris, who's now a tenant with his supplement store."* I was ready to keep going, but The Consultant stopped me with the palm of his hand.

"You call that LUCK?" he said, looking genuinely surprised. *"I call that being READY. You were READY to leave the old place. You were READY to work with the best Trainers and RMTs. You were READY - mature enough - to ask questions and learn and embrace change. That's a ton of hard work. You can call it smarts or foresight, but calling it luck? That's bullshit."*

He was right. Change is hard, but as you tell your clients every day, "do it anyway."

STAFFING

When they open a new gym, most entrepreneurs look first to their friends for help. It makes sense: you know them well. You know their motivations; you don't need to interview them. Perhaps you partner, or hire, your girlfriend.

Frequently, one Coach at a gym will make the jump to Owner of another, and several coworkers will desire to join him. Seems like an obvious win at the starting line.

However, if you aren't working from a written contract – a mutual understanding – then you're going to trip coming out of the blocks. *Friends don't need contracts* is the typical thought of the new businessperson. In reality, if you want to keep your friends, you'll write your expectations for each other down. A contract keeps your business separate from y our friendship.

What causes breakups? Is it huge blowouts over large issues, or is it the day-to-day simmering of low-level resentment over small issues? Think about your last roommate: did you split because they stole from you, or because they never did the dishes?

Avoiding confrontation and distrust isn't the issue. Dealing with those things in a predictable way, as quickly as possible, makes relationships last. Passive-aggressive behaviour does not. Upfront confrontation, when it occurs in only one direction, does not. As the saying goes, you can climb mountains, but you'll be taken down by the pebble in your shoe.

Solid contractual agreements are a collaborative process. "I'll be at the Box these specific 30 hours. You'll be at the Box these other 30. Here's what we'll do if one can't make it. Here's what we'll do if we run out of money. Here's what we'll do if we MAKE money. Here's what I'll be paid, and here's what YOU'LL be paid. These are MY cleaning tasks, and these are YOUR cleaning tasks...."

The more specific your agreement with your partners and staff, the better the long-term relationship, because there won't be any room for doubt. Few doubt the need for contracts when it comes to money; unfortunately, few write contracts concerning the day-to-day business of their Box. It's not a measure of your trust; it's not symbolic. It's a clear discussion on your expectations for one another, ending in a document that you can use for reference later.

Stop me if you've heard this one. Three partners open a new gym, agreeing to "split the work evenly." When they start, they break the classes up into even numbers. For three months, things work out fine.

One day, Steve can't make the Saturday class. *I'll take it!"* says Ann, thinking that Steve will make it up to her later. Ann's keeping score. Steve may not be.

Later, when the plumber mentions that he'll have to finish his work on Monday, after hours, Marnie offers to stay late to lock up afterward. She spends 3 hours on facebook, including posting pictures to the gym's page. Steve goes home at 7pm without mopping, figuring that since Marnie's staying late anyway....

Meanwhile, Ann takes the accounting home with her. Learning as she goes, she spends hours of 'home time' balancing payroll. Eventually, she's painted herself into the 'bookkeeper' role; she thinks, "I can do it faster than the others, because I've done it before." There's no extra pay, but it's a lot of extra work...unseen by Steve and Marnie.

With equal check-signing authority, Marnie and Steve 'vote' to take advantage of the Again Faster 20% off sale after the Games, and buy some new boxes. Ann panics when she finds out, because she knows they're struggling to cover rent next week. *Why wouldn't they ask me first?* She wonders. *Haven't they seen our checking account?*

Clear, specific roles, written in advance, and mutually accepted, can avoid ALL of these problems. Want to keep your friends? Write a contract.

SEPARATING ROLES WITHIN YOUR BUSINESS

The Ghost Runner
When kids play baseball, they don't waste time organizing teams. They start with what they have available to them: *"Timmy, you take second base. I'll pitch. Sherry, you're up."* With huge holes in their lineup, they play as if each side were still fielding 9 players.

Hit into the outfield? No problem....Timmy will eventually get there. Pop fly? Open sky for the pitcher. Strike? The batter picks up her own ball, and throws it back to the pitcher. They simply make do with what they have.

The only gaping void appears when Sharon hits a double. She gets on base; her little brother, Aaron, hits a single. With runners on the corners, Sharon should be up again...but she's stuck on third plate.

"Ghost runner on third!" she yells, and trots back to the batter's box.

While the 'Ghost Runner' can't be found in any official softball rulebook, its presence and rules of behaviour are widely understood among kids. The ghost runner can't steal bases. When the batter hits a single, the ghost runner advances by one base. A home run, with a ghost runner on second, means two points for the batter. Simple.

When starting a gym, one of the most important things you can do is to clearly delineate the different jobs required to make your business successful. Breaking down responsibilities by using job descriptions is immensely helpful in the long run, as more staff are added and areas of responsibility are negotiated at hire. In our Affiliate, some of the job descriptions include:

⚓ CEO

- Personal Trainer
- CrossFit Coach
- Cleaner / Janitor
- Equipment Maintenance and Repairperson
- Bookkeeper
- Case Manager
- Tutor
- Social Media
- Writer
- Editor
- General Manager
- Specialty Coach (contractor)
- Gym Staff
- Photographer
- Ignite NeuroMotive Coach
- Ignite NeuroMotive Therapist
- Ignite Curriculum Writer
- Ignite Director of Education
- Ignite Case Manager
- Webmaster

These are all jobs with their own unique list of tasks to be done. Some bleed into another, and my own name appears in several of the boxes.

Why write the descriptions if you're going to fill them yourself - some for now, some forever? Simple: the Ghost Runner. The position is there, clearly spelled out, for when you find the right person.

In a not-uncommon example, one of your Coaching staff will request more hours. You'll present them with three options: Cleaner (here's a job description!,) Gym staff (here's a job description!,) or Social Media (here's a job description!) This means a clear outline of duties and responsibilities, with no overlap, no wasted time, and no gaps.

If you've said one of these:

> *"Well, Chastity is supposed to do the cleaning....but I didn't tell her to wash the windows, so I do them."*

> *"Michael is supposed to close the batch every night, and take a picture of our whiteboard, but sometimes he forgets to do one or the other. Neither are in his contract, so I can't really hold him to it."*

> *"When we started this business, I was supposed to do the coaching, and my partner was supposed to do the business stuff....but they're never around, and I'm here all the time!"*

...then you need job descriptions for your staff. It's much easier to write these in BEFORE they're hired, and ask them to live up to the expectations (clear and manageable) than just hope that they do a good job.

Our other High Level Goal: get you outta there. When reviewing life goals and answering The Big Question, most Affiliates tell me that "time" is a high priority, but in short supply. With prewritten job tasks, it's easy to plug the right person into the right job when they come along, without wasting any time or being unclear about expectations. These also minimize (and standardize) training time. If a new staff member has a question, they can refer to their

Staff Handbook (which we'll build in the next section.) If they're unsure about something, they'll have documents to reference BEFORE calling you at home.

One more thing: don't put anyone's name in any task box yet (I know, I know...but be patient.) You're writing descriptions for people to fill, according to tasks that need doing. You're NOT trying to piece together jobs to best fit your staff or partners. They're human; they'll adapt, and do better work with less guessing. Describe what your business NEEDS, not what your business HAS.

JOB DESCRIPTIONS

Breaking down roles within your business is a simple task. There are three which are easy to identify: Coach, Cleaner, Bookkeeper. Dig into each and pry them apart, simplify down to the very basic level; write checklists for each that are as specific as possible, and then use those checklists to create staff contracts. It's not a complicated process, but it does take some time.

When consulting with a gym, I typically ask questions to allow owners to draw out roles and name them in their own terminology. This allows you to take full ownership over each position, and make your business model specific to YOUR gym.

For example, consider the case of the CrossFit Coach. This is perhaps the one position that EVERY CrossFit gym will have. If you don't own a CrossFit gym, replace 'CrossFit Coach' with Class Coach.

Question #1: What's the FIRST thing a Coach does when he arrives in the morning?

Typical answer: Writes the WOD on the board.

Question #2: Where does he get the WOD? Does he make it up, or is it pre-programmed?

A: It's programmed weeks in advance.

Q: Who's responsible for the programming?

A: It's a collaborative process....

Q: Who's responsible for the process being completed? Who sets up the programming meeting? Who sends the day's WOD to the Coach?

A: The Head Coach. **[Create position: Head Coach.]**

Q: How does the first CrossFit Coach of the morning receive the workout?

A: He can take it from our site, or the Head Coach sends it to him.

Q: If from your site, who put it there? **[Create position: Blogger/Website.]**

A: The person who runs the site.

Q: Is that the same person who handles your facebook page, twitter account, Pinterest board...?

A: Sometimes. **[Create position: Social Media.]**

Q: Before he can write the workout on the board, does he have to clean it, or is it already clean?

A: It's clean from the night before. **[Create position: Cleaner. Add 'clean whiteboard' to Cleaner checklist.]**

Q: After the workout's posted, what's next?

A: The Coach logs into the tracking software, and turns on the stereo.

Q: Who has set up the class booking/billing structure in your software?

A: The Head Coach. **[Add to Head Coach job description: scheduling and tracking]**

Q: Where does the music come from? What is played pre-class, during instruction, and during the WOD? What's the volume level? **[Create Opening Checklist]**

A: We stream through an online service. We play the same station all day, but turn it up when the WOD starts.

Q: What time is the door unlocked before the first class?

A: 15 minutes beforehand. **[Add to Opening Checklist.]**

Q: What's the coach doing as people enter?

A: Standing by the door, greeting them and signing them in **[Add to Opening Checklist.]**

Things, obviously, are getting very specific. What I'm trying to get across here is that there's always room for differentiation between coaches, but the basics – the things you care about most – are always met in a consistent way. People are ALWAYS greeted at the door. The music is ALWAYS from Radio Station X, and played at Volume Y. Everyone is signed in BEFORE class.

Unfortunately, people need to be instructed at this minute level. If it were you, would you greet everyone at the door, or spend your time texting your friends in the cleaning closet until 1 minute before your class? Would you like people to be milling around aimlessly until class starts, looking at the clock? Would you like them to follow a warmup written on the whiteboard? What if someone new arrives; would you like them to stand awkwardly at the front desk until a veteran member engages them and goes looking for a Coach to help them?

These aren't meant to turn your staff into robots. They're meant to take away misunderstandings in advance.

Now, consider your class flow structure. Who sets up the necessary equipment – the coach, or the athletes? How much time is spent on warmup? How much on mobility? At what time does the WOD begin? Is there strength or skill work before or after, and how much? Is there a debriefing time afterwards? Find what works best for you, and write it down. This can be a collaborative process with your staff instead of a dictatorial one, but it must be done in order to provide consistent service.

Members will always have favourite Coaches. It's critical to make sure that the same high-level service is provided to everyone, regardless of the Coach. Let members choose their favourites based on coaching style, NOT based on their ability to start class on time.

A final point of consideration: dress code. Dress code is never a problem until it's a big problem. No staff member ever shows up one day with a big change in appearance; rather, it's a slow downward degradation. Decide where you draw the line for standards.

Q: What does a Personal Trainer wear?

A: Collared shirt. They don't have to get sweaty, or down and dirty.

Q: Does a CrossFit Coach wear the same?

A: No, a T-shirt is fine.

Q: Does the T-shirt identify them as a Coach, or is it okay to merely have one of your Affiliate's shirts?

A: Affiliate's shirts with Coach on the back.

Q: YOUR Affiliate shirt, or ANY CrossFit shirt?

A: Ours only.

Q: What if it's a Games shirt?

A: Ours only.

Q: What if they're going to be outside?

A: They can wear a hat.

Q: YOUR hat, or any hat?

A: Ours only.....

Q: Shorts?

A: Sure.

Q: Colour? Length? Logos? Types?

A: Colour doesn't matter, but I don't want big "TapOut" logos on there....

Making these decisions in advance helps the staff member KNOW what's appropriate. It solves one of their problems: What do I wear today? It stops an issue before it becomes an issue, and creates a standard of professionalism in your business.

WRITING STAFF CONTRACTS

Now that you've broken down your business into a dozen roles or more, and written checklists and responsibilities for each, we can use those to write contracts. Contract-writing is scary, and that's where attorneys capitalize: that intimidation.

Contracts are simple, though: record what you expect, not just what you require; review with your new staffer; and then you both sign. You can download templates from 321GoProject.com to help, and just plug in your own points.

When you're hiring staff, you have responsibilities in three directions:

1. Do the right thing for your clients;

2. Do the right thing for your new staffer;

3. Do the right thing for the business. For a happy, productive relationship, all three must be met. Agree?

To that end, you owe it to everyone involved to provide the staff member:

> ⚔ A staff handbook, to remove the variables and let them be creative and independent;

- A staff uniform (or specific guidelines), to help them maintain a professional appearance and carry the confidence of their clients;

- Clear, written expectations about behaviour in and out of the gym, to eliminate 'grey areas';

- A tool for performance measurement that doesn't change;

- A nonsolicitation contract, in case they're not sure how to tell you they're leaving;

- Scheduled arrival times before clients;

- A key, to symbolize your trust and their independence;

- Clear rules about after-hours use;

- A clear view of the road ahead. Most Coaches leave because they can't imagine making a career of being a Coach. They leave because they want a FUTURE, not necessarily a business.

- Ongoing education, through instruction, books, collaborative lecturing, rip 'n read files, and Certifications

- Opportunities to be entrepreneurial (let them start their own new program within your Box.)

- A clear wage, as well as the potential to earn increases in the future;

- A healthy, strong business behind them;

- A contract that spells out all of these elements.

You're not forcing them to do uncomfortable things. You're helping them do the job they want to do, without worrying about all the tiny decisions that surround that job. You're empowering them to make their own decisions by removing the little bureaucratic hangups. You're freeing them to be as creative as they like, without worry of *"how Jim would do it...."* because they'll already know the answer.

We have sample staff contracts available at 321GoProject.com.

What's the best way to behave with staff and members? This is was a frequent topic on the old Affiliate blog. How do you inspire confidence, avoid conflict, and keep people coming back?

You don't need to be everyone's best friend. What you need to be is consistent.

Readers of parenting books will recognize this bit of advice. Readers of business books may not, as it's frequently lost in policywriting minutae and rewards systems.

The best gift you can give someone is the knowledge that you're going to react the same way today as yesterday.

SCALING YOUR STAFF

Forty years from now, this will be accepted logic. It will also still be controversial.

It took Elliott Jaques nearly 50 years to develop his theories around stratification of job tasks. I'll try to sum it up in five minutes. If we can do it with a split jerk.....

Disclaimer: this is not a commentary on anyone's intelligence, potential, or raw brain power. To the contrary: the purpose here is to identify friction and cognitive dissonance. If you're using people to their full potential, they'll be happier, love their work, and attract more people. If they're placed above or below the level at which they're most productive, they'll be unhappy. Who wants unhappy staff?

We're going to arrange the jobs in your Box by level - that is, by the mental processing necessary to do the job.

Level I - analog. "I do THIS and THIS and then I do THIS." Step-by-step. No further processing required. In our Box, we've been lucky enough to hire Sean to do the cleaning. Sean loves a good checklist: first, I sweep the 'big room.' Then I sweep the hallways. Then I mop the big room. Then I mop the hallways. Sean LOVES to clean. He's passionate about it. He's loyal to a certain brand of toilet bowl cleaner. He doesn't question his wage, or dread coming to work. He's excited to be part of our 'Team,' and if you give him a new t-shirt, it's like a slice of sweet Mango. This is a front-line worker.

Level II - binary. "I do this. IF this happens, THEN I do this." The algebra of the task expands, but the paths are still linear. Decisions are automatic (predetermined in your staff handbook) but enforced by the Level II worker. This may be a Shift Supervisor for Level I workers, or a call centre employee with a large textbook on their lap. No need to see the big picture, just fill in the gaps. All the answers are before me; no need to question them, or their motives, or their origins.

Worth noting: most McFit gyms consider their Personal Trainers 'Level II' workers. IF Mary wants to lose weight, THEN she must walk on the treadmill. IF Jimmy wants to gain muscle, THEN he must do 3 sets of 8-10 reps on the bench press. However, some gyms may even treat their staff as Level I workers: To lose weight, Mary AND Jimmy must do the circuit AND dance when the bell chimes AND buy these supplements AND do this low-calorie diet.

Level III - more algebraic. This is where a great Personal Trainer lies: they see the long tail. They recognize the long-term plan that dictates the short-term programming. This would be the General Manager of most businesses, responsible for not just scheduling and tracking, but also some forecasting and planning. It is at this level that most of the Delivery portion of your business is managed (or should be.) This is where a great Personal Trainer is most happy: if I take care of my client's needs, the business owner will keep getting me more clients, and do the administrative planning stuff that I don't like.

Up to this point, the system has been mostly algebraic. The transition from Level III to Level IV, however, is like the transition from ice to water: the Entrepreneur is quite different from the great Coach who wants to make a living at coaching.

Level IV - the business owner. Planning, long-term forecasting and oversight. A view of 'the big picture.' An understanding of HOW and WHY.

Example: a client is dissatisfied and wants their money back.

Level I: *"Not my job. Ask my supervisor."*

Level II: *"Our policy says no refunds."*

Level III: *"I want to keep you happy. If I keep you happy, you'll tell your friends. Maybe you SHOULD get your money back...."*

Level IV: *"If I give this person their money back, it sets a precedent that may hurt ALL the Trainers in the next few years. We want to grow out AND up, and we need a solid foundation and rules from which Levels II and III can draw, so they don't have to stress about this stuff."*

Jaques' levels actually go up to 12, but for your business, let's end there.

Now, the most important part: making sure people are where they SHOULD be. How often have you seen one of these?:

- The Coach who loves his job (Level III) so much that he decides to open his own Box (Level IV.) He's miserable for the next three years, because he hates bookkeeping and scheduling and lawyers and cash flow and overhead. Worst of all, he coaches less than ever, because he doesn't have time. His own fitness suffers...

⋏ The Coach who's so great at showing up on time and cleaning up after their groups that they're put in charge of all other coaches. NOW their job is managing people and doing math, instead of doing the job at which they shine.

⋏ The high-quality, educated Coach who's asked to stay after the gym closes and handle the mopping every night. This is a tough one, because mopping needs to be done, and if you don't have Sean....

All of these are examples of Cognitive Dissonance. There's a 'best' place for people in your organization. Can we all avoid the trap of mandatory promotion? Can we please stop moving gifted Coaches into positions where they're frustrated and less effective?

Putting a person in a job that's below or above the level at which they're comfortable and most happy is not going to end well.

IDENTIFYING THE BEST

Now, you've got a great Box. You're building a Family, and some of the members show great promise as athletes; some as Mavens; some as supporters; some as grinders; and some as Coaches.

Alternately, you could be hiring from outside your Box. It's not my favourite method, but it's occasionally necessary. Let's imagine that you're hiring a General Manager - not a coach, but someone whose job is to handle the Delivery of your service, with a little bit of insight into the future of the company.

What will you consider? For most, their Education (Skills)

and Experience are the biggest factors. However, in a meeting with The Consultant, he suggested that we're only looking at a quarter of the whole picture. There are four 'Lenses' through which to view potential staff:

BRAIN POWER – do they have the intellectual capacity to do the job?	Skills and Knowledge – acquired education and experience.
Value/Commitment – Do they recognize the value in what they're doing? Would they do it for free?	The 'X' Factor – Personality. Debatably defined as the absence of NEGATIVE traits.

The first square, BRAIN POWER, is likely going to get me in trouble. There are those who may find the idea that smarts=good to be discriminatory. It is: you're smart enough for this job, or you're not. (Without trying to pander to my audience, I've found that the vast majority of CrossFitters and Affiliates are much smarter than a slice of the average population. Have you noticed the same? Does CrossFit self-select toward the more intellectual...or do I just know a LOT of people who are smarter than I am?)

Frankly, without enough Brain Power, all the charisma ('X' factor,) commitment (if they don't get the job, they don't eat) and education in the world won't get the job done. I think we can agree that education and intellect aren't the same thing. I'm also not talking about IQ here: 'BRAIN POWER' means the ability to draw on experience and education to extrapolate a course of action.

Skills and Knowledge :the bulk of a person's resume, but probably least important. You can teach a person anatomy; you can't teach charm. When I was returning to Canada after a few years of coaching in the States, I applied for a job at a local ski resort. Interviewees were screened in one room; if they passed, they were sent through to the second room, where the 'real' interview took place. What was the first-room screening process? *"Stand on your chair and sing, 'Happy Birthday'."* Luckily, I'd done a similar interview in Wisconsin a few years before: finalists were taken to a restaurant to 'celebrate.' Before the meal - or any drinks - each was egged into doing a Karaoke solo onstage. The shy folk were eventually turned down, education and experience notwithstanding.

Value/Commitment: I have a Coach who would do this CrossFit gig for free. That's rare. However, the trick is not to devalue the financial part of the job, but rather to increase the value of what the Coach GETS from doing his job. Trust me: money is not the principal motivator for people. This guy is motivated by the ballet of the barbell; he lives to see people sweat. He's well paid, of course, but he's not committed because of the money. If the staffer VALUES their work - and sees how important it really is - they're closer to self-actualization than the highly-paid Coach who hates their job. Maslow got that part right.

The 'X' Factor: Charisma. Radiance. That stuff's all great, but your concern is primarily the absence of negative habits: does the interviewee talk a lot about drinking on facebook? Do they have a bad habit of swearing in front of kids? Are they overtly sexual with other members? Weed out the negative traits first - they're easier to quantify than the positive ones.

The big question: how do you measure this stuff in advance? Luckily, you're smart. You're going to recognize BRAIN POWER when you see it. Evolution has provided us with tools to identify the smartest of our species, as borne out through a ton of psychological research. The 'X' Factor is nearly obvious, too, but requires a bit more digging (for instance, if the email address on their resume is *'rearmountie69@sex.xxx,'* you can probably move on.) Ontario Police interviewers now require recruits to relinquish their facebook password, so that the employer can search their friends, comments, and likes....

Skills and Experience - most of that is coming from you, friend. But if they've coached elsewhere, they've got some. Heck, maybe they've got an Olympic-level snatch, but if no one can stand to be in the room with them for an hour, they're not going to succeed.

Working backward, if you take the previous section about Scaling Staff and apply these four Lenses when hiring, you'll be in better shape.

UP, UP AND AWAY: STAFF PROMOTION

Promotions and Happiness

How do you become a firefighter?

Go to college, says your high school counselor. *Study firefighting. Get a degree or a diploma, then hand in your resume.*

Wait, says the recruiter from the Fire Department. *Go learn a trade. You'll be more useful to us.*

Good, says the Chief. *Now go get married or something. Get some life experience, and check back in a few years.....*

This isn't a publicly-shared process, but it's usually what happens for young adults trying to become firemen or police officers. As it turns out, a 98% on your final exam in

Police Foundations doesn't really make you a great cop.

Let's consider some things that we know to be true:

⚲ A great student doesn't necessarily make a great athlete.

⚲ A great athlete doesn't necessarily make a great coach.

⚲ A great coach doesn't necessarily make a great 1-on-1 Trainer.

⚲ A great 1-on-1 Trainer doesn't necessarily make a great Head Trainer.

⚲ A great Head Trainer doesn't necessarily make a great General Manager.

⚲ A great General Manager doesn't necessarily make a great Partner.

⚲ A great Partner doesn't necessarily make a great student.

Each of the above jobs - call them 'levels' - requires separate training, motivation, and desire. If a CrossFit Coach loves coaching classes, but doesn't educate himself beyond the Certification weekends he attends, he may not be a great 1-on-1 Coach. And that's fine.

If your Head Trainer loves finding new information and sharing with your other Coaches, great. If they like organizing the Coaching schedule and helping to determine the programming at your Box, fantastic. If they don't care to think much about cash flow, they're not going to help you as a General Manager. And THAT's fine, too.

When people are happy - fulfilling the tasks that give them joy - it sometimes seems as if a promotion is a nice reward. It's not. Adding unfamiliar tasks for which staff aren't properly trained will be exciting at first, and then demotivational and frustrating. Money won't bridge that gap.

SENSE OF PURPOSE

A video producer at the 2012 Canada East Regionals shared this insight with me.

When Jewish prisoners at Nazi internment camps were finally liberated, many were debriefed on the terrible persecution techniques they'd endured. Some of their answers surprised the interviewers.

When trying to break the stoicism of the Jewish adults, the Nazi guards would put them to work: breaking rocks, building houses, stringing fences. Given a task, no matter how onerous, the prisoners would work toward the goal with resolve. Guards commented that the work seemed to strengthen the will of the labourers (we now recognize this as the 'Flow State' that comes from physical work.)

When they dug latrines, they didn't complain. When they dug graves for their own dead - later, for themselves - they set about the job with a surprising sense of purpose. Only when they were forced to dig ditches and immediately fill them in again did they despair.

When everyone on a team is working toward a common goal - be it trying to avoid bankruptcy, building an underdog Affiliate from scratch, or scrambling to learn as much as possible - they work hard. They find fulfilment. They sleep well. They push.

When they're not sure of your goals, challenges, obstacles, and horizon, they drift. We're wired not to find comfort and solace, but to find reward. That means we seek challenge. If your staff isn't being challenged, or can't find a common rally point, they'll seek another.

Do your staff know your *intent* as the Owner? Do they know your plans for the Box next year, or two years from now? Do they know your story? Do they see you fighting, and know your enemy?

Will they leave, forsaking your warm fire to seek their own dragons and glory?

SEEING THE HORIZON

You know this tune by heart: over the years, you've worked to develop your Coaches. You've had them Certified, protected them from liability, carried the burden of risk for everyone. And now, they'd like to start their own Box.

Or maybe it's a member: they're so inspired by your coaching, your philosophy, and your business that they think they'd like to be more like you. The romantic dream of entrepreneurship beckons, and they apply for Affiliation. Ironically, they're convinced that you'll be flattered - after all, you're clearly raking in a great living, and there's more than enough to go 'round....right?

This is a popular topic lately - Lisbeth Darsh brought it up on the A-Blog, and by no coincidence, I've been talking to Affiliates all over the United States about this very thing. Growth, overall, is good for CrossFit. Growth on your block, or splitting your membership, or the new induction of weak coaches into entrepreneurs...those are debatable. The worst occurrence is the transition of a fantastic Coach into a poor business owner. That's sad, and many who wind up discouraged didn't really want to own a business in the first place; they just couldn't see the next step.

We're brought up in a system of promotion: if you do a good job (merit) or simply stick around long enough (attrition,) you'll be rewarded by being placed in front of your peers. Our parents worked within this system, and theirs did, too.

If you already own a gym, think back to the moment you decided to open your CrossFit Box or Garage Gym.

Now, think back to five minutes before that.

What was in your head? WHY did you want to move from Trainer, Coach, or someone outside the fitness industry and open your own business?

In my case, I had more than one reason. I needed to make more money, and couldn't see a way to do it where I was. I felt unappreciated: the gym where I worked had grown immensely since I'd signed on, and I wasn't getting credit. Frankly, I thought I was smarter than the owner...or maybe I just cared more. Finally, and perhaps most of all, I didn't know where else to go from where I stood.

Ten years ago, there weren't any 40-year-old Personal Trainers. Ten years before that, there weren't ANY Personal Trainers. I simply couldn't imagine that my advice would still be relevant when my hair turned grey.

The only logical step up, then, was to become an entrepreneur. Self-employment was the only promotion possible. I wanted to test out my mental wheels, sure, but would never have taken the risk if another option had presented itself.

MANY new CrossFit Boxes are owned by passionate, inspired Coaches who saw only one possible way forward. When they asked themselves, *"What's next? How do I move UP? How do I make it possible to keep doing this until I retire?"* the answer came back: *"Open your own gym."* In many cases, it was the ONLY answer they heard.

If you can create a future - a next step, a way for your Coaches to 'move up,' or a way for them to be entrepreneurial - there's no reason for them to leave. Human nature mandates exploration and novelty. If they have itchy feet, and want to move, challenge them to look up instead of dead ahead.

Some other ideas to consider:

- A 'Head Coach' position, responsible for the oversight of other Coaches; programming for your Box; running monthly training sessions for your Coaches; making decisions on Cert attendance and new programs;

- A 'General Manager' position, to replace you - as owner - when you feel like taking that long-overdue vacation time (or just staying home occasionally);

- A 'Case Manager' position, who oversees individual training plans AND customer retention, client satisfaction, and social media;

- An 'Events Coordinator,' who sets up your events and works for part of the gross;

- The developer of a brand new part of your business. Intra-Entrepreneurship. I'll explain that concept in a moment.

Each of these positions should create the revenue - and more - to cover the increased wages that follow increased responsibility.

INTRAPRENEURSHIP

Charles Schwab - the first man in history to draw a salary of a million dollars per year - did well not because he was a great industrialist, but because he could lead people. Schwab was Andrew Carnegie's right-hand man when the steel giant was at his peak.

As the story goes, Schwab had a mill manager whose crews were lagging behind. The mill manager couldn't figure it out: he'd tried bullying, cajoling, pleading, yelling; still, his was the slowest mill in the Carnegie empire.

When Schwab visited, he asked the manager for a piece of chalk. As the day shift was finishing up, he asked the first man he came across, "How many heats did your shift make today?"

"Six." The man replied, defensively.

Schwab knelt down, chalked a big number '6' on the ground, and walked away.

When the evening shift arrived, they asked about the big '6.' *"The big boss was here,"* said the workers. *"He asked us how many heats we'd made, and we told him six. Then he wrote it on the floor."*

The next morning, Schwab took another walk through the plant. The night shift had erased the giant '6' and replaced it with a big '7.'

When the day shift arrived, and saw their number beaten, they enthusiastically attacked their work, finishing with 10 units for the day. The mill had quickly gone from one of the slowest in the Carnegie line to one of the fastest.

A large part of CrossFit's charm is that it's objectively measurable: you're faster at 'Fran' than you were last month, or you're not. Coach Glassman created his own measurement criteria, specific to CrossFit, just the way Schwab created measurable outputs specific to a steel mill.

In the business world, 'objective and measurable' usually means, *"how much revenue did it generate?"* While there are other ways to determine success, this is the simplest and has most resonance. More money from staff means more cushion for the business, and better job security. It also means more time off for the owner, and more self-satisfaction for the staff member building her 'own' program.

When a Coach has an idea for a new program – let's use the example of starting a CrossFit Kids group – evaluate it objectively. Share that evaluation with the Coach; show her the numbers. *"It will cost X for your Certification and travel. If your wage is 4/9 of total revenue, it will take Y months at Z members per month to repay that cost.*

"If we have to make room in our schedule for that class, it costs us A in lost revenue from the cancelled class. Can you replace that lost revenue within 6 months; repay the cost of the Certification; make enough money to keep YOU happy; AND generate more revenue than we're currently earning in that same time slot?"

If the answer is 'yes,' and you agree, then it's win-win.

EXAMPLE: THE IGNITE PROGRAM

You've already read the story of Ignite. Tyler, a Trainer and Teacher, wanted to build something from scratch. We went through the cost-revenue valuation process above, and were both confident that we could make it work.

Our plan:

⅄ Get Ty into schools to run some CrossFit groups;

⅄ Book some 1-on-1 sessions to help with reading and math;

⅄ Progress to groups for different ages at our Box;

⅄ Develop a weekend course for teachers;

⅄ Run a study or two;

⅄ Develop a web-based curriculum;

⅄ Approach insurance companies for funding;

⅄ Develop our own Certification process for others who want to help.

The reality, Weeks 1 through 6:

⅄ Booked into schools on a weekly-recurring basis;

⅄ Clients booking sessions a year in advance;

⅄ Waiting lists for the FIRST IGNITE GROUPS offered after one little Pilot class

⅄ Three clients, fully funded by insurance companies;

⅄ A 'How-To' short-form Cert weekend for teachers;

⅄ Participation in the Provincial Math Curriculum Development Group;

⅄ Inclusion in new research on improving EQAO Test scores;

⅄ One study on attendance in a high-risk school;

⅄ Calls from physiotherapists, Occupational Therapists, and Speech Pathologists for information;

⅄ Two new consultations each week.

Ignite today:

⅄ Weekly referrals for long-term MVA claims, with preapproved plans for between $3200 and $18,000

⅄ Two full-time staff members, with more in the development process

⅄ "Innovation Company of the Year" Award for 2012

⅄ Ignite Affiliates in MA, MI, TX, ON, FL, and South Africa, with others on the way at time of writing

⅄ A half-dozen Tutors with various specialities

⅄ A concussion-testing program (concussionpro.com) to help better assess cognitive skills pre- and post-concussion in kids and adults.

Does it help business? That's obvious. Does it help kids read better? Oh yeah. And move better. And do math, and complex drawings, and box jumps and cleans, too.

PAYING STAFF

Not everyone wants to change. Don't force anyone; let people be happy. If you can't create a path of development and personal growth, though, don't expect them to stick around.

When we started out in 2005, I received some great advice from our bookkeeper: don't have employees. Instead, have subcontractors.

These tips are legal and relevant in Ontario; it would be a logical extension to include the rest of Canada. However, if you're in the States or Europe or Australia or Africa, you'd be wise to check first. There ARE ways to make it work, and 321GoProject is working on sharing that information. Stay tuned to the site!

How it works: every staff member registers themselves as a business (about $60.) Weekly, they submit an invoice for hours worked, which I pay immediately. Some, who make over $30,000 per year, have to charge me HST (a Goods and Services Tax,) which flows right from the HST we charge members. There are benefits to the business owner, more benefits to the subcontractor, and even a few for your client.

For the subcontractor:

⋏ They can deduct expenses that they'd normally incur for work - like some mileage, gas, car repairs, work-related 'toys' - and pay for them with pre-tax dollars. Given that our income and other taxes add up to over 40% of our gross income, that's a significant savings.

⋏ They own their own company, creating one more layer of liability protection.

⋏ They get to own something instead of just showing up for your sake.

⋏ They can minimize their income tax burden by paying themselves an actual wage only if and when they feel like it.

⋏ They can set their own schedule without being

hamstrung by the legalities of the 3-hour pay minimum.

For you, the business owner:

⅄ Some of the rules of termination no longer apply; you can cancel a contract instead of going through the legal hoops of firing someone. However, this can also be interpreted as breach of contract, so be careful.

⅄ You can let subcontractors take a client here and there (nearly an industry necessity) instead of having to pay for a minimum 3 hours of work each time they show up. While I can understand the value of this rule in the retail world *("Can you come in for an hour?")* it really hurts a Trainer's potential revenue stream. If you're charging $50/hour for personal training, and the Trainer makes $20, and you have to pay them for two extra hours after the session's over, you don't have much reason to give them the client, do you?

⅄ It's easier to manage payroll and track performance.

⅄ You'll also enjoy an extra layer of protection from liability. In fact, though I choose to insure our subcontractors, you can require that they have their own insurance.

⅄ Either way, you don't have to pay WSIB (Workplace Safety Insurance Board) for a subcontractor, which in our case would be over $300/month.

⅄ If they (or you) don't work, they don't eat.

⅄ The old, "whose clients ARE they?" problem is largely solved, making it easier to switch 1-on-1 clients between trainers during vacation times or in the event of one trainer's exit. Spoiler alert: they're the clients of the business, NOT the individual.

For the Client/Member:

⅄ Being accountable to someone other than the Signor Of Cheques gives the Trainers a greater interest in your progress.

⅄ You want your Trainer well-fed, rested, happy, and making lots of money. It's in your best interest.

⅄ They'll never know the difference, but they WILL know that their Trainer is among the highest-paid (read: best) around. They can feel good about supporting a professional, instead of hiring a kid.

This has been a big boon to us, personally, as well:

⅄ It's much easier to share income with my wife;

⅄ Some household space (around 10%,) and the proportional share of utilities and consumables are paid with pre-tax income;

⅄ I was able to 'sell' some personal sporting assets to the business, reducing its tax burden;

⅄ Maintenance of one family vehicle (up to 50 cents per kilometre) is payable with before-tax income;

⅄ Retirement plans and health care are paid by our Holdings company; again, pre-tax income. That means a 40% savings in some instances. Canada's a tax-heavy country.

We got lucky, at the beginning, to have shareholders who knew the difference, and Trainers who saw the light. It may help you, too.

HOW MUCH?

Here's the rub: on a day-to-day basis, your staff (and contractors) should be doing the vast majority of the work.

With proper systems in place, you can perform your REAL job – as leader, visionary, and planner – and leave the more routine matters to those who are best suited for each task. This is part delegation, but primarily optimization. Put your best coaches on as many classes as possible; put your best Trainer with as many clients as possible.

When negotiating staff contracts and pay levels, many staff – and some owners – look only at this day-to-day and think, *"The Coach is doing 90% of the work...."* or worse, *"Any extra training the Coach does is just a bonus to my bottom line....."*

Neither is true.

The Coach-Client-Business relationship isn't linear. At any one moment, the client's perception of the business can change, based on the Coach; their perception of the Coach can change, based on the business.

When working in your facility, whether at 6am, noon, or midnight, the Coach is representing your business. They are working on your behalf. They are not "training their own clients" - because they don't HAVE clients. The business has clients, and they are training the clients of the business. Where the clients came into the picture is irrelevant. Referred to you, referred to the Coach – doesn't matter. The business makes the Coach even more than the Coach makes the business.

You are providing the space. You're providing the insurance, perhaps. You're providing the schedule, the billing system, the brand, the reliable source of revenue. You're providing clients who wouldn't find the Coach on their own. You're their buffer against bill collection and late-paying clients. You're the backdrop of credibility against which they do their art. More importantly, you're providing the opportunity. Opportunity created through your hard work, reputation, and most importantly, your risk. RISK is the undiscussed, unconsidered, and undervalued portion of the equation.

What separates a staff person from an entrepreneur? Risk. You have taken the risk; they haven't. YOU have put things on the line. They have not. The hurdle is largely mental, yes, but you've made that leap. If you're like me, against the best advice, you'll pay your staff before you pay yourself (see the next section.)

Risk is not a good idea for everyone; this is why, as a species, we're risk-averse. If many of your staff members tried to start their own business, they'd fail; it's statistically true. Most, if given the full picture of ownership, wouldn't WANT your job. That counts for something...but what?

It's challenging to take a subjective, conceptual factor like 'risk' and apply it objectively; to create a value to be entered into a spreadsheet for calculating wages. I'll share my model. While, at first, it appears that the percentages are slightly higher for the business than for the Coach, the value of 'risk' – a very, very conservative estimate – tips the scales.

THE PERCENTAGE-BASED PAYROLL

If we consider the Trainer/Coach and the business as equal partners in the endeavour (the business gets the clients, tracks their account, schedules them, delivers them to the Coach; the Coach delivers the business' programming via their own expertise) we're still missing something. There are really THREE parts involved: The Coach, the Business, and the Cost.

In most situations, the Business carries costs associated with employing a Coach. Insurance, payroll, software, lights, phone...while the Coach bears no responsibility for expenses. If pay per session is an even split, the Business is on the losing end, because all expenses are deducted from the Business side. 50/50 can quickly become 50/20/30, where Coach/Business/Costs are split apart. Without even considering the value of Risk, as mentioned above, the Business is at a distinct disadvantage.

It's very tempting, given the above rate of loss, for the business owner to take as many classes, clients, and groups as possible herself. This costs the Coach money, ties up the Entrepreneur's time, and increases the Business' dependency on the owner's presence. It's not a good model because it's not sustainable in the long run.

If we consider the third part of the equation – Cost of Service – as an equal part of the pay breakdown, the equation changes. What was once divisible by two – *this is my part, this is your part* – must now be broken into three parts...at least. That middle part – Cost of Service – is where the Coach and the Business meet. Within that third of revenue is where negotiation occurs.

Setting aside 1/3 of Training revenue for the Coach, and 1/3 for the business, a $60 Personal Training session looks like this:

- $20 – Coach
- $20 – Business
- $20 – Cost of Service.

A CrossFit Group, based on attendance over the week, looks like this:

60 Attendees for the Coach's Group, at $10 per visit = $600

1/3 for the Coach: $200

1/3 for the Business: $200

1/3 for Cost of Service: $200

Did it cost $200 to have the Coach onsite last week? It may well have. In our calculations, though, it's more like $130 per week (or about 2/9 of total revenue.)

To make the math simpler, let's break everything into ninths.

Coach – 3/9 of Revenue

Business – 3/9 of Revenue

Cost of Service – 3/9 of Revenue

Of the Cost of Service portion, if 2/9 of Revenue is the actual cost of keeping the Trainer onsite, then 1/9 is still free. We allocate that to the Trainer / Coach. In effect, our breakdown looks like this:

Coach – 4/9 of Revenue

Business – 3/9 of Revenue

Cost of Service – 2/9 of Revenue

Considering only the Coach's share (4/9), it would appear that the Business – who created the opportunity through risk and business infrastructure – takes a larger share than the Coach does. However, considering all costs, the Coach actually makes the largest share of gross revenue.

This 'middle third' is negotiable, of course. If the Coach is covering his own insurance, paying for his uniforms, subtracting VISA and Debit terminal fees for the transactions of his clients, and sharing in fees for your scheduling/billing software, it may be viable to increase their share of gross revenue to 5/9.

In some cases, where the Trainer /Coach takes on responsibility beyond normal Coaching duties, such as oversight of other Coaches, we've increased their percentage to 5/9 of gross revenue per session. In one example, a Coach took over Head Coaching duties and made the jump to 5/9. This could be done in other ways, too, including a dollar or two made per training session performed by other Coaches.

A typical subcontractor enters our business at 4/9 of gross revenue. Long-term staff cost less than speciality staff, who require more time, can't do their own checkout and billing, and may require speciality equipment. We've NEVER had a disagreement at 4/9 of gross revenue after a discussion on Cost of Service.

OTHER WAYS TO SPLIT RISK

The class Coach can earn money in several ways.

First, they can be paid per head – they make $5, for example, per attendee. This is a nice model for the Business Owner, because it encourages staff to boost attendance at their classes.

Second, they can be paid per class - $25 flat rate, for example. This is nice for the staff, because it's a guaranteed wage regardless of attendance.

The differentiating factor: who's willing to shoulder the risk of a low-attendance class? The risk-reward equation can fall to the Owner, if the Coach requires more stability. On the other hand, an enterprising Coach can build themselves a great income.

Key to this understanding is a solid contract, with expectations laid out in advance. Bad feelings over pay levels can be avoided when this discussion takes place at contract negotiation. The two main complaints of Coaches who leave, when discussing their pay, are:

"I was only making $5 or $10 per hour!" - their attendance was too low, or

"I was bringing in all these people, and still only making $25, no matter how many showed up!" - their attendance was high, but they were being paid the 'safe' method.

While I advocate for allowing the staff to choose which method they prefer in advance, I also encourage the business owner to set a solid time frame for renegotiation.

If, for example, the new Coach chooses $25 per class, come what may, write a six-month contract, and ask them to abide by that rate for the duration. At that point, you may want to negotiate a per-head rate, if their attendance is low. Conversely, if their attendance is high, they may want to move to a per-head rate after the six-month mark.

The only mistake you can make, when negotiating rates per class, is to allow one side to flip-flop from one model to the other depending on what's best for either the Coach or the Business. "$25 per class, or $5 per head, whichever is higher" is unfair to the Business; "$5 per head to a $25 cap per class" is unfair to the Coach. Whoever bears the greater risk deserves the greater reward.

PAYING YOURSELF

The question: *"How much should the Affiliate owner make every year?"* comes up regularly on the Affiliate-owner discussion Board. Usually, the advice given is to pick a number (*"How much do you WANT to earn?"*) and work backward when setting up your fee structure (*"How many members, paying X, will I need to pay myself Y?"*)

I don't disagree with this method, but I don't fully agree either. While the test will help the new Affiliate draw up a framework for her business and pricing, and helps with goal-setting and revenue objectives, most people undervalue what they're worth. They think, "what SHOULD I make?" instead of, "what do I WANT?"

Since most are coming from a Personal Training background, where top earners average around $40-50,000 per year, they lop another $10,000 on top for their bank risk and shoot for that number. These folks are, in the words of Michael Gerber, "buying themselves a job."

On the other hand:

Last weekend, I was sitting on my back deck, which I built

with rough cedar that had been discarded by a local mill. I'd been working extra hours all week (a 5am start, instead of my normal 6am) to paint the new space we've added to our Box. My kids were towelling off after dipping in our new pool (a T-frame, it's inexpensive, but big, level, and I work hard to keep it crystal clear for them.) I was drinking beer and barbecuing. In the field next to our yard, the kids' grandpa was cutting hay, and I could smell it when the wind changed direction. My wife had just finished her run through the Valley where we live; I had done the day's workout with a few friends before I left work; my kids had ripped up their Rumble/Tumble group at the Box that morning.

I was thinking, "By God, we're billionaires!" Your pay is more than your cheque.

That said, your wage should grow continuously with your Box.

WAGE VS. PROFIT

Many new businesspeople see the revenue-expenses=profit equation and think, *"There will be lots left over! I'll just take the profits, and as they grow, my income will increase."*

There are several reasons why it's better to just pay yourself a wage.

1. You need to eat. An unfed, exhausted coach doesn't help anyone.

2. Expenses, at home AND at work, expand to fill the space allowed.

3. You can't survive on a variable income for the rest of your life. You'll never sleep.

4. The business is there to serve YOU...not the other way around.

Especially at first, when most financial experts would advise you to pay down your loans, save 3 months' worth of expenses...*I'm* telling you, pay yourself. Your loan rates, at time of writing, will never be lower than they are now. Your business MUST pay you a wage, right from startup, or you'll always find a reason to NOT pay yourself. It will be tempting, over time, to view yourself as the greatest expense in your business. *"If I didn't have to take a cheque this week, we could pay off all of our credit card debt!"* is going to cross your mind. You MUST be paid, every week without fail, or risk losing context on the business. You're a Coach because you love fitness, and CrossFit; you're a business owner because you love your family. Get paid.

At first, it will be tough to validate paying yourself (and your partners) anything, especially when cash flow is negative. Even if it's $20 per week, though, write the cheque. It's MUCH easier to increase a payment than it is to start a new expense stream. There will always be a reason to put self-payment off for another week. You must pay yourself.

Using the cash flow forecaster tool (free at 321GoProject.com,) plan regular wage increases for yourself. It's much easier to write another $100 into your cheque each week than to write $400 on top at the end of the month, so break it up as small as you like. If you don't plan for increases, and forecast expenses to match, they simply won't happen. You'll tread water forever.

Planning wage increases for the Owner also serves to stimulate growth. If your expenses are going up $400 per month beginning in September – no matter WHAT the cause – you'll scurry to sell more memberships, packages.... you'll rise to the occasion. You'll make ends meet. Why wait until another expense is thrust upon you? Plan for personal improvement as a salary, and forget the 'profit' line.

INCREASING 'NET' WITHOUT INCREASING 'GROSS'

PAY

If you're like me, you want to pay fewer taxes. Entrepreneurs routinely pay up to 50% of all the new revenue they generate – revenue that wouldn't EXIST without their risk, intellectual capital, and investment – to the government.

We're taxed on our staff wages. We're taxed on profit, and THEN taxed on our pay, taken out of the leftovers. Before we show a profit, we're taxed on property, consumables...and asked to collect sales taxes on their behalf. If, at times, it feels like you're just a tax-collection machine for the government, you're not alone.

For this reason, we urge gym owners to Incorporate their businesses. Though rules differ around the world, there are benefits to business owners, not the least of which is the choice of WHEN to pay taxes – before, or after expenses. In exchange for a bit more knowledge about your business, and a more formal tax return, you'll be able to use expenses as leverage against revenues.

Talk to your accountant for more information. It's important. Here's a simple chart to illustrate the difference:

Revenue -	$100	Revenue -	$100
Tax – 25%	$25	Gas,other eligible expenses -	$18
Net after tax -	$75	Net before tax -	$82
Gas, other	$18	Tax – 25%	$20.50
NET TOTAL	$57	NET TOTAL	$61.60

Difference: $4.50 per $100. $45 on every $1000. $4500 on every $100,000 – and there's FAR more than just those expenses available as deductions.

This is as far as I can advocate on this particular issue, for obvious legal reasons. However, talk to your accountant about the legal ramifications of incorporating.

TAKING IN NEW CLIENTS

You're probably ready to start reading about how to GET new clients. The #1 question of most gyms is always: "How do I get more clients?" Before we get there, I think it serves us well to consider how we'll KEEP those new clients. That way, when they arrive, their place will already be set and waiting for them.

The psychology of a new client – be they new to exercise, or CrossFit, or just your gym – is predictable. Human beings share commonalities, and that's incredibly helpful for building communities. In a tribal setting, humans were finely attuned to similarities and differences between themselves and others. Awareness of these habits and feelings can help us retain our members. Here's where they're coming from:

Functional fixedness is the inability to see a use for a common object other than the most 'traditional' use. An example, stolen from Wikipedia: if someone needs a paperweight, but they only have a hammer, they may not see how the hammer can be used as a paperweight. This inability to see a hammer's use as anything other than pounding nails, is functional fixedness. The person couldn't think of how to use the hammer in a way other than its traditional function.

If you offer 'open' gym hours to non-CrossFitters (as we do,) or you see a lot of walk-in traffic without CrossFit knowledge, you're going to be asked, *"where are all the machines?"* At this point, you'd better have your elevator pitch ready....and some groundwork to back you up.

Their perception of CrossFit is less important than their impression of the social atmosphere. At first visit, your main concern is to make someone feel welcome and unchallenged by the tribe.

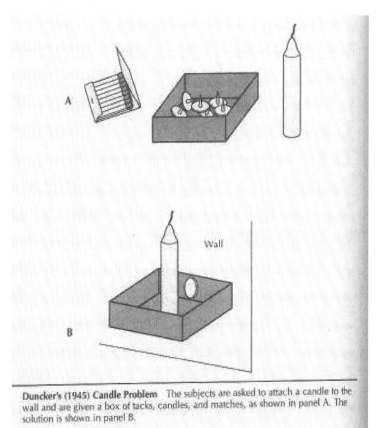

Duncker's (1945) Candle Problem   The subjects are asked to attach a candle to the wall and are given a box of tacks, candles, and matches, as shown in panel A. The solution is shown in panel B.

But first, a delicious example of functional fixedness: Carl Duncker's Candle Problem, from 1945.

In a classic experiment demonstrating functional fixedness, Duncker (1945) gave participants a candle, a box of thumbtacks, and a book of matches, and asked them to attach the candle to the wall so that it did not drip onto the table below. Duncker found that participants tried to attach the candle directly to the wall with the tacks, or to glue it to the wall by melting it. Very few of them thought of using the inside of the box as a candle-holder and tacking this to the wall. In Duncker's terms the participants were "fixated" on the box's normal function of holding thumbtacks and could not re-conceptualize it in a manner that allowed them to solve the problem.

The problem for CrossFit Affiliates is that most people aren't just seeing a lot of empty space, but the equipment they do recognize is out of their familiar context.

At GloboGyms, squat racks are the domain of the do-ragged, tank-topped meatheads. Take a woman unaccustomed to venturing far from the treadmills, and plop her into a CrossFit box unexpectedly, and what does she see? MeatheadLand. Take a teenager from their high-school Pec Palace, and look through their eyes: those plywood rectangles must be for doing lunges on 'leg day.' Take a male bodybuilder who's interested in "cross-training" and show him the kettlebells, and you'll get, *"what muscle groups do THEY work?"*

OVERCOMING FEAR OF CHANGE

A few years ago, I lucked into Chip and Dan Heath's book, *"Made To Stick: Why Some Ideas Die and Others Thrive."* I loved it, and so when their new book, *"Switch: How to Change When Change Is Hard"* was released, I was eager to hear their newest message. They didn't disappoint.

One great story, from the guys who underlined the importance of telling stories: Genentech sells front-line treatments for cancer. They invented an asthma drug called Xolair; it worked very well, and had properties that worked better than anything else out there, but wasn't selling well. Xolair isn't an inhaler, or a pill. You only need one dose per month - but you have to get it through an IV drip at your doctor's office, and asthma docs weren't used to administering medication that way. *"Nurses didn't know how to handle it,"* says Heath in the book. The successful sales reps smoothed the elements on the path toward the solution: they held classes for nurses and helped people figure out how to submit their claims.

Amazon.com has a patent on one-click ordering for a reason. When people are ready to commit, you've got to be ready to accept them right away, or risk having them change their minds.

In Seth Godin's now-famous series of posts about the Lizard Brain, he makes it clear that it's easiest for anyone to remain the same; to protect the small sphere of competency they've already developed. Change is painful. Self-exposure is embarrassing. NOTHING about joining a gym, enrolling with a Personal Trainer, committing to your OnRamp program, or doing PVC thrusters is enjoyable. Unless, of course, you make it so.

Removing barriers to entry may require some time, but it's time well spent. Amazon's decision to develop one-click purchasing came after a year of tracking how many consumers filled their online cart, and then abandoned their site before paying. *"Your job,"* says Godin, *"is not to be creative. Your job is to ship."* How many clients make it to your door, and then abandon?

Some good ways to remove barriers to entry:

⚔ Offer online bookings. Just the act of avoiding human interaction for one more step down the path helps.

⚔ Make your online bookings require as few clicks as possible - there should be a direct link in your newsletter to the checkout screen for the program mentioned.

⚔ Teach your staff to take ACTION, not messages. If they're not aware of a program you're offering, that's your fault, and it's costing you money.

⚔ Continuously showcase others in the gym - not just the firebreathers - to reinforce community acceptance.

⅄ Introduce people every chance you get. I'm a classic over-introducer. Reinforce the net.

⅄ When introducing, mention an interesting accomplishment by each. Brag 'em up. For instance:

"This is Glen. He's got our members' snatch record. Plus, he looks like a Ken doll." Now they've got something to talk about. Bonus: Glen's a huge fan of our Fraternity Barbell Club, and he's quick to invite others to join, if you get their conversation onto the subject of weightlifting.

You don't need more exposure. You certainly don't need more advertising. What you need is to lessen the fear.

THE ANTIHEROES

What happens to the misfit? When the introvert, the thinker, the shy new client leave the gym, where do they go? Place an intelligent person inside a GloboGym, and they'll be understimulated. There's no thought required; no necessary gain in intelligence to keep going.

Place a real athlete in front of a mirror, and have them do biceps curls. The challenge is too undaunting. What's a concentration curl after you've landed a double backflip? Take a skateboarder and dress him up in that corporate spider silk, UnderArmour. Watch him squirm. Watch him leave BigFitness and never come back. Quitter.

What happens when these folks meet up? You create a new culture. The gymrat normal becomes the outcast. Suddenly, the posing isn't the norm. The sweat-soaked, tattooed, scrawny guy is at home, while the designer-label shake-eater feels left out.

It's hard to fit in. The same feelings of community that make us - the outliers - feel welcome can feel like a barrage of arrows to those familiar and comfortable in the GloboGym. It's not just a new experience; it's a different tribe, and they don't speak the language. They're no longer running for President; they're wondering about the possibility of cannibalism. Our religion is foreign and scary. CrossFit is the Black Candle to the bodybuilder.

The train of thought of most potential new clients is going fast in one direction, and has to be turned to another. You'll never turn it around quickly, though: you'll need more than one turn.

First, when asked, you've got to be ready with an answer that's simple, 'sticky,' and friendly. Something that starts the train moving to the left.... just a little bit.

Something like, *"We can combine your strength training AND your cardio work if we choose exercises that use all of your body at once."* Nothing about anaerobic training or anything complex - yet. Use words and phrases that are familiar to the visitor ("strength training," "cardio.")

Second, you need some reinforcers. We use a brochure, just so we have something to put in their hand. The brochure can contain more complex information...but not too much more. You can introduce the concept of anaerobic training; you can give other references (like crossfit.com, or the Journal) and you can give some testimonials. The job of the brochure is just to further arouse interest. Move the train from North to Northwest.

This quote, by Mikki Martin of CrossFit Kids, has always been a favourite: *"We don't have a lot of machines. What we DO have is a gym full of knowledge, and world-class coaching."* We use the explanation, *"We change the gym every day to match your workout. The facility conforms to the exerciser, not the other way around."* Or something similar.

Third, you need deeper explanation available to the newbie without you as a middleman. Reinforcement works best if it comes from a third source; it's more likely to be internalized. If you're the only source of information, you're more questionable. If the rookie can find a TON of information on CrossFit.com (which she can!) you're much farther ahead. This process may take 24 hours, or it may take months, but this is where the train really starts heading West.

Example: We provide exercise videos on our site - both extreme examples, and basic barbell movements, demonstrated by 'average' folks. We also provide links, in our brochures and on our site, to other CrossFit sites we admire. We're demonstrating that we're not alone here.

Finally, you need a program like OnRamp to provide experience in the exercises most commonly used by CrossFit. Participants in our OnRamp program stick with CrossFit much longer, show up more often, and progress far more rapidly. They're also huge advocates of the program. Their train is headed West, young man, at full steam.

One more interesting note: in 2000, the German researcher Defeyter found that 5-year-olds show no signs of functional fixedness, because they have less experience with the use of various objects. They're not stuck in the 'traditional use, ' because they're not familiar with tradition.

EXTREME PERSUASION

There are 5 elements of persuasion that, when put together, are nearly irresistible. The author of "*Flipnosis: The Art of Split-Second Persuasion*," Dr. Kevin Dutton, created the SPICE acronym to help us remember:

  1. Simplicity:
Most of the brain's processes are automatic. That means that we 'skim' information and put together puzzles with many pieces missing; we 'infer' the missing pieces based on our perception of the big picture. We automatically fill the

'gaps,' as discussed above. This is partially why so many fender-benders occur so close to home: the driver looks in their rearview mirror at the same street they've seen a thousand times. The brain 'inserts' a picture of the empty street, even if the driver doesn't actually see the street; the car behind him becomes invisible.

For our sake, the take-home lesson: keep your message as simple as possible, so there are no gaps to be filled with the wrong information.

2. Perceived Self-Interest

People decide what's important for themselves based on what similar people are doing. Of course, "similar" is determined by the individual, NOT by their coach or teacher. An example: a Beijing study showed that adding the phrase, *"Our Most Popular Dish"* to any item on the menu would increase that item's sales by 20%. The closer the peers were related to the individual, the more likely the individual would take on the characteristics of the peer.

For us, this underlines the necessity of telling stories about the AVERAGE client, instead of just posting pictures of the genius students or athletic firebreathers. The more commonalities between the viewer and the subject, the more likely the viewer will be to take ownership of the same ideas. This is called, "social proof," and people tend to trust it more than data.

3. Incongruity

This is true of tonality of voice, "non-verbal communication," and typical cliches used in advertising. Cliches, as I've often complained, are dismissed by the brain and never permeate (partially for the reasons in #1, above.) When you're using cliches, the listener automatically "fills in" the gaps, "solving" the puzzle. And once the puzzle has been solved, it's discarded. It requires no further action and is thus not stored.

However, when we start with a familiar model, and allow people to infer what comes next....and then throw in an unexpected curve, we're demanding attention. Partially because of Lowenstein's Gap Theory, people can't stop themselves from watching until the end. Mozart was a master at this. But so was Vic Bloom, who wrote Archie comics.

In a book from my childhood, Bloom was talking about writing for comics, and he used this example over four frames: Souphead is skateboarding, and slips off. The skateboard continues down the street, unseen by Jughead, coming around the corner with a huge burger blocking his view. If you had to guess the next frame, you'd likely guess it would feature Jughead on the ground, covered in ketchup.... but Bloom's recommendation was to have the skateboard pass harmlessly between his legs. Start with the familiar, then throw a twist. In the final frame, Souphead, chasing his skateboard, rams into Jughead, and they're both splattered.

4.   Confidence

There's a difference between being *in* authority (you're the boss) and being *an* authority (you're a trusted expert, often removed from the immediate situation.) For us, this is why a client who reads our blog daily and finds information, delivered for free, to a large audience, is more likely to commit for the long term   than a client asking questions in our office. Any client who accepts you as an authority, instead of just the holder of their long-term contract, will be more likely to become a part of your gym family or Ignite Academy.

The old adage that 'a clipboard will get you anywhere,' is absolutely true. Speak with confidence, and you can talk your way into (or away from) anywhere.

5. Empathy

Empathy has more in common with similarity than sympathy. If you can demonstrate commonality (*"that workout killed me, too!"*) it's more effective than, "*good job! That   looked hard!*"

There IS no fixed 'sales' process that works: those who are most successful are the ones who can apply situational context to recommendations for services. For instance, *"Great time on that shuttle run! The only thing that helped me get better was getting some running coaching from Mike, last June."*

The SPICE model makes a lot of sense. Does commanding have any place within that model....or does it take away from the messages you're trying to deliver?

BRIGHT SPOTS

One of the major problems people have, when making changes or starting new habits, is that they focus too much on the negative. *"I'm fat. I'm out of shape. I have no willpower..."* we hear these all the time in the fitness practices. People perceive that they're starting to push a heavy car from a dead stop, and fail to acknowledge that, most of the time, the car is either already rolling or on a downhill slope. Chip and Dan Heath (*"Switch!"*) believe it's a mistake to start the goal-setting process from that negative point.

Instead, they recommend that the student identify Bright Spots first. Chances are, a new fitness client isn't doing EVERYTHING wrong; they're just doing the right things infrequently. Even if they're reading about exercise, but not acting on it, they're doing *something*. Your first job with a new student, or with yourself, is to identify a few Bright Spots in the past, and then try to isolate some small Bright Spots in the future.

Q: What are you doing right now that's working?
A: Be specific. *"Well, I'm walking the dog every day."* That's good. *"I'm trying hard"* isn't specific enough. *"I really WANT to this time!"* is too vague.

For a student: *"I'm reading my textbook on the bus ride home."* The bus ride may be too distracting, but the student has already formed a positive habit, at least.

Build on that first Bright Spot. *"OK, let's keep that going."*

Next, try to duplicate that Bright Spot. *"How do you feel while you're walking your dog? What do you think about? What do you enjoy about it? Where do you go? What do you enjoy seeing? What's the best part? Do you prefer to walk your dog at the end of the day, or in the morning? Do you enjoy seeing your dog have fun?"* Find out WHY. It's important to make an emotional connection, rather than just a logical one.

For a student: *"I read on the bus because I don't have time when I get home. The bus ride is boring. None of my friends are on the bus with me..."* Questions to ask: what part of reading on the bus do you enjoy – the pictures? The uninterrupted time?

THEN do goal-setting. Let's say that the fitness client would like to lose 10lbs. It would be nice if a client came in and said, *"I want to improve work capacity across broad time and modal domains."* That doesn't happen. So let's go with what's more likely.

Q: How will that goal make you feel when it's attained?

What made you choose that number, specifically? How do you think you'll look / feel / act?

You're getting the client to 'try on' the goal, and as anyone in retail knows, if they try it, they'll sell themselves on it. Practising success is as important as practising ping-pong. The phrase, *"fake it 'til you make it"* is relevant and effective when a student practices the art of winning.

One day, while riding the bus, you'll read the last page of the textbook. How will you feel then? Someday, you'll see something toward the end of the book, and relate it to something you read earlier. How will that feel? How will you know you've made a connection?

Q: What will be your first sign that you're succeeding? Let's say that you wake up tomorrow, and 10 pounds have melted off. What's the first thing you'll do that will be different? How will you come to realize that the weight is gone? What will change in your life? What will you have for breakfast on that day? How will you dress?

At this point, a coach is trying to establish their first milestone. Be specific. Don't accept, for instance, *"I'll know I'm succeeding when I get on the scale and two pounds are gone."* Instead, *"I'll know because I'll feel lighter when I wake up. I'll know because my husband/wife will comment that I look better. I'll know because my pyjamas feel loose."* THAT'S your first milestone : loose pyjamas drawstring. Write that down for them.

When they've achieved their first milestone, a coach can revisit the questions and establish their second. This short-circuits the three-month conversation you're likely to face if you don't break down the goal-setting process:

Client: *"I feel great. My clothes are loose. I'm stronger and more flexible and my back pain is gone. My wife can't keep*

*her hands off me. My hair is even coming in thicker! I
don't drink as much coffee, I'm more alert, I'm not
depressed. But I still haven't lost 10lbs!"* If you're like me,
this is one of the most aggravating conversations you can
have.

Student: *"I read the whole book! I figured out how
chemicals help move a molecule across a membrane. I got
an A in the class – my parents are jacked, and my
University application looks WAY better! But...I still don't
see how this is important to me..."*

The small goals, in this case, don't even have to be
objective. At the three-month checkup, you can go down
their list with them: has your spouse noticed a difference?
Are your clothes looser? Do you feel better when you wake
up? Check, check, check. Goal attained. On to the next.

Big problems aren't solved with big solutions, but with a
bunch of smaller steps. The magnitude of the solution
shouldn't try to match the size of the problem. If a new
client is 400lbs, they may believe that they require more
change than someone who weighs 200lbs. That's not true;
in fact, the opposite is true. It's easier to lose 50lbs if you're
400lbs than if you're 200lbs. You don't have to lose 200lbs,
but two pounds...a hundred times. Just keep focusing on
the two pounds.

It's common, if you're a teacher, to hear this distressing
sentence: *"I want to be a (insert scientist title here,) but I
need to take physics to get into the program, and I'm SO
BAD at math!"*

Now, we know that the real problem isn't the grades
necessary to get into the degree program at the University
of the student's choice. The real problem is that the student
is afraid of failure. In this case, the stakes are so high that

the fear is nearly paralysing.

Think about your fear of falling off the bottom step in a staircase: it's not terrifying. Yes, you may bruise your hands or knees, but that's the worst-case scenario. Now, pretend you're at the top of the staircase, and you fall down one stair. Much scarier? Of course: the magnitude of the fall hasn't changed, but the aftereffect changes the context. If you fall from the top stair, you're unlikely to stop until you reach the bottom. If you fail a physics test, you may not be able to recover your grade to a high enough level to be accepted into University. If you're not accepted, you'll have taken physics for nothing; wasted a semester of study; risked isolation from your social group by not graduating with them; risked your ego integrity by failing.

Later in this book, we'll talk about the practise paradigm and the growth mindset – two tools we use to short-circuit the paralysing fear of failure that's rampant in our educational culture.   Using Bright Spots, though, we can encourage the student to seek knowledge from the physics course, and use that knowledge to leverage career choices later on.

A SELF-FEEDING MODEL FOR SERVICE DIFFERENTIATION

The flow of a typical CrossFit intake process:

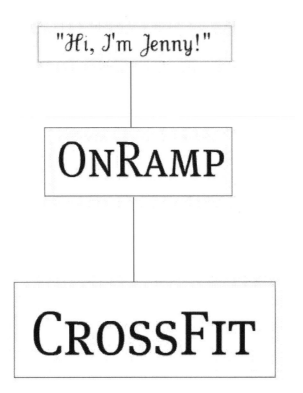

Good. Now, many people won't get bored with CrossFit. Some, though, will seek to improve particular skills, and won't want to wait for the day when 'Snatch' comes up in a workout. They've just bought Starting Strength, or an OLY book, and want to spend a few weeks perfecting THAT technique. Nothing wrong with that, right?

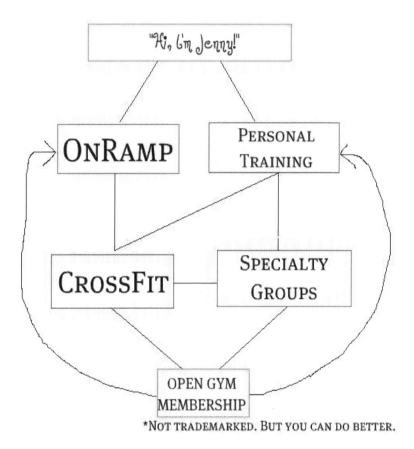

*NOT TRADEMARKED. BUT YOU CAN DO BETTER.

Better. In this model, they have a tiered option toward improvement: personal training, special-interest groups (for instance, our Barbell Bettys group, or Enduro) and open gym time to practice skills. Of note: not many skills are CREATED or DEVELOPED during open gym time, but practice - and failure, and play - are necessary in the pursuit of excellence.

DRAWING A MAP OF ALL OPTIONS

When I was fifteen, I was shipped - with a small group of other 'gifted' kids - to France and England for a whirlwind tour spanning a total of about 10 days. We were met at the airport by a guide; shown to our bus; dropped at our hotel; met by the guide in the morning; taken to lunch by the guide....for ten days. Our days were scripted down to the last statue, from the wakeup call to curfew. There were a few very short periods of exploration on our own, and of course, those are the times I recall best: getting served beer in a pub; following a monk through his island monastery; jumping to see over the sea of heads surrounding the Mona Lisa at the Louvre.

A few years later, I went to Australia for a month. Our vacation included a rental house and car...and no itinerary. We saw a bit of the coast, spent a day walking around Old Sydney Town, and checked off the typical Touristy things...but also spent many days watching television in our rental. Without a clear plan, we stagnated. Sure, we climbed the Blue Mountains, and had a few other highlights, but the time between those was....well, inefficient.

Though I didn't refer to it as such, you just read about the theory of Perpetual Motion: keeping people engaged by letting them specialize, prioritize, and play. The idea has one scary downside: it's not simple. There's no clear path through the garden, no recommended road. People are free to do anything: personal training, CrossFit, special groups for Olympic Lifting or Gymnastics or Running, or just play on their own. All of these things are fine - I'd argue they're necessary for long-term success.

This system could easily confuse people, if you're not careful. A map, and guides, are necessary because our Gym isn't simple. However, I believe it's better to catch people in a web than to send them up a rope.

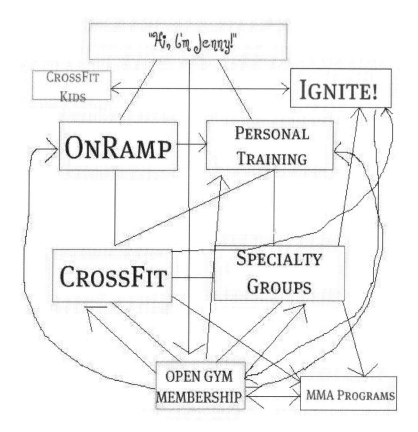

Our current model. Yes, it appears confusing, and for that reason we still have folks who choose the easiest (and cheapest) option: the Open Gym membership. Years ago, I believed that this was a negative tendency, and told them so. NOW I realize that, for new members, 'Open Gym' may be the safe option to keep them in the pool.

There's a tendency, in January, for newcomers to sign up. Their intentions (and motivation) are every bit as valid as your top firebreather's are. In GloboGyms, they shyly drift toward the treadmills and bikes to "scope things out" - and that's fine. For a first step, anyway: confidence doesn't come naturally to everyone.

First, new members go through OnRamp: the same introductory class as all our new CrossFitters. That lays the foundation for movement efficiency.

The CRITICAL step is what happens next: they can drift backward (quitting,) sideways (try the exercises they see others performing,) or forward (get some help.) We, in the CrossFit world, tend to view only the forward path; many forget that sideways movement, out of the mainstream programming, is important for improvement and engagement.

We advocate the creation of a New World: full of discovery, and ripe for exploration. Sure, the terrain may be confusing for newcomers - but you'll just have to draw a better map . Make the START easy, but allow them to wander....

THE PRIVATE ELEMENT

If there's one thing a potato farmer knows, it's this: diversify.

Potatoes are subject to disease, pestulence, and the frivolity of the weather. Not enough rain? They wither. Too much? Late blight. Fungus? All the Yukon Gold are susceptible.

There's a growing tendency among CrossFit Affiliates to limit their service offering. *"We don't want just anyone,"* they say. *"We want committed people only."* Leaving aside the argument that it's our job to *build* commitment, setting a pricing model around only one offering - the 1-month unlimited package - means missing out on potential revenue AND an opportunity to do the best thing for your clients.

Offering Personal Training at your Affiliate satisfies the 'premium' service problem. We'll expand on the need for a 'premium' offering later, in The Three Boxes.

Try as they might, some clients simply don't respond well in a group setting. They're too socially aware, maybe; they're too scared of making a mistake to take a risk, perhaps. They require much more attention than others. The best service you can give them is more of your time.

Offering Personal Training at your Affiliate means they can get the one-on-one time they need to get better.

The small-group-training model, popularized by strength coaches like Zach Evan-Esh, is a good one: given that you have limited time each day, it makes perfect sense to try and make the most revenue per hour spent. If every hour of your coaching time is filled, the only way to increase revenue is to encourage clients to train together. What if every hour is NOT filled?

Offering Personal Training at your Affiliate allows you to derive income at non-peak times.

CrossFit is for everyone: soccer moms to Navy SEALs. We scale by load, but not by type. One of the greatest services we can provide is the arena of sport to those for whom fitness has seemed inaccessible....until now. For some clients, though, modifications are SO great that they can't smoothly scale up or down on their own.

Offering Personal Training at your Affiliate means you can help those who don't fit the mold.

You have GREAT Coaches, I'm sure. They're educated. They WANT to help people, first and foremost. They also need to eat.

Offering Personal Training at your Affiliate means your Coaches can work as much (or as little) as they like, without fighting for class time. They can also take more ownership of their income, their clients' programming, and their time, by being responsible for a stable of private clients.

If it isn't raining in your market now, it eventually will be.

The all-or-nothing approach means that some of your best potential clients are being turned away at the porch. If your class schedule isn't completely filled, Personal Training offers a convenient way to sell your services....and do the right thing for many of your clients. Hey, it's how Glassman started....

MULTIPLE OPTIONS FOR MEMBERSHIP: BEYOND 'ONE-MONTH UNLIMITED'

When choosing your membership rates, you have two options:

1. Monthly unlimited

2. 2x/week unlimited.

Right?

The trouble with the 'monthly unlimited' model is that revenue growth can only be accomplished through a larger head count. As membership increases, so must space and equipment, decreasing net client value and increasing exposure to risk.

As the fitness industry becomes commodotized, and gym access moves closer to free, some gym owners are looking for another way. I offer these as examples of OTHER models, currently being used by CrossFit Affiliates successfully. Some are amazing; some are incomplete. Some are experimental. Some are risky. Some will provide a more enriching model than the one most Boxes are currently implementing; some will not.

3. The lower-priced 'base membership' with optional premium services. Yes, you can run your CrossFit gym on a base gym membership, and charge per CrossFit class. In 2008, many Affiliates were following this model, and some of the older Boxes have reverted to this method. It's generally assumed that every member will seek coaching

eventually, in some way, shape or form. The client paying the base membership fee may or may not cover the costs of running the Box, but they form the community of potential coaching clients, who pay a small premium for individual attention. Taken alone, the gym membership base may not support the gym on their own; the membership exists as a potential client pool for premium services.

4. Ad-supported content. Don't scoff. Just like newspapers and many other 'free' distribution models, ad-supported content is hitting the fitness industry hard. There are obvious examples in the CrossFit world: Reebok subsidizes the costs of some newer Affiliates for top-level Coaches; they can provide custom shirts with your logo (and theirs) for less than you'd pay elsewhere. Supplement companies are quick to cut the owners a deal in return for promotion.

Some gyms take it to another level, selling ad space on the walls above the televisions. This sounds crooked, but can be done tastefully, with ads that are relevant to your target audience and make life easier. Google's argument is that the ads it sells are a boon to its clientele, because they're relevant to the reader's interests and simplify the search process. If a local chiropractor, whose son was in your CrossFit Kids program, offered you $100 per year to post his name and phone number on your wall, would you object? These revenues are a substitute for membership fees, which can then be decreased to achieve the same net revenue. It also encourages your clients to seek outside help for mobility/pre-injury issues before they occur.

5. Externally-funded /supported services. These can mean a government subsidy for providing the service, a break on rent from a landlord who sees potential crossover revenue, or a breakeven 'side' business that will provide clientele for a larger one (a CrossFit Box attached to a chiropractor's office.) Sometimes, these are done out of love: *"I don't care if I make any money at this, I just want to give people the*

gift of health."

At the other end of the spectrum, non-CrossFit Affiliates are trying to manipulate the system. Some gyms, providing a base membership fee, will begin to provide free CrossFit knock-offs - Cross-TRX, anyone? - to their members. *"I already do CrossFit at MY gym....."* will become your obstacle in the next 3 years. As I wrote in 2011, our challenge has gone from, *"What's CrossFit?"* to, *"I already do that, but my gym calls it something else."*

6. 90/10 - 90% of clients pay for the 10% who can't. There exist at least five Affiliates, to my knowledge, where underprivileged youth attend for free, and their membership is covered by a portion of fees from others.

In one sub-example, youth are provided the opportunity to pay for their own membership through the design and print of t-shirts for members and nonmembers alike. In another, members' fees cover a given amount of 'scholarships' for kids who can't afford to pay.

There are other models, of course. Some operate their Box at a loss, and make up the difference doing expert courses and coaching, maintaining their gym as a 'home base' from which to practice and publish. This is more common than you'd think, and here's why: would you buy a book on powerlifting from someone who didn't run a powerlifting gym? Would you buy a Reverse Hyperextension from him? Would you buy a prowler from someone who had never trained an athlete? A runner who didn't train other runners? A physiotherapist without a clinic? When the majority of their revenue comes from outside their immediate circle, it doesn't matter how the gym makes money; it's enough that the gym exists, even as an expense within the overall business model.

I have spoken with clients of the 321GoProject who operate under each of these models, and my own Affiliate uses one of the above (not the large-fee monthly "CrossFit Standard.")

Some gyms, of course, do very well with the monthly fee. If you're looking for something different, though, the world is your oyster. There's more than one way to run this show, and if you're within a market saturated by other gyms, you can help clients by offering something different.

How to choose? Do what you believe is best for the client. As a result of our Ignite research, we believe very strongly in the value of practice - play, if you will - and so offer Open Gym for MANY hours, every day. You may prefer to cast your shadow of influence over a client every time they visit your Box.

While it's important to understand that there are more options open to gyms than the standard, it's equally important to make these options simple for your members. Rather than offering ALL of the above, choose up to  three, and offer those. In our case, we sell CrossFit, Personal Training, and Open Gym in a tiered system by price.

Personal Training can be a big part of a gym's revenue

stream. The industry has been aware of this for decades. For a CrossFit gym, where pricing attempts to bridge the gap between high-priced personal attention and low-priced group classes, simply having PT prices listed can serve to frame the CrossFit rates.

20 years ago, when you were standing in line to buy a Coke at the movie box office, you had two choices: large, or small. Most people - around 80% - bought the small. Then, someone enterprising introduced small, regular (the old large), and super-sized. Now, 20% bought super-sized, 60% regular and 20% small. The super-sized buy-in was actually a surprise; no one expected buyers to drink anything that big. It was just there to add a 'bookend' effect to the large size.

If you only have one choice, then it's a choice between "yes," or "no." Nothing else to think about, so the buyer focuses on price. With two choices, they'll usually take the small because, (a) they'll save money, (b) they're playing it safe (if they don't like the flavour, they haven't wasted all that soda and money.)

With three choices, you – the buyer - start at the large because it's dazzling, beautiful and huge, but perhaps too expensive. Then you consider the small, but it looks puny next to the large - it appears cheap and unappealing. So, the middle is juuuust right (and a safe bet).

Now, the super-sized was created just to sell more regulars, so when you do sell it, that's a bonus. You can also charge more for your regular because the super-sized is so much more. For example, if a super-sized cost $10, and the old-large was $5, well in the new system you could easily sell the regular (the old-large) at $7.50.

When you offer 3 choices, it's not about charging too much. It's about giving the customer choice - and marketing is about choice. But, 4 or more choices is bad. It starts to get confusing (it is easy not to decide if there are too many choices to make; to be paralyzed by indecision) and there's no clear middle option (don't forget, people like "safe.")

When I was selling treadmills, we carried three lines: Bodyguards for $2500 and up(made in Canada, very expensive, feature-laden but not clearly better,) Visions for $1400-2100 (well-made, higher price than a department-store model, easy to assemble and deliver, stuck to the basics and did them well) and Horizons from $900-1700 (department-store quality that benefited from being on the same floor as Vision and Bodyguard.) We'd start people at Bodyguard; they'd look at the price tag and move on. Then we'd put them on a Vision. They usually loved it. They'd look at a Horizon just to check, and come right back to the Vision. We were selling 8 Visions to every single Bodyguard or Horizon (8-1-1.) On a week when the Bodyguards were taken off the floor, though, the Visions and Horizons sold equally (5-5.) This WORKS.

In CrossFit, you have a good chance to fill your OnRamp program, or your coached groups, if you offer private, one-on-one training. Using our model as an example (we also have a membership-based gym in our Box), if you frame your offerings this way:

1. Open Gym Membership ($50)

2. CrossFit Group Membership ($185 per month)

3. Private, 1-on-1 PT ($320 per month for 8 x 40-minute sessions)

...most will pick CrossFit. Good coaching, WODs that aren't tailored to the individual, but good attention in a tight group. Alternately, if your Box setup is more traditional:

1. Basic Unlimited ($250/mo)

2. Per Visit ($20, guaranteed fewer than 5/group)

3. Private 1-on-1. Training.

It's important to note that all prices are put into the same time context (monthly) rather than asking clients to compare prices per month to prices per session. It's too much math. Choose the time context of the service you prefer to sell, and base other prices around the same, even if you have to describe averages. In other words, you can still charge per session for PT, but post an average price per month when comparing to CrossFit classes.

...you may not sell more Personal Training (you probably will!) but you'll definitely sell more small-group sessions.

For more excellent advice, get *"How To Sell A Lobster"* by Bill Bishop.

TOO MUCH CHOICE

I read a lot of psychology and sociology research. My purpose is to get to the underlying rationale behind the business plans, marketing, and even programming. If we can, we want to help everyone in the world, and that means increasing our appeal. We'd also like to do the best job we can when we do have a person's attention.

While the perception of choice is critical for asking consumers to commit, too much choice - or a lack of clear choices - is paralyzing.

"The Art of Choosing," a great book from Sheena Iyengar, is a more in-depth look at the surprisingly limiting effect of having too much choice. To prevent overload, the brain will often take the path of least resistance - the one with the fewest choices, or even no choice at all.

Given one or two choices, a prospect doesn't have much

trouble. But give them five or six, and the most attractive option may be: *I'll come back later, when I have more time to consider all the options.* Rarely is the choice to NOT choose overt; they may actually believe they'll be back at some future date. We know better, though, don't we?

It seems to be the sum of choices that matter most. For example, a newcomer may only see two choices on your site:

1. OnRamp

2. Personal Training.

However, if they encounter more choices downstream, the effect may be the same. In other words, it doesn't matter where in the buy-in process the choices can be overwhelming; what matters is that you set a path as early as possible, and keep them on it.

Good example:

1. OnRamp (click!) - Next OnRamp Class is MWF at 8am. Click HERE to sign up!

2. Personal Training (click!) - Meet with a Trainer for Free! Click here for a FREE consultation!

Bad example :

1. OnRamp (click!) - For more information about OnRamp, click here. Three Classes available - Beginner, Intermediate, or Advanced! Click an option for more!

 - Intermediate (click!) - How to tell if you're intermediate: click here. Read about our testing process: click here. Intermediate groups run at 8am, noon, 3pm, and 7pm. Need to mix and match classes? Email us here.

2. Personal Training (click!) - Benefits of Personal Training: click here. Most people start with private sessions. Book a free private consultation here! Want nutritional advice, too? Click here! For prices, click here. Save money with

packages! How many sessions do you need to start CrossFit? Click here!

...it's so boring, you can barely read it! How does a newbie feel on your site?

Remember: three options at a time, and a maximum of three levels of choice. This increases your service offering by the power of 3, but only has your clients making simple decisions.

Tier #1 Options: Personal Training – CrossFit – Open Gym Membership (select one. Let's use 'CrossFit' as our example.)

Tier #2 Options (CrossFit): OnRamp – Punch Card – Unlimited Visits (select one. Let's use 'Unlimited' as our example.)

Tier #3 Options (Unlimited): Single $185 – Partners $299 – Family $380

In this example, we've guided the client toward a decision by breaking the options into threes, and offering no more than three levels of qualifiers. We could break the 'qualifiers' down into these questions:

Tier #1: What level of service (coaching) would you like? 1-on-1, group, or none?

Tier #2: How much time can you commit? Short-term, a few times per week, or a lot?

Tier #3: Are you coming alone? When?

There may be dozens of other choices available to your clients. Don't present more than three options at a time, and structure your tiered system to lead them toward a simple decision.

Dorothy, for example, didn't like The South Beach Diet. She found The Atkins Diet too questionable. She dropped out of WeightWatchers twice...but thinks she could do it after

January.

This is my third 'Free Consultation' with Dorothy. The first time, I had to break off for another client after 90 minutes; the second time, she met with another Trainer, but wasn't satisfied; this time, frustrated, I was determined to get her started on something.

"So," she said, *"I think I might do OnRamp. But is everyone as out-of-shape as I am?"* I spent ten minutes reassuring her that everyone in OnRamp was reborn as a newbie on Day #1. I extolled Coach Whit's ability to smilingly deliver you right to the very Gates of Hell, and then casually bring you back to life the next day.

"Oh." Then: *"Does Whit do Personal Training? I didn't see that on your site."* Uh-oh. Ten more minutes on the value of Personal Training.....

"Whitney seems really, really strong. Isn't she scared of gaining a lot of muscle?" Aaaack! Backtracking into biochemistry....

"I'm premenopausal, though. My doctor says my metabolism is really low, and I should try being a vegetarian." Falling! Falling onto philosophy!

"Well, you've certainly given me a lot to think about." Downed for a 10-yard loss. Sigh.

It isn't Dorothy's fault. The problem, as I now understand it, was that I gave her too much choice.

People believe they want more choice. But when confronted with choice, they're paralyzed. The example of selling jam, in an earlier section, is one illustration. Another terrific example, mentioned by Derek Sivers in a post on the same subject:

Surgeon Atal Gawande surveyed patients, and 65% said that if they got cancer, they'd like to choose their own treatment. But among people given the same survey who really DID have cancer, only 12% wanted to choose their own treatment. People don't trust their own judgement, be the decision over chemotherapy or table jam.

Your solution: the Three Boxes. Iyengar goes so far as to recommend that if your depth of choice is too large, you're better to organize in a hierarchy of three (she even calls it 3x3, as if it were written in a strength training program!)

This is important, so let's run through the example in a different way:

Level #1: choose between Personal Training, CrossFit, or Other Group.

Sample questions: Do you require individual attention? Do you prefer privacy, or a group? Do you have specific weak links that you can identify that need to be addressed?

If the answer is yes to individual attention and privacy, PT is the obvious answer. Stick with it. If cost is a concern, though, or if they'd relish the chance to participate with others, CrossFit is more appealing.

Now give the client three choices under the CrossFit category:

Level #2: OnRamp, Full Immersion, or Free Trial?

Do you need to see if you like it first? Would you like to be guided, step-by-step, up the exercise hierarchy? Do you think you're ready to jump right in?

*note: you and I both know that no one's ever ready to 'jump right in,' but most think they are. This third option is like choosing "Jalapeno Tango" as one of the jam flavours in the study - it's going to appeal to someone, even if it's not the best answer.

Level #3: Right now, tomorrow, or the next day?

OnRamp starts on Monday. Are you ready to start right away? Next month? January?

Dorothy is still floating around, looking for the 'perfect' plan. There isn't one. And I'm partially responsible: by letting her become paralyzed by choice, she hasn't gained any ground in six months.

PRICING, DISCOUNTS, AND SALES

If you charge Bob a lower rate than Phil, for any reason, Phil's going to find out about it. And when he does, he'll either:

1. Leave, or

2. Wait until he can get Bob's rate before renewing.

If you drop your rate, ever, even temporarily, for any reason, that's your new rate. You've gone there once; it stands to reason that you'll do so again. I'll wait until that happens, thanks, instead of missing a deal. And I'll resent you until it *does* happen.

We'd been in business one month when ███ opened. This is a small town; ███ had a good location, hundreds of thousands of dollars behind it, amazing networking (it was owned by a local surgeon's wife,) an attractive layout, and a decent manager. Their video-game bikes were featured in *Maclean's* (a national Canadian newsmagazine) as the 'wave of the future' for kids' exercise programming, complete with a picture of the local facility and quotes from the owner.

We had a shareholder's loan for $16,000, a renovated office space (our floors were carpeted, and we painted over the grey wallpaper) and we probably stunk of desperation.

Twelve months later, the owners of ███ asked us to buy them out. We agreed to meet.

I grabbed my shareholders (I had two others back then,) and we paid a preemptive visit to the other gym. At first glance, it was formidable: small, but very neat and clean; brand-new machinery, and lots of it; a private 'Personal

Training' space full of bright balls and balance boards.

But it quickly became obvious where the problems lay. First, there was no way to pick a staff member out of the throng: no one was in uniform. We waited almost 5 minutes before anyone greeted us, though we were surely noticed when we came in. We didn't identify ourselves as potential owners, just as potential members. We got the 'tour.' We got the 'pitch.' And then I asked how many members the gym had. "A hundred and twentyish." Was the response from the Assistant Manager.

When I paid a solo visit the next day, and asked the same question, the answer was much different: "A hundred and seventy-one," the Manager said, confidently.

The next evening, the "night" desk person reported grimly, "about ninety."

As it turned out, they had no idea how many members they had. Their tracking system was nonexistent. Worse, they had no regular contact with their members. No one was checking cards. No one was talking to anyone. No one could even tell us who was paying what rate for membership, since some had joined at the 'old' $40/month rate, some had joined at various "sale" rates, and some were paying full ticket - over $60/month! The best part: if I had to renew, and didn't remember what I'd paid last time, the staff couldn't tell me, either! Imagine paying $60/month for a year, and then finding out that you could have been paying $40 all along....

You're unlikely to find this level of incompetence in your competitors. More than likely, they're looking for you to make simple mistakes like this one. We passed on the deal. The gym closed its doors, paid its debts (over $300,000, according to their books) and the owners moved to ███ for six months.

Never, ever, ever drop your rate. Ever. If you absolutely

must, throw in other things for free. Make sure you advertise the actual value of the 'free' stuff (don't undervalue it either.)

For instance: instead of offering 10% off membership, throw in a free Personal Training session ($55 Value!) for new signups. You maintain your rate, give greater value to your deal, and preserve the value of the "bonus" at the same time.

In one of the very first posts I wrote on DontBuyAds.com, I urged readers to know their rates, and stick to them.

This was a lesson learned the hard way by a former employer, who runs a small network of fitness equipment 'superstores.' In my first month as her manager, I was struggling to sell ANYTHING, and asked when we'd be having a 'sale.' She fired back, in her typical machine-gun style:

"Chris, you never, ever, ever cut your rate. You drop your price once, you can't ever come back from it. What's Bill gonna say when Ted gets 10 percent off? I want 10 percent off, too! You drop your rate 10 percent for one guy, you do it for everyone. Now quit drinking free coffee and reading T-Nation, and get back on the sales floor!"

That was a decade ago. Last week, she offered to sell me the local store. I drove past their new location during my 5am commute.....and saw windows full of *'SALE! SALE! SALE!'* signs. I saw a dozen different brands, instead of the three flagships we bragged upon back then.

And then...another example from our own Box. Lately, we've been packed with sports teams, from whom we require a minimum 10-week commitment. We've been after one special girls' hockey team for three years; though we train the age group younger than this team, and the age group older, the team of our desire has been 'training' every winter at a local boxing club.

This year, their coach offered us an opportunity - again - to quote for their business. Throwing it to the wind, I said, *"Look, Mark, we really want your team in here. Tell me what you're paying elsewhere, and I'll try to beat it."* The rate was ridiculously low ($150/month for a group training session every week.) Can we do it for less? Yes. After all, the lights in the gym are already on; the staff is already there; the insurance is already paid.

BUT. It's unconscionable to undercut every other team. Pretend, for a moment, that there's not a single parent with daughters on two teams; that there's no conversation between coaches and players of *this* team and *that* team; that we're not a town with one degree of separation. Pretend no one would ever find out. It would *still* be wrong. If we're providing Sally training for $8 per session with her team of 17 others, and Megan will pay $4, is it wrong to take Megan's $4? You bet it is. It's robbing Sally.

We don't operate on a 'pay-what-you-think-it's-worth' model. We sell a professional service, that costs money. We can't control what they're selling.

WHY WE RUN OPEN GYM
Most CrossFit boxes don't offer a membership option; members just pay per class.

Besides the obvious cash boost on the first of the month, a membership option helps:

> ⅄ Build the community. Interaction outside the group format is important, too.

> ⅄ Make time to practice skills without running on the group's schedule, or at their pace.

> ⅄ Members to bring friends to 'try' the gym more discreetly.

> ⅄ Members expose themselves to foreign activities,

like Strongman, that are happening while they're in the gym

⚔ Members prepare for events

⚔ Members do their 'homework' from your Trainers and Groups

⚔ Members meet new people. Folks walk in all the time. I like to talk to them.

⚔ Crossover athletes into the CrossFit fold. For instance, most football players here didn't do CrossFit Football WODs when they started; now, they all do.

⚔ Expose beginners to the more advanced.

⚔ Members learn by watching and repeating.

⚔ Your mavens meet your meek.

⚔ The competitive aspect is built among those who seek it.

THE STRATIFIED PRICING MODEL

You've done your homework, and you've set your rates. You've bracketed your CrossFit Group rates to give them context, setting your high rate and your bargain-basement rate at high and low ends of the spectrum. People understand WHY CrossFit Unlimited costs $200 per month, and they no longer ask, *"Why?"*

What's better: to have 300 members pay $200 per month, or to have one member pay $60,000 per month? Though the risk of serving only a single member is higher, the other benefits are huge: less required space. Less wear on equipment. Less time spent at the gym, working. Better progression for your client, and an easier time programming their workouts. If only we could meet that client...

The ideal number of clients is somewhere in the middle, of course...unless you remove the risk factor. If the $60,000 client would sign a lifetime contract, the decision would be easy. Fewer clients, paying more, creates better life for your equipment; more time for you; and more predictable cash flow. So why not raise your rates?

You already know the answer: paying $300 per month for CrossFit is a big lump to swallow. That's a car payment, after all, and though we know it's worth more than a car, CrossFit doesn't fit into the normal "gym expense" line on the home budget spreadsheet. There's also the family to consider: a client may be able to justify the cost to themselves, but explaining to their spouse may be another issue.

The answer is something the retail, auto, and electronics industries have known for decades: sell accessories. I'm not talking about products, like supplements, with low return; I'm suggesting that you broaden and improve the CrossFit service, in bite-sized increments.

For example, if I attended a gym where Unlimited CrossFit was available for $135, I'd be at one of the least expensive CrossFit gyms in North America. If I could add 'Open Gym' time - an hour before and after each class, available to Unlimited members only to practice skills, do mobility, or play, for another $35...that's one of the cheapest gym memberships available anywhere, including GloboGym. If I can add individualized programming, with homework to do during these Open Gym times, for another $35 per week, that's among the cheapest 30-minute Personal Training rates anywhere. Yes, I have to sign up for 10 weeks at a time, but that's what a solid program requires for results anyway...

My rate, taking advantage of the above attractive options, is $310 per month. I'm not paying $310 per month for CrossFit classes; I'm just adding "a little more." Later, you'll read about Lowenstein's Gap Theory. This is how you apply that Theory to your pricing model.

It's also a good method of providing dream-level service to your best clients, and making a living with more free time, more revenue, less space, and less equipment cost.

SCALING SERVICE

If you're like me, you've noticed more Boxes adding products for sale:

⚔ Equipment (rings, boxes, etc.)

⚔ Supplements (their own, a large brand, and even MLM brands)

⚔ Clothing brands (Skins, etc.)

⚔ Expanded lines from their OWN Box (CrossFit Catalyst wear, etc.)

I think it's great to diversify your revenue stream, as long as you're careful about the quality of the goods provided. Everything you sell is a reflection of your own values, and if you've got a great product that you truly believe will help people, you'd be crazy NOT to provide access to your Family. Unsure? Don't sell it; something else will come along. I promise.

Some Affiliates, after realizing that they can't possibly work a longer day than they already put in; can't fit any more people into their classes; can't add any more Personal Training clients; or can't figure out a way to take more money home, will seek to create more revenue from clients they already have. There's absolutely nothing wrong with that: if you can produce even more value, then charge accordingly. Help more people, or help people more. That's a great plan in life.

You CAN scale service, though, and not by losing more sleep, or adding more Coaches, or building a bigger Box. Your lever? Relevance.

The more relevant you can make your message - in other words, the more important your message to a given member at a certain time - the more it's worth to them. Relevance is created by the environment and events of the member, not by you, but if you can provide a timely solution to a problem, it's worth far more than your typical fee.

Examples:

⋏ When we do Ignite Coaching - CrossFit and brain training - on head-injury victims, we're paid by their insurance companies. Ethically, I can't bring myself to charge more for these sessions than a normal PT session, even though a corporate entity is paying the bill. However, we can (and do) find that Ignite clients can progress more quickly if we see them five times per week; we also charge for the extra time required for the highly technical programming necessary, and for meetings with other Therapists involved on any given Treatment Plan, and for time spent on documentation.

⋏ A local Massage Therapist with a full caseload leaves one appointment slot open every day. Her normal rate: $80 per hour. Want to get in today? Sure: there's one appointment slot open at 5pm (prime time) for $100. If it's an emergency, it's worth the price. Who among us hasn't been there? If it's not worth $100, then wait a few weeks.

*some call this gouging. I disagree. She fills that spot 90% of the time, and always with a client who REALLY needs massage right away. If she didn't have a price bump for that spot, it wouldn't exist for clients at the 'emergency' level, and she couldn't help them. Win-win.

> ⚔ Most chiropractors have a different rate for "maintenance" appointments and "First-time visits." Obviously, the intake process for new clients requires much more time and research than a monthly tune-up. I can personally attest to a willingness to pay DOUBLE for any chiropractor open on a Sunday morning.....

> ⚔ We also have a few Ignite clients whose disability limits their ability to leave the house. Though we stayed away from in-home treatment for years, we've reintroduced the practice for these cases. We charge more because the time required for travel is time that could be booked otherwise. In addition, a client in a level-3 coma requires some extra preparation time and coordination with other Therapists.

How can you increase the relevance - the relative importance of your time - for each of your services? Yes, it's important to me that I learn how to catch a power clean better, but it's not critical TODAY. Hint: the smaller the knowledge Gap, the more imperative the urge to fill it.

COMPETING WITH 'FREE'

There are many different ways to deliver your service that don't revolve around the "1-month unlimited" model. You may not be interested...but your competitors (Globos and McGyms) certainly are.

1) In Ontario, teenagers can attend GoodLife Fitness for 'free' in the summer. The service is attractive to parents, who can't spend the time monitoring their child's comings and goings. At least if they're at the gym, they can't be.....*finish the sentence*. Right?

This is a prime setup for service sales, however. For me, I

wouldn't want my teen running amok in a new weight room; I'd get her some personal training sessions. It ain't free anymore!

2) As fitness becomes more commoditized - with tracking apps, 'personal training software,' GPS-enabled shoes, and calorie counters - we'll see a split between access (free) and attention (highly-priced.) Some gyms have very minimal monthly rates - $15 per month - but high signup fees that discourage changing gyms. *"I don't want to cancel by Pump membership...I'm only paying $15 per month!"*....yes, $15 per month. Every month. For life. These gyms are dependent on new clients signing up to maintain cash flow. When that stops....

"Information wants to be free..." is the rallying cry of pro-access groups like WikiLeaks. It's a quote, taken out of context, by Stewart Brand. This was the original:

> *"On the one hand information wants to be expensive, because it's so valuable. The right information in the right place just changes your life. On the other hand, information wants to be free, because the cost of getting it out is getting lower and lower all the time. So you have these two fighting against each other."*

Your opportunity lies in the split. Charging for one-on-one attention, or attention within a small group, is your key. Don't like the one-on-one model for total time spent? Fine...do CrossFit, but make sure every member has personal time with a coach every month to review goals and make recommendations.

Offer speciality groups for people who want to work on specific elements. Offer premium Attention services, like Personal Training, even if you don't want to do it YOURSELF - through subcontracted coaches. Spend TIME with people - something that's hard to do in a simple class-based model. Build relationships with clients, not groups. Demonstrate the gap between 'free' and 'expert,' and offer both. Celebrate the gap; widen the gap.

You are in a unique position to help people: by publishing quality free content, and then offering personalized solutions.

GAINING NEW CLIENTS

Why CrossFit?

Every week, thanks to the 321GoProject, I'm fortunate enough to chat with 3 or 4 CrossFit Affiliates I've never met. I also get to share with at least a dozen Mentoring clients through the same program.

First, we talk about high-level goals: where do you want to GO in life? Who do you want to BE? What's most important to you: is it time? Money? A sense of purpose?

Then, a pivotal question: why are you choosing THIS method - a CrossFit gym - to satisfy those goals? It's a rhetorical question, of course. I already know that owning a CrossFit gym can satisfy any of those three, and others. I just want to hear the answer.

Invariably, I get a speech from the heart about how CrossFit has changed THEIR lives; how they want to share that change, joy, and benefit with others; how they're empowered to take some risks in the pursuit of that delivery. I hear, most days, a great story about discovery, inspiration, and self-actualization. Most often, they're opening a CrossFit Affiliate because they believe *it's the right thing to do.* And they're not wrong.

Then we look at their site. We click on, "What's CrossFit?" and we see a message about work capacity. We read about 'functional' training across broad time and modal domains. We see the "What Is Fitness?" link, right where it's supposed to be. Logical arguments for doing CrossFit?

Check.

Nowhere is their story.

Write your story. Put it up. Help us to know you.

THE THIRD PLACE

Ray Oldenburg talks about
"The Third Place," in the
book, *"The Great Good
Place."* This concept is
starting to gain in
popularity. Oldenburg
posits that most people 'live'
the vast majority of their
lives in one of three places:
the Home (place #1,) the
Workplace (#2,) and .... the
third place.

This "Third Place" is necessary for creative interaction
(hobbies or sport,) and typically features a high percentage
of regulars, as well as access to food and drink (at least,
according to Oldenburg.)

Starbucks has seized upon this idea: while Tim Horton's
was posting their "No Loitering" signs, Starbucks was
installing couches and free WiFi.

Several years ago, I floated a topic on T-Nation message
boards entitled, *"What Can A Great Gym Do....That It
Doesn't Yet?"* I offered a free Catalyst Gym t-shirt for the
best idea. Some great stuff came forward, and I was
extremely proud that we were already doing 90% of the
good ideas. The t-shirt went to a user named "sumabeast"
for his idea of a "study lounge:" couches, tables, and some
textbooks.

Would this be a great idea for a GloboGym? No way.
Square footage crammed with revenue-driving, complex

machines; a membership interested in burning calories, not reading. In fact, this library idea doesn't fit the fast-food-fitness model of compartmentalization and "No Loitering" at all!

A great idea for CrossFit? Absolutely. Since many of us rent industrial space, our ceilings are very high. That leaves the potential for a small space over the bathrooms. A couple of dorm-room-style couches, some free coffee, and some texts laying around provides a heavily-fertilized seed bed for growing your CrossFit community.

At 10am every Saturday, 16-30people crowd my doorway. They're on their way out of the gym, and they're getting checked in while they juggle their "outside clothes," sign up for other groups, chat about Paleo, commiserate about the WOD, debate Sunday's Hopper WOD...... The discussion is great. But what if they were sitting down for a half hour? These folks would never leave.

As I wrote back in 2008, nothing attracts a crowd like a crowd. You are hardwired, in fact, to seek belonging and sameness among others.

When I'm doing a speaking engagement, my first priority is to find commonality: a link with someone in the audience. If I can make one person laugh, I've made a link; I have empathy with an insider (part of the crowd, or the group I'm trying to join.) I'm in. I have an advocate, or a sponsor within the group.

We've been taught, through evolution, that safety resides in the middle of the herd. The weak and sick are pushed to the edges, where the wolves wait in the darkness. We struggle for acceptance because a lone deer is easy to corner; a big family or group lowers our odds of capture. You've heard the phrase, "safety in numbers?" How about, "herd mentality?" Both are extremely accurate. We can't help it.

Part of recruitment and retention means showing a client

that others in their peer group - or the peer group they desire to share - are also members. Demonstrating that large numbers of other people also trust your judgement - or visit your place - is a straight line into the reward centre of the brain.

By reinforcing the notion that, *"Your friends are here!"*, you're confirming two things:

1) that the 'group' comes here, and attendance is part of what defines the group

2) that the individual is wise for making the same choice as the 'group'

Each trigger a positive reaction in the brain, and that confirms the choice to stay at your gym.

How can we put that into practice?

1) Mention friends who have done the workout (*"Melanie was here this morning, and she had a great score!"*)

2) Fill your scoreboard, and post pictures. You can be as in-depth as beyondthewhiteboard, as simple as posting pictures of your own scoreboard (as my friend Funbobby Kwasny does every day at CrossFit SubZero) or using a really simple tool like SocialWOD.com, which combines both.

3) Show pictures. Tag people on facebook.

4) Demonstrate sameness rather than infallibility. (*"I had some cake on the weekend and felt like garbage!"* is better than, *"I don't eat cake."*)

5) Fill the gym. Even if it's for free. Skip Chase has a great video on this in the CrossFit Journal.

6) Arrange and rearrange your clients in as many ways as possible. Food groups on facebook, outings to the movies, reading groups, charity events, Team WODs on Saturdays.

7) Write 'athlete profiles' about your members.

8) Write personal messages on their facebook walls.

9) Celebrity name-drop. Hint: every member is a celebrity.

10) Form your yearbook committee. At each event, nominate a picture-taker (we have an athlete awaiting knee surgery who steps up EVERY time, and takes hundreds of pictures. She's amazing.) Then let athletes tag and share pictures.

Confirm what they believe, and you're in the circle with them. Draw them to the centre.

WHY WE DON'T USE MEMBERSHIP CONTRACTS

"So, to sum up," I said, unbelieving, *"you automatically renewed my contract for three years at the end of May."*

"Yes, sir."

"Without my knowledge or consent."

"We assume consent, sir."

"You're wrong to." I clicked over to another page on my browser, shifting the phone to free my mouse hand. *"I'm looking at a CRTC ruling from 2003 that says you're required to notify me before renewing my contract, and then again afterwards."*

"But you were notified, sir. It's on your bill."

"I get four bills from you per month. I have them here. No mention of an involuntary contract renewal."

"It would be on your April 2011 bill for...." she pauses, searching for the reference, and then gives me the account number for a telephone at one of our facilities. *"You go to page three, about halfway down the page, and there's a line of text..."*

She's right. In non-bolded type, a warning that my contract for four services - two telephones, two internet connections for two facilities - will be automatically renewed for a three year term unless I opt out, in writing, before May 25.

"One of these facilities will no longer exist after September 1," I say, but I already know her response.

"You can cancel, Mr. Cooper, but there's a cancellation fee for the 34 months that you have remaining."

A cancellation fee, for four services, that would amount to over five thousand dollars.

"Do you think I'm wrong to say that I've been tricked into this contract?" I ask. I'm blunt.

"Uh...." that's not on the script, sir, and I get off work in fifteen minutes.....

Perhaps in an attempt to smooth the waters a bit, she follows with:

"But, Mr. Cooper, you own a gym. You know how these contracts work...." she smiles down the line. Nudge-nudge, wink-wink, inferring that we're all in the screwing-people business...and what's a little on the side, between friends?

"Actually, we don't have contracts. People sign a sheet of paper that says I'm not responsible if they hurt themselves, and that they promise to be nice to everyone. That's it. So - no, I don't understand."

She lobs one, slow and low: *"But why?"*

Good question. Maybe it's because I want to be able to sleep at night. Maybe: because if you don't want to be here, then it's in no one's best interest to have you around. Or maybe I just don't want a client who's as loud as I am to ever get angry. Loud people just get louder when they're angry....

THE SOCIAL CONTRACT

People aren't rational.

When you meet them, people are defensive. They're

defensive because they're scared: scared of looking stupid; scared their gut will flop out of their new lululemon shirt; scared they'll be told that they shouldn't be wearing *that*; scared you'll tell them they've been doing it wrong for the last ten years. They're trying to stand there and grin bravely, PVC over their heads on their first visit to this scary concrete torture chamber, frightening acronyms written messily on a dirty wall, surrounded by strangers who are experts, Lizard Brain screaming to duck and cover, and you're saying, *"3,2,1...."* and they think they may actually pee a little on those box jumps....

And yet...people can get over it. The brain's ability to adapt, even to stressful circumstances, is remarkable. We talk about plasticity a lot in Ignite seminars, but it never ceases to surprise me: any objection, no matter how logical, can be overcome by a strong emotional trigger. For instance: *"When I saw your dirty bathroom floor, my skin crawled. But I stayed for a class, and thought you guys were really nice and the group was really welcoming. So I stayed. I still hate your bathrooms, but...."*

What people require from you is the establishment - and constant reinforcement of - an emotional baseline. *"No matter what else happens, at least THIS will be true...."*

> ⚔ *"I'm having a terrible workout. This might be my worst 'Helen' time ever. But I know Coop won't tell me not to come back...."*

> ⚔ *"I'm out of sessions, and I forgot my wallet at home. Class is about to start. But they'll let me in today, because they trust me and I trust them not to embarrass me about it."*

> ⚔ *"CrossFit Flashbulb just posted on my facebook wall. I won't block them, because they won't tell me to lose 20lbs in front of my friends....or at all."*

> ⚔ *"I can bring my friends with me, because even if*

their bathroom is dirty, I think they'll love the coaching enough to tell me I was right to come here. I'll be socially validated....I think. I wish they'd clean the bathroom! Maybe I'll wait a month...."

When there's no telling HOW low you'll stoop; when the relationship between you and your client doesn't appear to have a firm foundation; when you act differently toward them on different days of the week...you don't have a relationship worth sharing.

A final note: I'm talking here, of course, about your social contract. Just as emotion can overcome logic to help you, it can also harm you: no matter how good your coaching, or how much you've changed their lives, if you break that contract once, the rest won't matter. The foundation has to remain solid and strong.

THE EVANGELISTS

The only thing better than reading a story online is hearing it told in person. Me, I'm building a campfire.

Your job: build raving fans. Tell their stories to others. Brag them up in public, and they'll brag you up in private.

As your family expands, you'll be able to identify the 10% who are full-on evangelists. To these folks, you assign jobs. You keep them busy, because if they're bored, they're finding other stuff to talk about.

One of the greatest 'gym tour' videos you'll ever watch is by Zach Evan-Esh. On his front desk, he casually shows his photo album; visitors to the gym, if kept waiting, have a place to sit and browse his pictures. If you're like us, you have thousands, taken by participants. We usually have a 'best picture' contest after each event, and I'm usually tagging people on social media for hours the next day to build up the support web between people.

Luckily for me, I have some members who built their OWN project. They chipped in and purchased a smart little frame by Kodak (it's called the Pulse.) It's on the front desk. Visitors to the box can see dozens of pictures (it's pretty common to have a group gathered 'round, post-WOD.) And the real beauty? No work on my part!

The frame is linked to our Affiliate's facebook profile. Any member with a picture they'd like to share can just tag me on facebook, and boom! It's up in the frame on the front desk in less than 15 minutes. It's automatically linked. If I don't like a picture, I remove the tag and it's gone.

You have a lot on your plate. If you can automate any part of your workload, so much the better. Why not let the yearbook committee take over?

SPINSTER ELK

There was a time, sixty years ago, when elk covered Northern Ontario. On the little Island where I grew up, my grandfather would hunt elk regularly, in the fields and swamps on his own land, and usually be successful. They're gone now - my grandfather was a great hunter - and my father is part of a movement to reintroduce them to their native area.

Yesterday's technology - hunger and bullets - wiped them out. Today's technology - RFID collars and helicopters - is slowly bringing them back. And we're learning some interesting things about pack behaviour; mavens; and fear of entrapment.

As it turns out, the elk - renowned for covering great distances and spreading the herd far and wide - are mostly homebodies. ONLY the older females - past the age of childrearing - are the explorers. While the males stay at home with the food, it's the spinsters who roam. Radio identification frequently turned up older females hundreds of kilometres from the original reintroduction point.

Where are they going? What do they seek? How will they know when they find 'it'? We're not sure. We're not sure they know themselves...but it's their nature. Their role in the community is Discoverer. It could be that they're the bravest; it could be that they're considered expendable. Either way, they're the Seekers: the mavens.

How does a shivering elk help you grow your box? Well, if you're going to make a living at this, friend, you're going to need some good Mavens.

Mavens are Ladies Who Lunch; they're Water-Cooler Evangelists; they're the Early Adopters; they're the lead sled dogs. They want to experience new things, but their MISSION in life is to SHARE those new things with others. Their identity is *"the one who's always doing something new/crazy!"* - and to reinforce that identity, they have to show others what they're doing. Fair dinkum. CrossFit is *"something new/crazy!"* to most people.

 There are different types of mavens, of course. Some are content to do new things, and not share; for these, your job is to create unexpected glee *(first pullup? Here's a free hat!)* Some are more than happy to talk, loudly, for better or for worse - for these, your job is consistency. And some, perhaps the best, are happy to confide in a few friends who trust them. For these, your job is to create pride. Make Bright Spots. Give them a reason to stick around; they're magnetic.

A maven may not yet know what they seek. Let them lead; follow and give them Mangoes. More on the 'mango' concept later.

*I've used the term 'maven' in the feminine, because it's a female Elk who does the exploring. But there are plenty of male Early Adopters, too.

THE THERESAS

"I'd do CrossFit if I had more time for myself."

"I wish I had time to join the gym, but I'm too busy helping [parent/spouse/child/students] get to all of their [sports/appointments/jobs/homework]."

There is a small, golden subset of your membership for whom these aren't excuses: they're real conditions they've placed on their life. In short, they would rather help someone else than do something for themselves.

Perhaps it's an avoidance technique - they're scared, and procrastinating. On the other hand, perhaps their sense of fulfilment in life comes through the delivery of service to others. Perhaps yours does, too. It's noble.

We all know that these folks NEED exercise. They need it more than anyone: if not to keep themselves healthy and sane, then to better provide care to those who need it. Often, they need stress relief, and frequently they need to find a sense of self beyond the health and welfare of others.

Good scenario: they take time to exercise daily to stay strong and healthy for others.

Better scenario: they use CrossFit to build up strength and esteem; to develop their own sense of self-worth; to derive joy from their own accomplishments instead of the one-off triumphs of their kids or spouse.

Best scenario: they lead others into CrossFit.

THE TERESAS

There are some who don't care about the Open; who don't mind a smallish deadlift; whose lululemon don't match their Under Armour. They care about the community, though: they show up and post pictures when they can't compete; they send friends and family and talk about CrossFit on facebook. They invite others - each temporarily sick, weak, or lame - to do the Friday night 7pm group that no one else attends. And people come because it's Theresa asking, and not Coach.

The key to their consistency is their perception of need. You DO need these folks, the quiet leaders who reinforce the foundation of empathy (but not sympathy) in your Box. Your members need these folks, too: who will recognize when a member has been missing for a week; is having trouble at work; or simply needs an easy WOD to feel like they're winning at something. I'm lucky enough to have a few Theresas on duty.

Don't be afraid to ask for help. *"You know, T, I think Elvira is going through something. If you're coming on Friday, would you invite her?"* A hand up, offered by Theresa, is sometimes preferable to an invitation from Coach.

THE BARBELL BETTYS

One of our most popular groups of all time: The Bettys.

Initially, it was just a 'womens' weightlifting' group. But it's turned into a family.

You can see the original Bettys post at barbellbettys.com. Nothing to write home about – in the programming, at least. But you'll also see Tyler's letter to his Bettys after the first group ended; there's the group announcement second group, and there's the latest post, too.

As soon as the original Bettys group began to refer to one another as 'Betty,' to facebook one another and go out for drinks, I knew we had something. Soon friends started to sign up. They called Tyler, "Barbell Ken," and organized a facebook page.

They had a mantra *("I am strong. I am beautiful.")* to be repeated 10 times per day.

They went out for a Christmas party.

They bought Bettys shoes.

They did Bettys art.

After it was launched, all I had to do was join in the fun. *"Hey, Betty!"* I call when one arrives to do their homework during open-gym time.

When the Barbell Bettys faced a crux (too many brand-new Bettys!) we had to make a decision: should we offer beginner and advanced classes? How will we split them up? How will we deliver the news that some would move on to more advanced training, and some would not?

We're working on those problems now, but the Bettys are a great example of one group that we've done right.

Was it the coaching, or the legend, that makes this group attractive and successful?

THE OUTREACH COMMITTEE

You want the ultimate textbook on marketing, long-term buy-in and loyalty?

This makes sense, if your goal Is to build a fellowship. A community needs affirmation, communion, and repetition of its core values. Alcoholics Anonymous starts the same way, every time. Wal-Mart's morning "Team Meetings" always end with a cheer.

This is high-level thinking, and the original Mantra concept wasn't my idea. But we used it in our original Barbell Bettys group: they were asked to repeat, *"I am strong. I am beautiful."* ten times, three times per day. They didn't say, *"I'm a Betty, hear me roar!"* Nothing to reinforce that they were our clients, or that their group was great. The mantra was enough of a collusion to tie them together, and eight generations of Bettys later, we're still reaping the benefit.

Other than a mantra, you could use many different types of Affirmation:

While trying to stop swearing, my uncle kept an elastic band around his wrist. He'd snap himself with it every time he swore. Lance Armstrong stole the idea with his yellow 'Livestrong' bracelets. Well, maybe we don't have much of a case, but the idea was the same, except Lance's affirmation was positive feedback instead of negative.

When I was a kid, many adults kept a 'cuss can,' into which they'd drop a quarter when they swore.

In discussions with one of our wise members, himself a leader in his Church, he noted that CrossFit fills the 'community of spirit' need for many. This goes further than the surface-level cameraderie of "WOD-buddies." People need a spiritual outlet; a simple and coordinated way to GIVE to others. For our parents' generation, Church or other social groups filled that role. For many 25-year-olds today, CrossFit can do the same.

Charitable fundraisers and events are much more than a way to bring in new members, promote your gym, and help others. Doing charitable work also fulfils a deep human need to help. We do several every year, from very simple – a midnight 5k – to more complex. This was my favourite:

Last Christmas, a member approached me to sponsor a family for the holiday. We'd purchase three gifts – one each for three kids – and a local social service organization would deliver them just before Christmas.

I called the social organization (the Children's Aid Society) and they were thrilled to have even ONE family sponsored. "How many kids are in the program?" I asked. "One hundred and fifty-seven," was the answer.

"We'll take 'em all." I said, and we did.

For the next several weeks, hundreds of members from our Catalyst Family purchased gifts for little kids. Some commented that they hadn't purchased toys for years. Some had never bought for a little girl before, and asked for size recommendations. I got choked up when I read one of my favourite members post, "We went overboard. We got winter clothes like we were supposed to, but how do you NOT buy a little girl a doll for Christmas?" Gulp.

I cut a huge tree and put it up in the gym. On December 18, we had a big party, and the Children's Aid Society showed up with vans to deliver the gifts. We formed a human chain to pass them from the tree, through the gym and out the back door. It took over half an hour, moving gifts nonstop. I've never seen so much joy in one room, and that's no exaggeration. I wiped away a tear or two myself.

You think Gold's Gym can provide that for people?

You have a tremendous opportunity to help a LOT of people, and give your members a way to do the same.

Many social organizations use common causes to keep up the affirmation process: food drives, blood drives, fundraisers. We use events like Murph. We've ordered bright green wristbands for our OnRamp program, and bright pink for our Bettys. What are you doing to re-affirm the selection of your members?

MANGOES

Behavioural change doesn't come easy, but it can certainly come cheap.

While building your Affiliate Family is the best bet for RETENTION (people do what their peers do,) they're not going to sign up for the first visit based on the Community you've built. This would be akin to responding to a personal ad, picking them up at home, liking their father's handshake, and marrying them before 9pm when the chapel closes.

When animals are trained for the movies, the Trainers rarely use punishment. They realize, of course, that Bobo isn't going to learn to skateboard *today*. On Day #1, Bobo gets a reward - a piece of mango - if he allows the Trainer to place a skateboard in his cage without freaking out. This goes on for a week or so.

In week two, Bobo gets his mango only after he touches the skateboard. Week three, he's required to sit on the skateboard - unmoving - for a moment before the mango is produced.

As soon as you've read the section on Bright Spots, you'll recognize what's being done here: Bobo is taking very small, incremental steps, and building on them. He's rewarded, and though he may not be able to iterate how he's feeling, he knows what that mango tastes like, and how much he'd like to have it. He'll go to greater lengths to achieve the same reward next time - a trait he shares with his human cousins.

Most of your clients are looking for overnight change. That's nearly always a recipe for failure. Instead, start giving them Bright Spots:

"Hey, you made your appointment this week! That's a positive step!"

"This week, I'm going to give you some homework to do between our visits. OK?"

"We've got two solid weeks under our belt. You're even doing stuff on your own! Let's talk about tying everything together now with an eating plan." At this point, you've created enough of a foundation that you can begin to introduce your retention strategy. *"Hey, remember that lady we saw at the gym last week when you were stretching? She's coming in next. I'll introduce you. She lost 40 pounds last year!"*

Mango, mango, mango.

'NOW-THAT' BEATS 'IF-THEN'

Every year, after registration for the Catalyst Games has closed, we announce the Grand Prize.

No one expects the announcement. No one even knows there is a Grand Prize. By waiting until after the registration has closed, we're delivering an unexpected bonus, which triggers far more 'happy' chemicals in the brain than the typical perception of reward.

Daniel H. Pink makes a few key points on this topic in *"Drive: The Surprising Truth About What Motivates Us."* His idea is that motivation has changed; that the old ideas about 'Type A' personalities are antiques from the Industrial Revolution. Instead, he characterizes people as 'Type I' or 'Type E' - Intrinsic or Extrinisic.

Since what drives us has changed - he calls this new Era *"Motivation 3.0"* - it logically follows that our reward system has changed, too. People are more likely to seek an experience; to pursue novelty; to look for a point of differentiation. A sense of self-identity is now better satisfied by standing out from the crowd, rather than 'fitting in,' as would have been the desired outcome of the previous few generations.

Pink's solution to providing novelty as reward: the surprise prize. Reward that wasn't anticipated may have greater value. In 2010, we announced that we'd be giving away a 5-night cruise from a major line for two people. We'd be giving to a participant - not necessarily the winner - of the Games.

When my wife was with Enterprise Rent-A-Car, their behind-the-curtain motto was to set a high (but not perfect) expectation, and then over-deliver. They didn't sabotage themselves to delight, but they didn't over-promise, either; that meant that their service was always surprising (and delighting) clients, who believed they'd stumbled on a real secret gem. These days, "under-promise and over-deliver" is almost a cliche, but Enterprise was employing that same company policy over a decade ago.

We're trying it. We're giving the prize not as a reason to sign up (IF you sign up early, THEN you can *win!win! win!*) but as a reward for doing so, after the fact. NOW THAT you've enrolled, here's the Free Prize Inside.

Bonus: questions answered - Pink's Motivation 1.0 and 2.0 are best read in the book as background. The cruise was donated by a sponsor. And Enterprise Rent-A-Car is the biggest privately-owned company in the world, with a lot to teach us.

BENEFITS VS. FEATURES

Nobody buys drill bits. They buy holes.

They buy holes, 5/8" wide, in which to hang pictures of their new niece on their walls. If there were an easier way to get the picture frame stuck to the wall, they'd buy that instead.

Similarly, if an Affiliate is offering a Running Clinic, they may do well to consider calling it a "Speed Clinic" or "Go Faster Clinic" or even "Run Farther" clinic. Because nobody's buying "running" - they can do it anywhere, any time, for virtually nothing. They're buying running improvement. They're buying faster, or farther. So sell faster, or farther.

People don't buy:

Minty fluoride

500 horse power S-blade

100% cashmere

People really buy:

A clean, kissable mouth

A pool to enjoy with family

A memorable valentine's day

POSE clinics do this to some extent - the novelty factor will usually entice some runners a little - but we can do even better.

Good: Olympic Lifting Clinic

Better: LiftMore Clean Clinic

Best: Add 10lbs To Your Clean Clinic

Sell the benefit, not the feature. Drill bits are commodities.

REMOVING BARRIERS TO ENTRY

The people who need you most are calling to you. They're shouting your name. They're wearing clapboard signs with your Box's logo on them. But you can't hear them; you can't see them. And you may never meet them.

The fitness business has a tougher time finding 'browsers' than other industries. That's because seeking your advice means admission of weakness, and that's hard. Some folks, with solid ego integrity and happy lifestyles, have no problem reaching out.

And then, there are *your* next clients. They read your blog every day. They ask their friends about you. They resolve and decide and repeat, *"today's the day I'm gonna call...."* every morning. But they don't.

CrossFit is a big mountain. You may be the smilingest, happiest, knowingest sherpa around...but that's also intimidating, isn't it? By and large, the people who need you - and CrossFit - most are the ones who are least likely to work up the nerve to call.

I started lifting weights in my last year of high school. Dragged into the weight room by a friend, we tried to figure out the old Global Gym stack system (but didn't get much further than the biceps curl, leg press, and bench press handles, of course.) I'd never have tried if he hadn't pushed me into it. A skinny kid, I had a very limited athletic background; lack of knowledge was a huge hurdle; fear of doing something wrong in front of a gym class was paralysing.

The University weight room was the same story, but this time, I didn't have anyone to pull me. I had, back then, a tendency to blow things out of proportion (*"What if the machine looks different? What if I do something wrong and get yelled at? What if I get kicked out in front of other people? What if people immediately know that I don't know what I'm doing?"*)

Fortunately, this pit-style weight room had something I recognized: a treadmill. I sidled up to the door, clung to the wall, slowly squeaked my way onto the treadmill...and watched. I'd jumped from one safe lily pad (the doorway) to another, and I had a 'safe' place from which to plan my next move.

I'm making more of this than it really was, of course. I

wasn't paralysed by fear, but I was definitely anxious. Whenever a new person walks through your door, though, and sees concrete block; loud music; pullup bars....and no treadmill, they're going to have some anxiety. When the brain perceives anxiety, its response is flight. Duck and cover. Start the *"Dee-fence! Dee-fence!"* chant.

Let's consider the range of new joiners to your Box:

⅄ Jim's done CrossFit elsewhere. He's a part-time member at KleenexBox across town. He's not telling you that he dislikes the grip of your pullup bar because he's a jerk; he's just nervous.

⅄ Salvatore has done P90X for three years. Before that, it was GloboGym. His entire paradigm has never deviated from "Back and Biceps Day/Chest and Triceps Day." He's not asking you which muscle groups you're working with a power clean because he's stupid; he's just nervous.

⅄ Amanda has already lost 30lbs. She's finally got the courage to buy a gym "outfit" at a store...and guilt tells her that she's spent the money, and now she has to USE it. She wonders why you don't do more situps. She's not arguing with you; she's just nervous.

⅄ That guy who's been a member of your gym for two years...but never joined your coached groups? He's warming up with overhead squats because that's what he's good at. He wants to cling to the familiar. And he's nervous.

⅄ The Pilates instructor who asks why you push out on the abdomen, instead of drawing in? She doesn't want a fight, not on your turf. She's just nervous.

⅄ The firefighter who's top dog at the Station down the road? He's not doing half-rep back squats with 400lbs because he's a cheater, or has some other character flaw. He's just nervous.

⋏ The guy trying to lose weight, who doesn't take off his outdoor shoes when he goes into the bathroom? He's not trying to keep his socks clean. Just nervous.

⋏ The woman who praises the "supplement" or diet guru during her intake interview? She's nervous, too. Scared to death, actually.

Rare is the person who will stride through your door, plunk down their waiver, and ask for directions to the record board. Despite their bravado, if it's their first time, they're scared. They may be compensating; they may be arrogant. That's their defence. They're not taking a run at you; they're putting on a brave face for their own sake.

Recognize it as such. Agree with what they say, just like in the Improv Theatre. Give them reasons to see they're already on the right track (Bright Spots.) DON'T mention that you've noticed their truck circle the cul-de-sac three times in the last hour.

Fear is the barrier that's stopping most people from joining your Affiliate. Remove it as quickly as possible.

MIMETIC DESIRE

Desire is not a straight line.

Rene Girard, an anthropological philosopher, puts forward the notion that all of your desires are borrowed from other people. You want *this* because they want *this*, or they have it already.

Girard posits the model of desire as a triangle, not a straight line:

OBJECT

SUBJECT   MODEL

We desire something - an object, a characteristic, an attribute - because we see that others have it, and their possession reinforces the idea that the object is desirable. In this triangle, the Model is the current possessor of the habit or object.

Consider a woman, 40 years old, who visits your Box for the first time today. Her name is Mary. When she's searching your location on Google, does Mary desire to do a pullup? No; it's not yet in her realm of known possibilities. She doesn't care about pullups because she's never seen one done by a woman, perhaps. Mary just wants to lose 20 pounds.

When she's standing at your front desk, Mary still doesn't want to do a pullup. She wants to survive without "sweating too much" or committing another social faux pas. Her goal in session #1 isn't to make friends or experience "the community": it's to survive with ego intact. She doesn't want to embarrass herself. She's nervous.

And then...she sees Julianne hitting five beautiful kipping pullups in a row. Julianne is 40. Julianne has abs. Julianne puts chalk on her hands, and swings her legs *like so,* and can actually pull her chin above the bar in midair. Wow.

CrossFit thrives at providing behavioural Models, and providing clear paths to mimicry. Not only can we *show* you Julianne, but we can map you out the ways to *be* Julianne.

Successful businesses in all industries do this well: *here's Julianne. She likes this purse. You want the same purse? Here's how to get it.*

Interestingly, Girard takes the step further, suggesting that when the model and the subject become equals - when Mary can finally link 5 kipping pullups - they become rivals. They compete for acquisition of the object - they start to compare each others' max pullup numbers. As the rivalry grows, the value of the object increases. This, too, is where CrossFit shines: by offering the competitive element, clients can move up through the hierarchy of desire without changing their mode of pursuit (in this case, gyms.)

How does this affect you? Simple: pack the gym with models of behaviour. If you have to do it for free, at first, do it for free. Take one from Skip Chase's book, and invite every waiter and hairdresser in town - models who are constantly in front of people, chatting - and have them do CrossFit for three months. The biggest risk is inviting a new person into an empty gym: devoid of models, they have nothing on which to base their desire for CrossFit.

(You don't have to say, *"You can come free!"* Instead, give them a coupon for 3 free months. That way your rate is unaffected, and you're giving away a coupon, not a freebie.

Small difference in delivery, big difference in the psychology of your other members.)

I've referred to your job as a shoehorn before. But before you can start trying to fit a foot, you've got to get that foot in the door, right? And if the step outside is maybe a little high, that foot going to stroll right past.

SOCIAL BUBBLES

A long, long time ago - 2009 - I wrote one of the most popular essays to be published on our Affiliate's site: *P90X Vs. CrossFit.* If you search on Google, it's ranked second behind Mark's Daily Apple's excellent post on the same.

I'll be honest: my original plan was to write a post that would get a lot of hits, garnering 'rank' through search engines. It worked. Unfortunately, at the time, I perceived that the best way to convert the P90X crowd to CrossFit was confrontation.

I now understand that a train doesn't reverse course; it can't. In previous sections, I've discussed how to change someone's mind and help their shift their thoughts to parallel your own. This has helped enormously with our own client adherence (they're more likely to work out, more often, and with higher purpose.)

This takes time, though: a train must make a massive, sweeping turn to change direction, and you can consider each conversation with a P90X fan as one tie in that track. After all, they're just as convinced as you are that they're doing the best possible exercise program.

We know better, don't we? At least, our empirical observation - and perhaps, experience - tells us that CrossFit is better than P90X. Don't believe us? Ask Reebok. And the NFL, and ESPN, and...and...

None of that will work. If we continue to draw firm lines in the sand, we keep people OUT instead of drawing them "up" to CrossFit. Reading the first autobiography of the Dalai Lama, it became clear that our main job - in business, in coaching, in life - is to INCLUDE people. He was speaking of religion when he decreed that any act of inclusivity is religious; any act of separation is areligious. It's not much of a stretch to apply his ideology to fitness....

...and so, when speaking to the P90X crowd, I now believe we're better served if we mention the things that CrossFit has IN COMMON with P90X. After all, our likes overlap (intensity, short workouts, creativity,) and so do our dislikes (Globogyms, mirrors, machines.)

If we start a conversation with a P90X practitioner the same way we would with a normal client (cover things they're already doing right, or Bright Spots; show them that they've got a 20% head start, or bonus; give them verbal cues to keep them excited, or mangoes; and then show them that the wall between us is only imaginary) it's an easy transition.

Inviting a runner to do the first event of your annual CrossFit championship is an easy way to overlap bubbles of specialization. Taking your WOD to the pool may encourage swimmers to start training at your Box. Hosting a 'P90Xtra' night may do the same for the train-at-home crowd.

In the last few sections, I've been talking about the abutting 'bubbles' of athleticism that surround your Affiliate. For instance, runners tend to make up their own social 'bubble'- if you're a runner, you tend to know other runners; make new friends through your running contacts; and spend your free time in the company of other runners. In this way, social bubbles are insular: you spend time with people who do the same things - and, perhaps, believe the same things - as you.

However, these Bubbles can overlap. The fastest-growing segment of the endurance-sport world is the Triathlon. The growth is fuelled, largely, but runners who have been slowly introduced to the sport by triathletes they've met through running.

The sports of Triathlon and Marathon are quite different, but the preparation for each requires something in common: running. It's acceptable for Triathletes to belong to running clubs, because they must also be good runners. This creates a 'bubble overlap,' and a tertiary overlap exists with the cycling crowd. Though a marathoner may have no desire to ever try a Tri, they interact well with a Triathlete because they have the run in common.

That's an obvious example, right? Runners get drawn into Triathlons because it's not a quantum mental leap to buy a bicycle, try a Duathlon, and then desire to go for the 'full thing.' Bubble overlap creates an easy mental path from running to triathlon: *"We look alike. We wear the same clothing. At 8am on Sunday morning, we go to the same place and do the same things..."*

Dr. Shirley Glass, a renowned expert on marriage infidelity, talks about *"walls and windows"* - basically, the parts of your relationships that you make public, and the parts that you keep discreet. In a marriage, of course, it's important to keep some things 'behind walls' - that is, your squabbles; the bathroom tendencies of your spouse; his bad habits, her bad hair. When these things are made public - or a window is placed where a wall should be - the social contract between spouses is broken. Gossip to your best friend about his distaste for flossing? That's breaking his confidence. Tell your buddies her real hair colour? Should have kept that wall standing, friend.

I use this analogy to illustrate the opposite point: that, too often as CrossFitters, we place walls where we should have windows. We create barriers that restrict our sphere - or bubble - of influence, rather than open windows to expand our social circle.

Example: a new client - thin, ponytailed, wearing a race t-shirt and shorts with a high cut - comes in to ask about CrossFit. She mentions that she coaches a running group. Your response?

> ⅄ *"We do POSE running. Most people do too much distance. Have you ever read CrossFit Endurance? I'm certified. Do you have bad knees? You probably have too much heel strike. You need to get stronger hamstrings...."*

Count, if you will, the walls that I've erected in the above paragraph (I see seven points of difference that I've put up; seven things that tell her, *"we're different than you"*; seven things that identify me as *"not in your bubble, missy. Not in your Tribe."* If you squirm a bit, here, don't worry: I've been guilty of this type of thing for FIFTEEN years.

Is this better:

> ⅄ *"I run, but I'm not great at it. I did a few races last year, just for fun; I really like cross-country stuff better. My ADHD brain tends to like variety, so distances scare the hell out of me...."* ?

At this point, she may laugh and say, *"Me too."* When she

does, you may see a small shimmer around and above you; that's the merging of two bubbles. Emphasize your windows, not your walls.

By the way, the Powerlifting Bubble and the CrossFit Bubble have been rubbing against one another for so long now, they're bound to merge. Slowly, more blog posts have been showing up on Powerlifting sites that suggest that....well, maybe CrossFit is okay...sometimes. Dave Tate, Louie Simmons, and now Mark Bell are going to make the merger an easier one...if we keep the windows open.

On a final note, the best way to expand your bubble: shared love for the topic. Man, I love powerlifting, and I kinda have a crush on running now, thanks to CrossFit. Getting that across at the start of the conversation places you inside the same mental 'bubble' right away.

BLENDING BUBBLES

My wife calls me an 'over-introducer.' I introduce people who have met before. This happens often, in fact: *"Hey Philsy, have you met Andrea? She just finished her first Fran."*

"Uh, yeah, Coop. You've introduced us three times."

I'd rather make this mistake than risk anyone not knowing someone. To put that another (better) way, I want EVERYONE to know EVERYONE.

We're no longer in the Industrial Age. We can call our current era the Technological Age, but I prefer to call it the Social Age. Instead of building pricing structures and marketing plans, I believe we're better to build a safety net.

For instance, when a new CrossFitter stopped smoking this week, she was shocked to receive support from dozens of people she didn't know. When she put her challenge on facebook, she was encouraged by multitudes of Catalyst community members. How could she do anything BUT succeed?

When I started a Personal Training business in 1998, my clients were all teenaged athletes. Back then, 'Personal Trainer' carried a stigma: it was for wealthy families who would do anything to help their kids get ahead. Most kids competing in sport wouldn't admit that they had a Personal Trainer, because none of their friends did; as I built up a clientele, they were able to point to one another and say, *"...so does she."* Luckily, this is no longer a hurdle for new PTs, but it's still easier to KEEP clients engaged if other clients are doing much of the engaging.

You can't be everywhere all the time. If one client posts, *"...time to get back to the gym!"* on facebook, and thirteen others chime in with: *"See you at the 7pm group!"* your job is done. Moreover, if one mentions at lunch that she's *"Going to try Catalyst,"* and another friend in the group can say, *"I'm already there!"* then there's no need for a sales pitch at all.

If you come through the doors, we've got you. Come into our parlour.....

THE OCCUPATIONAL BUBBLE

One terrific group with which to become involved is nurses:

> ⅄ They're very close-knit.

> ⅄ They make decisions based on the recommendations of other nurses.

> ⅄ They share triumph and tragedy (...and that's more important than factual data. You believe your friends more than you believe the truth)

> ⅄ They're more likely to influence the behaviours of hospital patients than doctors are

> ⅄ They're mavens.

> ⅄ They're notoriously bad eaters.

⅄ Many smoke.

⅄ Depression is rampant among nurses doing night shifts.

Alas, nurses are typically overworked to the point of exhaustion, and faced with tragedy daily. They're exposed to a lot of workplace-related stress AND rotating shift work, which makes their cortisol levels extremely high, and they have a tough time losing weight. They're also more prone to low-back injury, since their job frequently requires bending and twisting, often following a long period of sitting. Hospitals invest in clumsy, clunky machines to help them lift, but nurses frequently choose not to use the lifts due to their awkwardness. If an infirm patient has to be shifted onto his side, a nurse will choose to perform an odd, uncomfortable lift than travel out of the room, down the hall (maybe to another floor or wing,) recover the machine, and still be required to set the lift properly for the patient.

Price tag for patient lifts? $600,000 and up.

This year, we're celebrating nurses, and offering help. We're going to do free 'Nurses' Week' CrossFit classes - nurses attend free, whether they've done OnRamp or not - and a free 'safe lifting clinic' on the final Saturday. Yes, it's a terrific way to get new nurses into our Box; it's also the right thing to do.

PROFESSIONAL BUBBLES

Again, the best way to attract new members who are likely to stick is through social 'bubbles' - groups of people who share something with your clients, or move in adjacent circles. For example, if one of your clients is a runner, they likely have friends who run. These are your next CrossFitters.

We've been involved in post-rehabilitation since we opened our doors in 2005. With the advent of Ignite, though, our interaction with healthcare professionals has gone from infrequent to hourly. Though you may not be getting calls from physiotherapists who would like to shift their rehab clients to CrossFit - yet - you've likely encountered a few clients with "issues."

Jane arrives at 6:55 with her friend, an excited CrossFit Maven. While signing the waiver, she mentions that she has a *"knee problem, but I know when not to push it."* What's your response?

Bill books a 1-on-1 consultation, and mentions frequent back pain. *"I've been going to a chiropractor,"* he says, *"and he told me I'm okay for squats, but not deadlifts."* What's your next question?

Dave calls with questions about his daughter. *"She just had a big growth spurt, and now her knees ache if she's sitting down for a long time or playing sports. I took her to physio, but they just gave her some stretches and nothing happened. Can you fix her?"*

Each of these challenges are huge opportunities to interact with other healthcare professionals....if approached properly.

Step 1 - ask the client who they've seen in the past. Physiotherapist? Chiropractor? When they give a name, ask permission to share their information with the therapist. Even better, ask them to sign a release of information form on your letterhead. Then tell them you'll call the therapist, "just to make sure I'm on the right track." If you know the therapist well, say so.

Step 2 - Create a blank referral protocol. Look professional, and then live up to it. When a RHCP (that's Registered Health Care Professional) shares a client, you won't want to waste their time (or wait too long) with multiple calls for small details. Put it on one form. This is how they do it, too.

Step 3 - Ask how you can help the RHCP give the client better service. The biggest highlight of Mike Michalowicz' new book, "The Pumpkin Plan," is that he recommends asking other service providers how you can make their job easier. Find a way to provide service that benefits the RHCP and the client first. Above all, don't create competition; they have to make a living, too. Even overworked service professionals love to give advice; asking, *"How can we help get Michael to his appointments more often?"* is helping both the RHCP and the client.

Step 4 - Make a suggestion, and ask for feedback. A physiotherapist isn't going to write a client's program for you. They're busy, and if you're worthy of their trust, you won't need their oversight. Our initial email, after mentioning the client, looks something like this:

"MS mentioned that he's been seeing you for patellofemoral syndrome, and he'd like to get back to playing soccer by the summer. I've recommended two sessions per week for quadriceps flexibility and hamstrings strengthening; is that in line with your treatment? Any contraindications we're missing?"

Other considerations - Use your letterhead. Don't use a client's full name in correspondence (use their initials, like 'MS' above.) Write professionally, even when you know the therapist personally.

Finally, take them sandwiches. A professional referral is a big deal. The RHCP isn't just sharing trust; they're risking their own reputation by recommending you. One of my favourite things is having a huge tray delivered, and sitting down with a bunch of therapists for forty minutes to talk about the book or the Ignite program.

A professional referral can open a LOT of doors. Therapists interact in a weblike fashion; a typical client case usually carries 4-6 professionals, working as a team. Each professional works on dozens of other cases, with dozens of other professionals. Entry into this world is tough, but if you've earned a place at the table, it's of great benefit to your business, to other therapists, and to your clients.

CONNECTIONS WITH OTHER AFFILIATES

The CrossFit Affiliate community is full of amazing writers, artists, and even songwriters. Oh...athletes, too. When Lisbeth posts essays on the A-blog in the morning, thousands of people click through to read. Sometimes, other CrossFit boxes will write amazing essays. You're wise, I think, to post to them.

Linking to others in the CrossFit community lets you deliver messages to your members from outside your own little family. It tells them they're not alone; reinforces the grand notion of CrossFit; gives them joy; allows them to feel like an 'insider.'

Last night, a member emailed me about this guy she'd just found online named Jason Khalipa. She couldn't stop watching his videos on YouTube. I sent her a link to the 2008 Games finals, and filled in some gaps in the Khalipa story. Less than six hours later, she emailed to tell me she'd taken an extended health care plan at work in lieu of a raise so that she could "...do more CrossFit."

There's a huge story out there. The macro version is about the Games, and the athletes, the Glassmans, and the stuff you read in the Journal. The micro version is the day-to-day in YOUR Box. If you can connect the micro- to the macro-, you'll have gone a long way toward reinforcing the decision to join CrossFit made by your members.

1) encourage your members to 'friend' their CrossFit heroes on facebook. It's easy. It's a direct line from lowly beginner to Superhero. Can you imagine writing to Babe Ruth, in his prime, and getting an immediate response? That's what's going on here.

2) post essays written by others in far-flung Affililates around the world. I love to quote a paragraph directly, with

a *"read more here!"* link to the writer's personal blog. Give credit early and often. A few years ago, I featured several CrossFit writers for a week each - including Jon Gilson, Lisbeth Darsh, Robb Wolf...and our members still talk about it. I asked their permission first, of course.

3) ask other Affiliates - or heroes - to join you for events. We're in a remote location; when athletes from other Boxes travel to participate in OUR events, it's almost overwhelming for me, and huge for participating athletes. How awesome would it be to have a high-level stud show up at Regionals to run a WOD for spectators between events?

4) Post pictures - with credit - from other Affiliates. Link to their site.

5) When a member visits another Affiliate, call the other Box and introduce the client in advance. Send a t-shirt for the Affiliate owner. When a member from another Box visits, let them train for free. There's no policy or agreement, written or verbal, around this practice, but we NEVER charge visiting CrossFitters, and I've never had our athletes pay when they visit other Boxes, either.

*addendum: some CrossFit Affiliates are overwhelmed with visitors. At the same time, your travelling member is STILL paying you. Why not offer to pay their drop-in fee at the other Affiliate?

6) Post events at other Affiliates on your blog. Invite them to yours. Heck, create events among Affiliates in your area. if you're remote, like us, offer up a Skype event (we're working on one now with another remote Northern Ontario CrossFit.)

7) Submit content for the Community page. This family has many levels, and very deep pockets of knowledge. Chances are, if you're facing a dilemma, others have already been through it. Coaching happens off the platforms, too. Ask for help.

8) Build up a regional Google Group.

9) Cross-refer. As the number of Affiliates per city increases, I believe we're going to see more specialization in Boxes. If the nutrition program at Cross-Town CrossFit is amazing, send your people there. If your OLY weekend can't be missed, they'll send their own to you. Expand the ocean, don't try to protect 'your' fishery.

10) Ask top-level CrossFitters for a favour. I've done this many times, and NEVER been turned down. In 2009, when we started FranFest - a fundraiser for our local soup kitchen - Jason 'Rhabdo' Kaplan was nice enough to send me 100 words of advice on Fran. Just for our members. They LOVED it. This is equivalent to Gretzky giving you 100 words on *"How to Score."* Jason Khalipa sent an autographed shirt for the price of shipping as a prize for another event; Chris Spealler autographed a limited-edition 'Speal 6' shirt for a member who was leaving town.

The more infrastructure you build, the more solid your practice. Nothing draws a crowd like a crowd. Go Speal!

RUNNING EVENTS
Richard is the 38-year-old manager of a Call Centre. 15 years ago, he was nearly killed in a motorcycle accident. He doesn't talk about it much, but until CrossFit, he couldn't run; couldn't  squat; couldn't press anything over his head. And if we didn't run an event called Catalyst Games, we'd never have known any of it.

After I requested his story, Richard sent me his "Athlete Profile" for the Catalyst Games. Seconds later, his wife sent the REAL profile, containing all of the above and much, much more. She wanted people - for good reason - to know the REAL Rich.

The Catalyst Games is a big deal around here. We run around 6 larger-scale challenges per year at Catalyst Gym, and the Games is their granddaddy. In 2008, 17 people competed at a bench press/truck pull combo; a max-effort Deadlift; and "Murph." A couple of dozen spectators milled around. In 2012, we expect over 100 to run over a ski mountain, and perform 4 other events within a day. They'll be driving up to 8 hours to get here.

Games Day takes months of preparation, endless hours of planning, and a lot of hoopla. But it's more than worth it for any Affiliate to host events like this one. Here's why.

Higher training goals mean better attendance at CrossFit Groups

August 15-September 15 is the slowest 30 days of the year in the fitness industry. That's because it's the busiest for most people *outside* of the gym, and there's a lot of lifestyle upheaval happening in most members' lives. What's going to keep people training? A good goal, especially one that causes a little anxiety. People are more likely to prepare for an event that makes them nervous than one at which they're certain they can do well. This is a core reason that CrossFit works (as discussed in one of our previous Journal articles.)

MiniClinics for last-minute panickers

According to Lowenstein's Gap Theory, people are curious enough about the unknown that they'll sit through a bad movie, finish a bad book, or listen to a bad story long enough to hear the punch line. For the Affiliate, this means that if you can delineate gaps in your client's knowledge base, and define them well enough, they'll scramble to fill them. Hosting an event like Catalyst Games puts a fine head on client weaknesses. We host four miniClinics, every second weekend, leading up to the Games: OLY lifting, Running, Powerlifting, and Gymnastics. These are two-hour "bird's-eye-view" slamfests that help clients out, but also show them how much more they could improve. It helps them for the Games, but also spurs requests for regular, more in-depth clinics, which we run in the fall. Tough events magnify weakest links, and show CrossFitters where they need to improve most.

Facebook posts leading up to the event

Facebook is a terrific motivator for a nervous first-time athlete; it's also great for spreading the CrossFit message. If your friend were involved in a high-level athletic event, and posting updates about how hard they're training, or putting up articles about themselves.... how could you resist checking it out? Filling your OWN knowledge gaps?

It would never be possible to purchase the kind of positive, personalized PR you'll receive from clients who have far more credibility with their friends than you, a business owner, do. Remember: an event like this is far from the norm for most people. This will be something they remember *forever*.

Athlete profiles are better than testimonials

People like to read about others like themselves *almost* as much as they like to read stories about themselves. Putting up Athlete Profiles gives them a story, and by default the

Affiliate has earned the advocacy of the 'Athlete' in question. Obviously, if they're letting you post their story, training strengths and weaknesses, and sweaty pictures, they like your Box.

Change the Lives of The Meek

The most-repeated phrase at the Catalyst Games in 2008? *"I could have done this. Next year for SURE!"* That, from the spectator gallery and media. They've seen regular people do extraordinary things. And if *they* can do it.....

If you can keep new folks paying attention, and encourage them to attend CrossFit groups, they'll compete the next year. Our numbers are testament to this fact, and so are CrossFit Games numbers.

Create hype for a month before / week after

Nothing draws a crowd like a crowd. People are training hard, comparing themselves to others on the Catalyst Games site, and talking about nothing else. They're guessing the events (we release the first two a week early, the rest on Games day.) They're excited. They're anticipating. Could a McFit gym get that if they tried? No way. CrossFitters get *jacked*. It's fun.

Division of client skills

Everyone is good at something. Likewise, everyone is weaker at something. This is a terrific opportunity to highlight the strengths of your various clients on a big platform. That newbie who's a slow runner? Bet she's got an awesome deadlift. By tailoring the events to be as inclusive as possible, you'll make heroes out of doubters.

Pride Artifacts

In 2008, we gave away massive gold belts to division winners. We had 6 belts for 17 competitors. They were as big as the ones worn by WWE Championship wrestlers, and though obviously novelty, they were engraved on both sides with "Catalyst Games 2008 Champion." Another year, we had dogtags and engraved bracelets for the women.

Running races give away t-shirts for a reason: you get to

wear your story on your chest. Face it: when you wear your "CrossFit Regionals 2012" t-shirt to the weekend BBQ, you

WANT people to ask about it. It's a great story.

Spectators

Inspiration is rampant at these events. At local events even more than at the CrossFit Games, spectators will see "regular, everyday people" doing things that truly astound. They'll see friends pile-drive themselves into the ground with an Olympic barbell; they'll see 'that lady from the coffee shop' thrust herself, gasping, across a finish line. They'll see the greatest true benefit of CrossFit: achievement through strife. Of the 60 competitors in Catalyst Games 2009, 48 were voyeurs first: they saw the event last year, or picked up on their friend's facebook posts.

Story

At the end of life, what matters most is the story you can tell. People remember great stories; they don't remember the guy who 'played it safe' and 'made a mediocre living' and had great aluminium siding. They don't remember the great deal you got on your car in 2009; they don't remember that time you made it across town in only 11 minutes because all the lights were in your favour. They'll remember *this*. They'll still see, in their mind's eye, that time that mom crossed the finish line. They may talk about quiet, reserved Uncle Ted, who could pick 400lbs right off the floor! at his funeral.

(note: we've actually had this experience, sadly. An article written by a CrossFitter about her experiences in running and life was handed out at her funeral in July 2009, and continues to be downloaded from our site almost 400x /day.)

Simple Setup

The template is already set: use the CrossFit Games. Treat people like real athletes. Do what the Games did, or what we're doing. Don't want to do a big event? Try a powerlifting or OLY meet or do a road race. We do a big variety of events every year, and each has met every criteria and benefit listed above. They were all simple to put together, created a lot of excitement for clients, and gave them a story to tell.

Our typical annual calendar:

March: Murph Challenge

April: Fight On Friday (FGB)

May: Baseline Week: Michael,Angie,Grace,Kelly, and Fran in 5 days, followed by a deadlift meet on Saturday and a client social Saturday night

June – Midnight 5k. A simple course, a $10 entry fee, and over 100 runners at midnight. Many had NEVER been to our gym before. Proceeds went to a local school to build them a new playground.

September: Catalyst Games

November: FranFest (a partner-based tournament, featuring 3 different variations on "Fran")

December: Catalyst Family Adopts Families – a Christmas gift-collecting extravaganza. In 2011, we were approached by a social services agency to buy a gift for a child in need. I asked how many kids there were; there were 124. I said, "We'll take them all." We cut down a massive Christmas tree, and members of the Catalyst family 'adopted' kids and bought them presents. The human chain, from our mezzanine down the stairs, across the gym, and out the back door to waiting vans, passed presents nonstop for over 30 minutes. I was close to tears the entire time. We sat down to eat dinner as a group afterwards. It was fantastic.

The Big Reveal

To keep interest high, it's best to save the Big Bang for the last minute. We don't announce the next event until the current one's over. We don't tell anyone the events for the Games until a few weeks prior (we string them out until the very last minute.) To keep people training intensely, it's better to push the unknown element than to show them what's required, have them try it, and either back out or rest on their laurels.   It's also easy to take a "pass" on this event if you know the next event's going to be more your speed.

HOW TO RUN AN EVENT

I advocate doing regular (but not normal!) events to keep interest high and training intense.

Here's what we do to build constantly-growing events:

1. Add the event on our site. Build up to it for a few days.

2. Don't release event details or rules all at once...or add a twist, in the case of something familiar, like Murph.

3. Stress, in all your posts, that you're encouraging competition of self. As one beautiful email read today, *"I now consider myself a competitor, but on my own terms."* Loved it. Our grand prize - a cruise, donated by a sponsor - goes not to the top male or female Rx finisher, but is randomly drawn from every person who finished all events (ie didn't quit, or 'tap out.')

4. For the big stuff, use a venue outside your box. We've used a giant waterfront Pavilion, right on the river, and a local ski hill. Absolutely gorgeous. Sound system, lots of room, bleachers....they're all bonuses. Can't do it? Change your box around. You have to let people know they're not just paying for another workout.

5. Despite having a time cap on every event, don't award a DNF; instead, make it clear that every rep counts.

6. Have scaled categories, right down to the very lowest level.

7. Pump up the kids.

8. Hold a 'best photo' contest - we had 2000 entries submitted on facebook for the Catalyst Games last year. Of the 7 new members gained so far this week, 6 saw pictures on facebook before calling.

9. Invite media. If you have to, make it a charitable event (winners of the Catalyst Games 2009 got to donate $250 each to any charity they wanted.)

10. Build excitement at the venue. We let anyone who owns a business and trains at our Box put up a banner for free. Lots of colour. And most wound up kicking in a prize anyway. We feigned surprise when they offered.

11. Build the family all year. YOU can't talk 50 people into participating; but their friends sure can. Our cruise winner was dragged in, kicking and screaming....but as soon as we said "3,2,1...go!" on the first event, she tried hard.

12. Create souvenirs that won't be duplicated. We've given away cowbells, giant belts, dogtags...put your logos on

them. They generate a lot of conversation. They also look great on people's mantels.

13. Drag out the suspense. We build things up to a fever pitch.

14. Reassure folks that there won't be anything they can't do. We trickle out the individual rules and events....but the last was only released 48 hours before the competition. Everyone knew they could finish, at least.

15. Offer online signups. We use MindBodyOnline.com. Pretty easy to commit to something online that you'd never do in person, and if there's money involved, they won't back out.

16. Set a rate instead of having each person do fundraising. I hate asking people for money, and if you took a poll, I'd bet that most people pay the minimum themselves instead of asking for help from friends.

17. Keep putting out philosophical articles, stressing the value of completion v. competition. Remind the most nervous that it's in YOUR best interest to make THEM look good on Games day.

18. Feature the athletes individually. Put up athletes' profiles for ANYONE who will answer a few questions. Use these to demonstrate the huge spectrum of athleticism that will be present; to build up the family by telling everyone's stories; to show who's endorsing your program with their participation.

19. Instruct referees to keep everyone fair, but when in doubt, to give it to the lifter. To that end, it helps not to have a high degree of technical difficulty; we use "ground to overhead" instead of "snatch," because we don't want to have different judging standards for different athletes.

20. Keep reminding people that they're a part of something bigger than themselves; that they're not alone out there.

We had lots of 'Catalyst' banners; we also had some awesome 'CrossFit' banners.

21. Get some high-level acknowledgement. When Lisbeth posts our pic on the A-blog, everyone hits 'like.' When we did FranFest last year for charity, Jason "Rhabdo" Kaplan wrote a nice paragraph on strategy. The guy holds the world record - 1:57 - and all I had to do to get him to contribute was to ask. No one's asked my opinion, but wouldn't it be amazing if we had a CF superstar at Canada East Regionals next year, running a WOD for spectators, or doing the first event with the competitors?

22. Get some graphics work done. Our shirts were great (we printed the poem, "Invictus" on the back; last year, we used Jon Gilson's "Don't Quit.")

23. Build continuity between events. We release the next event a few days after each event, because the afterglow effect is still big. We're also considering the addition of a points series for local high schools, and a 'league' system at the same time. More to come on those ones.

24. Include the spectators, if possible. Our photo contest is one way; these are the most likely 'next CrossFitters' around your Box. Grab them.

25. Give people a common place to reflect and share memories. Facebook is great, but if you're not 'friends' with everyone, you'll miss stuff. So I opened up the Games blog to comments, just for one day, for people to share stuff.

26. If you have athletes with special needs, GET THEM IN THERE. They need competition. And you need to deliver it to them.

27. If you see anything 'cool' in other sports, steal it! For instance, motocross - a growing 'fringe' sport - uses 3-digit race numbers instead of the standard two. So we did, too. They just look cool.

28. Standardize the judging. Miss a rep? Yellow card - repeat, please. Miss another one? Red card. Do 3 reps over. Take the subjectivity away as much as possible.

29. Use a microphone. Mention everyone by name during each and every heat. If you're comfortable doing play-by-play, that's even better.

30. Sponsors - if you want them, remind them that CrossFitters are an extremely loyal group. Mention to 50 CrossFitters that Dr. Chiro supports the program, and he's got far more value than in any other possible medium. Charge accordingly.

31. Use off-brand, 'insider' logos to maintain the sense of group differentiation. In the pictures from the event, you'll see a lot of 'Green Army' shirts. That's us...but there's no mention of Catalyst on there. Also, everyone here knows that anyone wearing a 'Sport of Fitness' hat has puked during a WOD. Think of the "third jersey" that many professional sports teams now sell.

32. One Affiliate in New Jersey (CrossFit Westfield) had the brilliant idea of inviting athletes' spouses to participate in their annual Murph event as "counters." To participate or compete, you had to

bring your own 'counter,' who would be placed inside the gym with 80 other newbies. They had dozens join afterward.

THE SPONSORSHIP LEVER

YOU, my friend, are quite a catch.

You are the leader - physical, often mental, and in some cases, spiritual - of your Tribe.

In 2008, while deciding whether to Affiliate or not, I was watching a lot of Greg Glassman speeches on YouTube. In one case, he was talking to a room full of Level 1 trainees about the nature of CrossFit coaches:

> *"We get in there, man. People tell us stuff they don't tell their spouse, or their preacher, or their shrink. We get invited to their weddings. They celebrate with us, and they want to cry on our shoulder."*

That's a paraphrase, of course, but it always stuck with me because it's true.

Maybe because of the 'war buddies' bonding that occurs post-WOD; maybe because people learn to surrender their own life, limb, and safety into the hands of the Coach; maybe because your social status is so highly reinforced by the feedback of their social web. In any case, people trust you to the core. When you say, *"Do me a favour, and go grain-free for twelve days,"* they do it. When you say, *"A 200lbs deadlift is NOT something most people can do,"* and give them a huge Bright Spot, they believe it. When you shake your head and pretend to curse because they've achieved a double-under on their first day in OnRamp, and*"....you know how many MONTHS it took me to do that!?!?"* you've earned it. They trust you. You have a social contract.

On one hand, you have to treat that contract with care.

Recommend a product, and they'll buy it. Recommend the wrong product, or for the wrong reasons, and that social contract is jeopardized. Use that lever for good, and the bond is strengthened.

For this reason, I don't sell supplements in our Box anymore. I hand out some free tastes, from my OWN jars...but make it clear that I don't profit from their sale. I don't allow others to advertise their supplements, unless they're sponsoring our athletes or our events. I'm cautious not to endorse something in which I don't personally believe. And I'd bet you're the same way.

In turn, this makes your Family a powerful buying group: if, on the rare occasion, someone DOES find something they like, thirty others buy one, too. In January, this was Buddy Lee ropes in our Box; in March, it was Again Faster Speed Ropes. Last fall, a member of the Catalyst family donated a week's cruise for two to the Catalyst Games; I advocate his service every chance I get (real estate,) because he's awesome at what he does. When Glassman settled on a title sponsor for The CrossFit Games 2011 - he had his choice - he chose Reebok, because they sent their CrossFitters instead of their suits.

Last spring, I was invited to a race called the Mountain Maple. I'd never done a 5k before, but I kicked the Lizard Brain aside and signed up. Of course, I invited my Support Group: about 40 other members of the Catalyst Family, several of whom had never done a running race before, either. This more than doubled the previous year's total race attendance.

This year, the Mountain Maple invited me to be a title sponsor. The price: bring all those people back! Because I loved the race, though, I offered to do more: a little cash to pay for the medals for the kids' race (featuring ribbons in Catalyst Green!); a facebook group to excite the masses; a dirt-cheap running group to 'train' first-timers for the race;

and use of our MBO software to accept online registration for the race.

Now, I'm invested in the success of the race, because I've promised big things: a beautiful lawn; shady trails; a long climb, but an antique apple orchard at the top. I WANT my Tribe to have a great time. Could you find a better sponsor than one who depends on the success of your event?

Conversely, what I'm gaining is attention: not drive-by, billboard, blink-and-forget attention, but context. I'm gaining a story in which the Family is central. I'm gaining a memory to share with people. On the more measurable/objective scale, I'm also gaining about 50 newcomers to our newsletter (part of the sign-up process through our MBO setup); a part of the memory of the event (the bright green ribbons,) and access (an overfilled "learn to run" group.)

Given a long enough lever, you can move the world. Just be careful where you pry.

THE NEWSLETTER
Part of the overwhelming charm of newsletter software (Constant Contact, for example): you know who's picking up what you're putting down.

A decade ago, I endured a long weekend of 'sales training' with a firm called Frank Foster and Associates. Frank's idea: the only 'bad' potential customer is the 'maybe.' A customer who says *"yes!"* is great, it goes without saying. A customer who says, *"no, thanks"* is your friend - because you can move on to the next potential member with your great idea immediately. But a customer who says, *"hey, maybe!"* requires a lot of your time and energy to try to turn them into *"yes,"* and you'll usually fail. They're just being polite.

Frank was talking about cold calling. I'm talking about your monthly newsletter. (If you're not putting out a monthly newsletter, go do that now, and then come back.)

For our first three years, we sent our newsletter to a growing list of recipients without ever removing more than ten people. Though they may have been tired of listening to us, the uninterested audience would prefer to just hit either 'delete' or 'spam' than reply and thus, offend us. Our first email list was drawn directly from a local Chamber of Commerce website, and chances were good that recipients would eventually meet us. So they'd trash the newsletter, and we'd never know. This is not good.

If a client wants to remove themselves from your newsletter list, that's fine. They should have that choice, so you're not irritating them (they'll find their way back eventually. Don't worry.)

IF, though.....

Mary receives the email. She's not interested, but she knows that Sherri will like the sound of OnRamp. She forwards the email to Sherri, who clicks from the newsletter to our site. After reading about OnRamp, she clicks the tab for the next Running Group. Maybe she signs up right away - after all, it's easy, because you're using MindBodyOnline now, right? - or maybe she'd rather call first, just to have her intuition stroked a bit.

....and you see it all. With tracking software, you know where Sherri got the newsletter. You know which offering interested her. You could, potentially, be ready for her when she calls.

Blog software is similar. Twice per day, I let myself check our hits. Hits aren't everything, but if there's a major spike, it's nice to know why. In the new marketplace of paying attention, don't you want to know who's reading the menu?

If I wasn't checking, I would never have known that CrossFitNYC has linked to us several times. I wouldn't know which type of essays our audience prefers to read and share among their friends. I wouldn't know who is visiting our site from a friend's facebook page. But I know, because I check.

Call me paranoid, or obsessive-compulsive, but if I'm going to perform, I'd like to turn on the house lights once in awhile to make sure the audience is still there.

GETTING YOUR NEWSLETTER READ

No one wants to read your flier.

Sorry.

That Instagram pic of the sweaty girl, passed out on the floor by the kettlebell? Awesome. To you, and to me, that is. Without context, though, it appears a bit *sideshow*. Freakish. S&M.

Yes, your gym Family is eager to hear from you. They want a letter every month. Everyone else? They got four fliers in the mail, five SPAM emails, and an hour's worth of television and radio ads today. They saw banner headlines. They had their search results analyzed, and 'relevant' ads printed on their search page and on facebook. They do NOT need another advertisement.

They wouldn't mind a story, though.

Give them stories. Tell stories about your clients. Show a broad cross-section: the new firebreather on the block. The 60-year-old who dragged her daughter in after three months because she loved CrossFit so much. The eight-year-old double-under whiz-kid.

In between, you can mention news, like when the next OnRamp begins. You can talk about the nutrition seminar next month. And now, back to our story....

The best part about writing stories: the effort required is small. Formulate 4 or 5 questions, email them to members (*"Hey, I'd really like people to know your story. Will you fill this out for our newsletter?"*) and wait for the thousand-word torrent to come back. It's like throwing one boomerang and gaining five kangaroos every time.

In your newsletter, give a one-sentence introduction. Let people know that the writing is in the highlighted athlete's own words, so you're not accountable for spelling mistakes. Then print their first paragraph, and link back to your site for the rest. Beautiful.

You've built context. You've created connections and relevance. You've broken the ice, and purchased Attention.

This works SO well that we've renamed our newsletter, *"Stories From The Park."* The rate of opens doubled almost immediately, and the 'trash' rate has dropped to zero. Even if people don't open it right away, they're keeping the email. No one can bring themselves to throw away someone else's story...

BEING THE EXPERT

In his great book, The Four-Hour Work Week, Tim Ferriss sets some guidelines for avoiding the addiction that we have to facebook, e-mail, Twitter, etc. I won't lay them all out here (just buy the book, already) but one was to check email only once or twice per day, on a schedule. He also suggested having an autoreply on your inbox, with a message to e-mailers that you reply to emails at 8am, 12pm, and 8pm, for instance; items that required faster attention can call your office number (given) or even cell (not given, but given on your office voicemail.)

Your email says a lot about you. Mistakes in grammar, spelling, and language in general become permanent, obvious, and glaring when you put them in writing. Over the phone, your lapses in good grammar can easily be missed. However, using the wrong form of "their/there/they're" in an email is the same as having your picture taken with food in your teeth.

People notice your mistakes. People *love* to pick them out. People will get a fleeting sense of superiority if, in your email, you write "alot" instead of "a lot." Maybe they'll get the idea that you're not as educated as they; that you're not as smart as they once believed; that maybe you're falling into this CrossFit rhetoric instead of speaking truth. Every email you send is your resume. Even if you've had the job for two years already. Whoever said, *"There's no such thing as bad publicity,"* said it before he had an email account.

On another note, people notice the time and date that emails were sent. If you're sending them at 6am, they'll notice. If you're sending them at 8pm, they'll notice. If they get an email with both date stamps from you in one day, they'll comment. Just grin and acknowledge how hard you work on their behalf.

Last week, I had a parent email me a 'crossfit' workout given to her daughter at high school. Now, we've partnered with many high schools in the area, but this particular high school has resisted our advances. There were three workouts, all featuring four or five exercises. Each exercise was performed for forty to fifty repetitions. For five rounds. That's a lot of volume.

The real kicker: the kids did all three workouts in a *day*. That's a thousand reps per workout, times three, *thank-you-may-I-have-another?*

CrossFit has been working hard to overcome the "dangerous" label for years. Information has been our slow weapon; knowledge has finally trickled down to the lower levels of gym culture. Unfortunately, there now seems to be a more ominous consensus: instead of *'CrossFit isn't dangerous when coaches properly',* it's now believed that *'CrossFit Is Dangerous And That's Okay'.* Any workout that kills a kid is, by definition, CrossFit. A little knowledge is a dangerous thing.

If you take the example of the gym teacher who does a little personal training on the side, has read one or two textbooks and has a silly certification or two, you'll see the potential issue. Where once the 'trainer' prescribed the same bodybuilding-style workouts for every exerciser, athlete or otherwise, he's now prescribing his idea of CrossFit. What was once "Chest and Tris" day for his hockey players is now "bucket day" - kill them by any means possible. Functional? Meh. Core-to-extremity? What's that mean? Pukie? Awesome.

This looming threat isn't the theft of our methods, because none of it is truly "ours" to begin with. You can't patent 21-15-9, or the name "Fran," or doing workouts for time. The real threat is the entry of the word, "CrossFit," into the common lexicon, like "zipper" or "Kleenex."

So what's our choice of action? This was answered succinctly by Pat Sherwood at a recent cert in Ann Arbor. One word: *community*. Your Affiliate community is what drives new members; what pays the rent; what makes CrossFit powerful. What makes them a community? The common glue is education. It's your job to make your community the most informed group of exercisers on the planet.

Writing essays, referring people to CrossFit Journal is a great start. The main site is a massive chest of great information. But you have to get your own face on it, or risk leaving HQ's message open to local interpretation.

"You coach CrossFit? Well, my gym teacher does, too, and he says something different....." Establish yourself as an expert. Video is better than text, and most of us speak better than we write.

Video is also easier to watch, and setting up a series of short, one-point videos is a great way to build a reference library locally. Correct naming will help Google find you easier, and you'll find you're explaining basic concepts less frequently to members. New members considering which gym is best will gravitate to you, because you've already demonstrated knowledge.

Don't worry, you won't run out of information to put out there. Information is already available to everyone; you're just the frame.

The best way to avoid theft? Make it available for free.

THE EDUCATING EXPERT

John Jantsch does a lot of one-on-one business coaching. He wrote, *"Duct-Tape Marketing,"* and its unique approaches to attracting and keeping clients have garnered a lot of fans.

In his last book, *"The Referral Engine,"* Jantsch recommends promoting your business as THE EXPERT by becoming the provider of education to your 'friendsphere' - in person, online, or in book format. He points to those who, like himself, have created the persona of 'expert' - and garnered hundreds of new clients - by publishing information that helps others.

In my own experience, publication of printed material has meant a 'shortcut' to credibility. When we meet a physiotherapist for the first time, their natural scepticism quickly becomes curiosity as soon as we mention that we've published a book on exercise and cognitive function. Our little white paperback creates a smooth ramp over the speed bumps usually involved in the feeling-out process of client referral. Though publication shouldn't necessarily mean instant credibility, it DOES imply that we've put the effort into researching and then concisely stating our views.

In the CrossFit world, you don't need to publish a book. Having materials available for the purpose of education, though, demonstrates that you're interested in the well-being of browsers who are paying attention; that you're invested enough to think, consider, and research; and that you have something to SAY on the subject. Moreover, in The Age Of Opinion, it shows that you're willing to say something, instead of attack the opinions of others.

Creating documents and videos on your site that people can use as a reference, share with their friends, or download and read, gives a better picture of WHO you are. Jantsch claims that merely providing free information - correct or no - creates a notion of 'expertise' in the minds of the readers.

Some things to include for CrossFit Affiliates:

⅄ Sample food guides (ours is available on DontBuyAds.com, in the 'Free Prizes' section)

⅄ Sample mobility sheets

⅄ Printable progressions for exercises, perhaps? (DontBuyAds.com,'Free Prizes' section)

⅄ Hotel workouts sheet

⅄ Links to educational videos (but don't get carried away!)

⅄ A *'who are we, and what is this?'* type booklet.

We called this a manifesto, and our earliest iteration was terrible: full of angst, a clear *'us against them at whatever cost'* mentality. Not good for trying to attract people to a service with which they have no experience or exposure. *"Hi! Everything you've ever done or believed is wrong! We hate what you've been doing! We're better than you! Come and try us!"*

Nah. Instead, I humbly suggest this little piece of heresy: suggest what makes us the SAME. Then point out the small points of difference that people are most likely to appreciate. Same: we do different things every day. We use barbells, kettlebells, medicine balls, and bodyweight exercise. We do aerobic exercise ('cardio') weight training, and everything in between.

Different: we rarely EVER repeat a workout. We don't like mirrors, because they distract. Our workouts are quick, but tough, and get results much faster because of their versatility and because you'll WANT to be here.

Use statistics:

> In the gym industry, 53% of the folks who sign up January 1st don't make it to the gym at ALL by March 31st. Conversely, only 7% of people who join Catalyst quit in the first three months. Why? - fun - novelty - education / learning curve - scalable workouts - excellent coaching - fantastic community - athletic approach.

Final benefit: the client who knows the most is your BEST client. While someone well-read is not the ideal target for GloboBilly's, they'll improve the community at CrossFit Bill. Teach.

FRESH HORSES
What drew your members - and what makes them stick - to CrossFit?

As we discovered in our two-year study on exercise adherence and retention, novelty plays a huge role. The 'unknown and unknowable' gift presented to your membership every day is exciting; creates interest; demands just enough stress to keep people paying attention.

In discussion with many CrossFit Affiliates through my role at 321GoProject.com, it's interesting to note that the majority of clients who leave your Box soon join another CrossFit Box. They're NOT quitting CrossFit. They're quitting YOU.

Novelty in the Affiliate can extend far beyond the day's

workout prescription. New Coaches always generate talk and interest; new phases of training (for the more enlightened clients) challenge their knowledge and thereby increase attentiveness; and, of course, the Open does more than its share to keep your Family engaged.

For a few months, I've been pushing Affiliates in more saturated markets to consider Specialization (and, also, to BE THE EXPERT.) Just as a CrossFitter can be pretty good at everything, so too can an Affiliate be pretty good at coaching everything...but not every CrossFitter makes it to the Games. As inter-Box competition grows, specialization in one aspect can help attract empathy from bubbles that are adjacent to yours.

Another avenue: bring in a Specialist.

Popular running coach in town? Invite her to lead a clinic. Accomplished Powerlifter? 8-week Powerlifting Group, starring Sammy Squat. Kettlebell? Gymnastics? Swim? Rowing? The benefits of inviting an 'outside' specialist are many:

> ⚓ More revenue for the Affiliate for the same amount of time spent (we usually offer the outside Coach a percentage of total revenue.)

> ⚓ More 'street cred' because of their experience, if not education

> ⚓ Overlapping bubbles - *"Oh, Sammy - YOU'RE coaching at that CrossFit place? Maybe I should see it, I guess....."*

> ⚓ Exposure to outside influence. CrossFit grew (and continues to grow) because it invites those coaches who are better at one element to ADD to the programming. It doesn't eat its own dogma.

> ⚓ Acceptance and referral from the guest Coach (*"I'm a part of this thing..."*)

⊀ Differentiation from other Boxes

⊀ Community-building - NOTHING establishes camaraderie like doing something at which you're terrible with other people who are equally terrible.

⊀ YOU can attend!

⊀ If you like, you can make it a charity event.

New blood, novelty, fresh perspective....adding solid building blocks to your foundation has many benefits. Reach out.

OUTREACH REDUX
My parents' church has a marketing department. They call it the 'Outreach Committee.'

(Of course churches need marketing. They don't buy ads, but they're better at retention than any gym. You could argue that a gym fills a need similar to that of a church - addressing a physical need, rather than a spiritual - but they're much better at keeping people around, from infancy through death.)

The 'Outreach Committee' hosts barbecues. They visit people who are sick, or just need someone around. They go places and invite people to come to church with them. If someone hasn't been there for awhile, they call the guy up and tell them they're missed. They don't hand out magazines, but some other Churches do, and it appears to work for them....

It was Zig Ziglar, arguing that salesmanship is a noble calling, who introduced me to the concept of Jesus: The Ultimate Salesperson. Ziglar, one of the very devout, meant it as a compliment. He was addressing the fear some novice salespeople possess: a fear of seeming slimy. Not at all, says Ziglar; you're performing a vital role as communicator, educator, and counsellor.

In the fitness industry, every single big fitness chain has been built on the Industrial model: fit people into boxes, apply the correct equation, and expect a certain outcome. The only weakness in the system is the human operator: Big Fitness believes that, if you can't make progress on Program #12, it's a sign only of your weak willpower. You don't like Combo #3? It's not the chicken balls - it's your taste buds! They're broken!

When we're looking for a model to emulate for promotion of our service, and attracting new clients, why are we looking to the standard McFit model at all? I suggest we evaluate others who are more successful, and I suggest that the religious machine is a good place to start.

Imagine this: you bring your infant daughter to your gym. Members welcome her to the 'family.' As she grows, she attends lessons for kids, explaining the fundamentals of your philosophy, using fun games and easy-to-remember parables. At the age of twelve or so, she's allowed to participate in a more formal indoctrination before being celebrated as a full member, with all its rights and responsibilities. The Gym family is strongly involved in her social scene; in her triumph and tragedy; in her wedding; in her battles and finally, a hundred years later, in her loss.

Baptism? Funny tshirts, or beanies. Sunday school? CrossFit Kids, or at least gym immersion (we let little kids sit inside our big tires and colour them with chalk while their parents are training.) Confirmation, or adult baptism? CrossFit Kids (graduating up the ranks) or a Junior Gym Membership. Tithing? Monthly fee for deliverance.

Keeping these in mind, then, with your Outreach program, you may find yourself tending more toward earning a reputation, and using that as your building block, instead of spending so much time *selling*." Are these short-term fixes? No way. But who wouldn't want an 85-year member?

The pastor/reverend/preacher man isn't on the Outreach Committee. The Committee is made up of social people who believe steadfastly that they're doing the right thing. I think that's critical. If you've ever been approached by a friend trying to sell you something, you'll know that you're more likely to trust them than any salesperson. You want them to be right. If they've stumbled upon something great, it confirms that you were smart to have chosen them as your buddy.

If you ask your members to recruit their friends, and they don't believe your core message, the coercion will be obvious. Pyramid-scheme supplement companies try to use this method, but peer-to-peer only works if your peer is a) a great sales person, or b) they're completely enamoured, but still sane, or c) they don't try to sell you every damn thing they try themselves.

Make your members aware of your core message. Find reason to repeat your Elevator Pitch in front of them, without overtly 'coaching' them. And then turn loose the Outreach Committee.

PS - megachurches have reinforced in me something

else: nothing draws a crowd like a crowd does.

PERPETUATION

Let's examine the goals of our marketing efforts:

    ⚔ Convince people that CrossFit works better

    ⚔ Convince people that we know more than other fitness 'experts'

    ⚔ Convince people that CrossFit is safe and fun

    ⚔ Encourage people to try it

    ⚔ Educate people on our philosophy

    ⚔ Save people from the alternatives.

In my case, the last point has always been my Achilles heel. I've spent a dozen years ranting about how belly dancing, for instance, doesn't *"firm and tone your core."* As it turns out, that didn't make me any friends....

Instead, I should have been working to leverage my passion into COMpassion. I should have been trying to help people. I should have been writing about how the body works, and how exercise works, and how food works, and how the clean and jerk is a marvel of kinesthetic engineering. As it turns out, people are smart.

Your greatest marketing weapon, then, in the Age of Opinion, is education. An essay about knee extension will go further to convince a runner to try POSE than any advertising ever can; in fact, the only tool more powerful than education is that of empathy (their friend brings them to class with them.) Demonstrate knowledge, experience, and wisdom.

Knowledge expands; opinion isolates. Sharing what you know - without hope for compensation - shows that you're passionate enough to put it all out there; that you're on the lake because you love to fish, not because you're trying to catch a trophy. That you care enough about me - a stranger - to help.

Write essays. Every day. Need practice before posting? Do a 30-day challenge at750words.com (heck, do it anyway - it's your brain's warmup for the day.) Inform, don't opine (and it wouldn't hurt to talk about stuff other than CrossFit, either.)

THE DIP

No, it's not the new donut at Krispy Kreme.

Seth Godin talks a lot about the initial spike in clients, the slow taper, and the slower buildup in his book, *"The Dip."* It's one of my favourite Seth books, because his thesis holds up to experience. Most business classes address the early part, or the pre-Dip (the initial bump in traffic,) but then don't take the theory any further.

My own addition, humbly submitted: the Dip is cyclical, not linear.

First, in a nutshell: any innovative new product or service will have a quick spike in attention from the market. These are the Early Adopters - folks who will try things just to be first, or to *say* they've done it first (there's a difference.) Then comes The Dip, as the Early Adopters fulfil their norm, and move onto the 'next' great thing. Some will stay, sure; in the meantime, you're building up your Mavens and expanding, slowly.

CrossFit has led me to this conclusion: if we drill down into that group of Early Adopters, we'll find a subgroup of Anarchists. These are the counter-culture reactionaries who love to be different for different's sake. They may have purchased the first iPhone, but now they're using Android. They may have started CrossFit to rebel against "the norm," but now they're already looking for something else. Don't worry: they're not going in the P90X direction, but outward, constantly searching for the Edge of The World.

It's hard for the majority of us - who have been CrossFitting for more than a couple of years, at least - to imagine a point where CrossFit will BE the norm. We look back at OPT winning the Games in '07, and it seems like yesterday. To us, CrossFit still feels like rock 'n roll, baby.

But in the 1960s, your dad wouldn't have worn jeans and a ball cap to work, either. Mainstream adaptation is going to happen. Two of our earliest influences - Mark Twight and CrossFit Greyskull - have packed up their black blogs and gone Seeking.

As we build, and grow, and creep toward a New Order of health, we're going to see some rebellion. Some will come from within the CrossFit world. Some will protest from outside. It's part of the normal process. Someday, when your grandson tells you that he's quit CrossFit because the "new science" tells him to split his workouts into one bodypart per day, you can smile knowingly and shake your head. Then you can beat him at pullups.

OUR DEBT TO THE BEST

...or, "Why You Owe Jason Khalipa 50 Bucks."

If you haven't seen the movie, *"Every Second Counts,"* you owe yourself the pleasure. It follows five favourites through training for CrossFit Games 2008, and it's a great story about the unpredictability of CrossFit, and the unlikeliness that we'll ever see a repeat champion at the Games (go ahead, discuss below.)

The last five minutes is the best: after spending 90 minutes building up Dutch Lowy, Speal, and Josh Everett and OPT, we're led to believe that the final event will be a showdown between Spealler and Everett. It's couched this way: will the little, fast guy win; or will the bigger, stronger, competitive OLY lifter?

Speal goes first (he has a head start via points earned from the previous events.) At around rep #15, he's caught by Everett, who picks apart reps like they're a pile of PickUpSticks. He slows a bit, but keeps moving; and with five reps to go, the judge starts counting backward to the foregone conclusion. I'm disappointed for Speal, but then.....with two reps to go, there's a loud noise off-camera. The cameraman quickly pans, searching...and here's this guy, Jason Khalipa, with his arms in the air and a small crowd of fans slapping him on the back. He had won CrossFit Games 2008.

"We didn't know who he was," said Dave Castro in the post-interview. *"We almost kicked him out of the briefing room, because we didn't think he was supposed to be there."* I'm paraphrasing, but that stuck with me.

In 2009, Khalipa got off to a bad start. Again, we were told that we should watch the usual suspects: Spealler, Everett, Khalipa, and a couple of others. But we knew, didn't we? We KNEW that anyone could rise up from the murk. We were smarter. So when Khalipa faltered in the run, I wrote him off. He lay, collapsed on the tarmac, dehydrated and semiconscious; I left the computer to go outside and get some work done, disappointed.

Over the next two days, I followed every Twitter feed I could find about the Games. It was obvious that Khalipa was making a comeback, but without high speed internet in the Valley where we live, it was like awaiting Morse Code from the battle Front. In fact, in the last event, where Khalipa capped an amazing competition with a huge effort, the last Twitter feed of the Games read, *"Khalipa's heading to the finish line!"* I thought he'd won.

The best thing you can do in your Box? Tell the stories of your Family. But there's a macro-story, too; it's about your Tribe's place in a larger counterculture movement. THAT story tells us about carrots, not sticks; it shows us what's possible at the upper end.

Imagine yourself, at age eight, playing basketball in your yard. *"Michael Jordan fades....time for one last shot...swish!"* You put yourself in those huge shoes. When Jordan was at his peak, David Stern (NBA Commissioner at the time) was touring eastern Africa. In nearly every city, town, or remote village, kids would have hats and t-shirts with "23" or the famous 'Air Jordan' logo on them. The kids didn't know how to play basketball, but they knew who Michael Jordan was. And when Stern showed them how to take a free throw, they willingly picked up the game over soccer, the perennial favourite. That was Jordan's reach.

I have a three-year-old. He's stocky. He likes handstands, tag, and building forts with our plyo boxes. Five years from now, can you imagine him doing pullups: *"Khalipa's got 3 left, now two; he's going for the finish line!"* ....

SUMMATION: HOW TO GET RICH
When you opened your CrossFit Box, I'd bet that your intentions were noble: you love CrossFit, after all, and believe that it's your gosh-darn-duty to get the message out. I think so too.

You thought you could do it better. Or you thought....maybe you could make more money as an owner than as a Coach?

Even though it's a cultural taboo to openly desire wealth (thanks, agrarian / industrialist/monotheist educational system!) I'm ready to come out of the money closet. I want to become rich with a CrossFit Box. And I want you to get rich, too.

There are a few things you'll have to do, and even some that may make you uncomfortable. But no laws or bones will be broken.

1. Outflow

Control your outflow. If you don't have a personal budget, create that first. If your box doesn't have a business plan, learn to write one. Most important: understand cash flow. While members may prefer to pay you later, your staff has to be paid now; what fills that vacuum?

Want a starting point? Download our cash flow forecaster tool from 321GoProject.com.

THIS IS BORING, BUT CRITICAL. If you don't have a plan for spending, it's not going to matter how much money you make: you'll just blow it.

2. Know the difference between an asset and a liability.

Just like a mortgage, many folks believe that their equipment is an asset. For our purposes, it's not. Let's define an *asset* as something that brings you money, and a *liability* as something that costs you money. Do you need equipment in your Box? Sure. Do people come because you've got new medicine balls? Nope. If the power went out, and you had to run a WOD outside without equipment, could you do it? I'd bet you could.

3. Start compiling assets. For instance, consider purchasing a building instead of leasing. This deserves its own post; tune in tomorrow.

4. Consider investing elsewhere. Trainer leaving, despite your misgivings? Why not invest in their new Box? They could use startup cash, you know they're trained well, and you've got a modicum of control into how they appeal to your market.

5. Incorporate. The reason rich people keep more money? They actually pay *less* in taxes than poor people. They buy things with before-tax money whenever possible. For instance, in Ontario, a corporation is permitted to pay the interest on a vehicle; the gas and mileage and repairs for a vehicle; up to 10% of the interest on your home (office space rental,) and 10% of the utilities for your home, too.

Paying with before-tax money essentially means that you're saving up to 40% at point of purchase, and you'll also be able to claim the taxes back.

6. Find a muse. A passive revenue stream that requires very little attention from you, that will pay into your account, even if in dribs and drabs. For muse help, read *'The 4-Hour WorkWeek'* by Tim Ferriss. Spoiler alert: his was a health/fitness product!

7. Make your business systematic. Read *"E-Myth Mastery"* by Michael Gerber and write a comprehensive guide to running your business. Chances are, you can make a better burger than McDonald's can; it's one of the most effective businesses in the world, and it's run by teenagers. Your trainers can leave; you can take holiday; staff can face crises on their own *if* they know the plan.

8. Have a mission. Not a lame 'mission statement' from the 1990s, but have an intent that's greater than money and make sure your staff knows it. One great example is SouthWest Airlines: theirs is to be THE low-cost airline. A staff member says, *"hey, I think people would like more choices for lunch!"* and their supervisor thinks, *"does a bigger lunchtime menu help us to become THE low-cost airline? Nope."*

9. Help others. Zig Ziglar's best line, in my opinion: You can have everything YOU want, if you just help enough other people get what THEY want.

10. Learn to sell. IDENTIFY your weakest business links. Why is it so easy to train your deadlift hard when you have a weak posterior chain, but hard to pick up the phone when you need business? This, too, can be done more easily, and I"ll blog about it on Friday.

11. Have variety. Don't limit yourself to the WOD groups. We have offshoot groups for barbells, tumbling, MMA,

running, and several sports.

I've focused on the more obvious: increase revenue. However, the most important on the list is #1. Without it, nothing else matters.

HOW TO RETIRE

Two years ago, I was sitting in a stiff-backed office chair in a tiny room with my business mentor. The lights kept going out. On automatic timers, they responded to movement, and I was so riveted that I wasn't fidgeting enough to keep the lights on. That office chair was beginning to feel like a therapist's couch.

"What's your biggest fear in business today?" he was asking, and I didn't have to think long at all.

"Retirement. I'm putting NOTHING away." I said. I'd been brought up at the feet of regular RRSP contributors, who maxed out their annual contributions for tax refunds. My parents had every conceivable form of 'safe' investment; I hadn't contributed to a retirement plan for 5 years.

"Well, don't worry about it. You're not going to retire." he said. My blood pressure spiked. *"You're not the kind to retire. You're always going to be doing something."* He said. Strangely, that put me at ease. It may not do the same for anyone else.

Tim Ferriss' first big seller, *"The Four-Hour Workweek"*, shared several novel ideas about the relationship between 'work' and 'time.' Instead of massing a lump sum over 30 years, and then stretching it for another 30, Ferriss advocates "mini-retirements" throughout one's lifetime.

Rather than trying to save $600,000 by age 55, take one whirlwind vacation and settle into a pattern of driveway-watering, Ferriss champions the idea of three-month "mini-retirements" while you're young enough to enjoy them. Twenty thousand dollars, spent judiciously, can get you out-of-country for a year at a time, if you choose. Ferriss goes into great detail in his book, which I recommend.

Rather than work stoppage, then, we may consider work abatement. We can think about rest time. Call it 'active rest,' if it makes you feel better about it.

For many entrepreneurs, a change is as good as a rest. There are two parts necessary for you to walk away from your business, a week or month at a time:

1. Solid business infrastructure, so that staff can run the business (no business runs itself);
2. Cash flow that doesn't depend on your presence (though cash flow from your LEGACY is fine.)

SELF-INVESTMENT

In the previous section, I started talking about what 'retirement' means for an entrepreneur. The fear of losing one's 401k, or the opportunity to cease work at some hard-to-determine future date, is a hurdle for many who might otherwise take the jump into opening a gym.

Initial Investment

Where will you get the money? Should you take a partner with cash to invest, in exchange for equity? Should you borrow?

A financial expert on a local radio station relayed this solid - but atypical - advice. I'll tailor it to my own experience:
Between 2008 and 2010, my stock portfolio, which consisted of maximum US investment in moderate-to-

aggressive stocks, lost almost 40% of its value. It wasn't huge to start, but the loss, if withdrawn in 2008 and invested into Catalyst, would have covered all of my debts. Bank loans - gone. My own income would have gone up by over a thousand per month; multiplied out over three years, I could have shown a net gain. If that money had been reinvested in Catalyst's growth, one dollar in 2008 would have been worth over three today. Catalyst outperformed the market by many, many leagues.

When considering investment, few entrepreneurs consider investment in their OWN company as equivalent to investment in secure long-term stocks and bonds. They give their money to a financial planner, or buy shares online. WHO will care about your money more than YOU will? No one.

Especially while the markets are showing very little growth, investment in YOURSELF is one of the best options out there. Stop looking for fast-growth stocks. Stop paying into your retirement fund for a few months, regardless of what your financial planner says about *"dollar-cost averaging."* Even if your stocks grow 50% next year - they won't - it still won't keep pace with a business that provides you with a new wage forever.

INVESTMENT IN PROPERTY

If you're seeking the best way to increase net revenue without increasing gross revenue - in other words, to keep more of your money - consider purchasing a building.

In the short term, ownership of a building doesn't cost much more than the lease price. One rule of thumb among landlords: the rent on one unit should cover the mortgage for the while building. Many of us pay triple-net (we cover utilities and taxes, on top of the base rent) and as such aren't saving much over purchasing.

Even better, if you can lease some of your space, you'll cover a portion of the mortgage at lower risk.

Best case, you're only paying your mortgage for the next ten years. After that point, your business can 'rent' the space from you...which means increased income without a higher actual wage. After the payment period has ended, you'll hold an asset worth $300-500,000.

Most people believe that their house is their largest asset. As Robert Kiyosaki (*"Rich Dad, Poor Dad"*) often affirms, *"a house isn't an asset. It's a liability. A building that pays you is an asset."* In other words, you can rent the building and derive cash flow for decades after it's been purchased. Compare your salary to the rent you pay; if they're close to the same, you could be making the same money from home...if you owned your space outright.

Real estate, we've all heard, is the only investment that always goes up in value over the long term. We're currently in an economic slump, though, and that means lower interest rates. Building loans have never been cheaper than they are now, and likely never will be again.

Is it risky? Sure. But with a building, you'll never lose your full investment (you can sell the building.) The revenue saved in rent can buy you...a trip. More equipment. More staff. Another building?

This can be your retirement fund.

BUYING VS LEASING

Recent experience has illustrated that most tenants don't know how much they're paying in rent compared to the actual cost of the building they're occupying.

In one building, the current owners were more than happy to give me this advice: *"Just rent the bottom floor! That pays the mortgage on the whole building!"* The building was 3 storeys tall, with over 24000 square feet; I wondered if the tenants on the bottom floor knew?

In another building listed for sale, this was part of the description: *"Tenant pays 100% of mortgage; owner responsible for property taxes and incidental building repairs as necessary."* If the tenant saw the ad, why WOULDN'T they purchase the property?

Fear. That's why.

In business, the taker of risk is the earner of reward. And there's nothing wrong with that. But let's take a really close look at that risk; let's drill down into the murky unknown here and get all the cards on the table.

Fear #1: Price. *"I can't afford to buy a building!"*

Really? Interest rates have never been lower (5% for a commercial mortgage in Ontario in July, 2012.) At that rate, here's what you'd be paying monthly (including interest) for your mortgage:

Building Value	Monthly Payment (10-year amortization)
150,000	1665.31
200,000	2220.41
250,000	2775.51
300,000	3330.62
350,000	3885.72
400,000	4440.82
450,000	4995.92

500,000   5551.03

If you're currently paying $3900/month for your facility, that means you can buy a building worth $350,000 for the same monthly cost.

Fear #2: *"I could be stuck with the building if the business goes bankrupt!"*

News flash: it's easier to sell a building than to get out of a lease.

Let's say that the worst does happen: three years from now, you're destitute. You will NOT go from $250,000 per year to $0 per year overnight, though, so you'll have a few months to sell your building before you're absolutely broke. Even if you sell it for only 40% of the purchase price(very unlikely,) you can still break even, because you've essentially just paid rent for the three years of occupancy.

Conversely, if you go broke on the third year of a five-year lease, you'll be paying out the remainder unless you completely bankrupt your company. If you're NOT an incorporated company, you'll be paying out the remainder with the earnings from your second job at McDonald's.....

Fear #3: The Building is a Lemon. *"I don't know anything about real estate!"*

Nope, that's not your job. Luckily, it IS the job of many others. Get help. In our Box alone, we have several contractors; electricians; roofers; painters; and a HVAC engineer.

Fear #4: You'll be house-poor. *"All of my cash flow will go into paying for the building!"*

Maybe...at first. But probably not (run it through your cash flow forecaster, which you can download for free from 321GoProject.com.) And ten years from now, all that cash that's paying for the building will be paying YOU. If you own the building, your corporation will still pay rent indefinitely, even when the mortgage is gone. You'll just be paying yourself instead of the bank. How's an extra $4000/month sound? To me, it sounds like a retirement plan.

Fear #5: Things will go bad very quickly, somehow, and you won't be able to make the payments....

You're wrong. They won't. You're GOOD at this, and it's not because you're lucky.

The Ontario government offers a program for just this type of jump, however: they'll insure 90% of the purchase price against business failure. Your responsibility is to provide a 10% downpayment, and they charge a small premium (around 0.75%) for the fee. But the ability to walk away with only $30,000 of debt on a building worth $300,000 is worth it for most.

Is a building purchase right for everyone? Well, if you've read *Rich Dad, Poor Dad*, you may believe so. In the long-term, it takes care of a lot of the things that worry entrepreneurs: retirement income, earnings growth, long-term space requirements....

PART II – THE RIGHT BRAIN: BUILDING A COMMUNITY

Don't Be Vanilla.

Vanilla is medium. Vanilla is safe. Vanilla is 'Plan B' - as in, *"if I don't like anything else offered, I'll just take vanilla."* Vanilla is average. It's not disappointing; it's not remarkable. It's worse: it's nothing.

Don't be vanilla with sprinkles. Vanilla with sprinkles is an average pig with Revlon lipstick.

People don't want average. People want dissonance. People want two things at once, each balancing the other.

Ever drive down the highway in the spring, window open and cool air streaming in, with the heater on? Absolutely.

Ever crave salty AND sweet? Absolutely. That's why *'Crunch 'N Munch'* is so popular: two competing tastes beats boring old popcorn.

Cliches are vanilla. Nothing about the phrase, *"we apologize for any inconvenience this may cause"* actually appeases the inconvenienced. Nothing about it is memorable; nothing sticks.

There IS such a thing as perfect vanilla, of course. Some people even like vanilla. There's also such a thing as perfect mediocrity.

Your blog - and all the information contained therein - isn't just a nice little service you do for free. It isn't window dressing. It isn't part of your marketing checklist. It isn't a menu, or a brochure.

Your clients - your CrossFitters - are paying to read your blog. They're not paying with money. They're paying attention.

In the 1960s, we were promised heli-cars, robo-slaves, and a 20-hour workweek. Instead, we got the death of the simple news, working spouses, and a clock with dozens of deadlines but no 5 o'clock buzzer.

You are competing for *"share of wallet"* - we all have more disposable income than we did in the 1960s. The problem is, we've never done without. We're used to having all this stuff, whenever we want it, the very second we want it.

Moreso, you're now competing for share of awareness. You already know that our attention spans are miniscule. What are you doing to earn the attention of your clients?

If you can't write well, that's fine. We all fantasize about being great writers and photographers, but we're not. We're great coaches. Someday we'll be great business owners. Let someone else write for you. Show CrossFit videos that you hijack from Vimeo or YouTube.

Best bet: show a picture of a CrossFitter at your box every day. No, wait: a story is better.

The most-read book isn't the Bible. It's the phone book.

Everyone wants to see their name in print. That's a small trick to gain the attention of your audience. How are you going to keep it?

You don't need to write it. Just distill it and post it. Fitness Business Canada reports that the biggest threat to the fitness industry is the proposed 'music tariff.' Essentially, music companies (ooooooh!) would like to charge a few dollars ($2-$4) each time their song is played in LunchTime Spin by McFit (aaaaah!)

In this month's issue, Fitness Business Canada reports on "The Future Of Fitness." The top 5 potential markets for the future?

1) people who don't exercise.

2) people with problems that need fixing.

3) fitness that is fun and enjoyable.

4) fitness that encourages personal relationship and shared experiences.

5) fitness using neuroscience (?) and nanotechnology (@#$ %*!!!!)

One more: 'The Future of Health Clubs' - "exertainment," "specialized centres" for chronic conditions, "information hubs." Yay sameness! Gimme more beige!

Meanwhile, back on the outskirts, we're exploding. Part of the reason people choose CrossFit: they recognize average. Their tolerance for the same-old-rhetoric is at an all-time low. Visit the GloboBang homepage, and it's as exciting as the Sears catalogue with the bra section cut out.

CrossFit   Bally Fitness   Gold's Gym   24 Hour Fitness

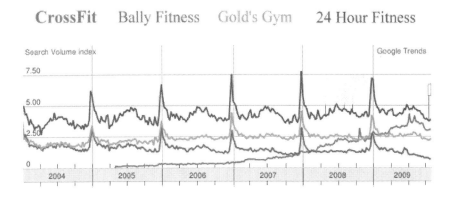

Part of our charm is that we're the alternative. We're growing among the more intelligent: the early adopters, the YouTube viewers, the Twitterers, the facebookies. Our members have tattoos and we sweat and collapse and bleed and vomit. We rumble in concrete boxes. We post videos of our workouts. We treat it like a sport. We don't stop trying to convert the mindless, madding crowd.

It would be easy to think, then, that the way to appeal to the most people is to be counter- well, whatever's popular. If they're for it, we're against it. If they're on BOSU, we're on bumper plates. Anything they say is immediately wrong, just because it's them.

In their book, *"Differentiate or Die,"* Jack Trout and Steve Rivkin offer a subtler approach: *take one step to the right.* Full-on opposition usually puts your audience on the defensive. What's more, if your message is too aggressive, you're more likely to attract the shorter-term, quick-to-move-on client.

One step to the right, in a nutshell: look at the basic message being delivered to a large mass of people. Then change one core element - not all - and make their transition easy. In this way are people led to your point of view: one step at a time.

If you think this sounds a lot like the Incongruity idea from the *'Extreme Persuasion'* section, you may be right. The 'Incongruity' idea proposes that if you take a cliche - say, walking on a treadmill - and change one small element, people will be drawn to it. They'll want to 'solve the puzzle': what's changed? What effect will that have on the end result? Can I predict the end result? Lowenstein theorized that the draw of the small mystery almost forces people to wait for the punch line.

That's where you come in.

Take a look at some of the best marketing endeavours from a few of my favourite CrossFit boxes. They're not "in-your-face." They're not aggressive. They don't try to change your opinion by 180 degrees; just get it to shift to the right. Just a little. Just one step. And they're very successful:

CrossFit Virtuosity - *'Why We're Different'* - no negative message about GloboGym, but a reiteration of the common message ('we train like people used to train....')

CrossFit Evolution - *"What We Do"* - *"We are unlike the regular gym, where you do your own thing. In our High Performance Gym, you will be coached each and every time you walk through the door."* No negativity, but a point of difference.

Use of examples is your best friend, say Trout and Rivkin. People can relate better to others than to a future version of themselves. If they perceive equality to the people in your example, realistic or not, you're off to a solid start.

As an example, if a dew-ragged bodybuilder comes in the door, telling him that 3-4 sets of 8-12 on the pec deck is disgusting is unlikely to start his conversion. However, pointing out that Steve Reeves, the Oak, and LaLanne trained in a way closer to CrossFit than to the modern chromey ideal may have that effect. Different than 24 Hour Fitness, but the same as your heroes.

left: Muscle Beach in the 1960s: gymnastics, calisthenics, overhead lifts. Familiar?

I think it's wise to illustrate our point of difference,   but illustrating   common points of sameness is a much easier way to get people in the door. Show them   the   foothills instead of Everest (they'll see the full mountain soon enough.) *"The same, but different"* doesn't quite cover it; how about *"Different, but the same?"*

THE PSYCHOLOGICAL CONTRACT

When a new member enrols, you have a piece of paper that lays out their responsibilities, and your commitments. It likely includes a waiver, a PAD form, and a couple of other ground rules (our fifth bullet point: *"I promise to be nice to everyone."*)

But the *real* contract - the one on which you'll be judged - isn't written down. It's the understanding that fills the space between the lines. The type of member you want is the one who doesn't need the contract. They don't need the burpee penalty, because they're not late. They take off their wet shoes at the door.

You promise not to cheat on your wife. That's not in your marriage contract; it doesn't have to be. It's unwritten. And these rules also exist with your members (*I promise not to embarrass you in front of the group,*) with other drivers (*I promise not to cut you off and potentially make you crash,*) and perfect strangers (*I promise not to spit on you.*)

Problems arise when the Psychological Contract isn't fulfilled. REAL problems - the divorce kind - happen when two partners are keeping two different contracts.

Change is uncomfortable. But if you're building a family in your box, you have a psychological contract with those members to address them like family. Changing your rates? Tell them so - but not as a corporate robot. Not as someone who reports to a Board, or appears rigid. Tell them as Coach.

(on the flip side, this is why psychologists decry the formal *"Family meeting!"* and suggest we all just eat dinner together instead.)

THE ELEVATOR PITCH

For time: *"What's CrossFit?"*

CrossFit is a social workout. It's a community. It's a revolution. And it grows ONLY through the telling of stories; the relay of excitement; the in-person experience.

Friends bring friends to CrossFit. Are your clients good at recruiting?

If someone walks in off the street with questions, can your staff sum up the experience in 30 seconds or less?

If you're stuck on an elevator and someone notices your t-shirt, can you recruit them before they reach their floor?

This is the notion behind the 'elevator pitch': a quick overview of the benefits (not features) of CrossFit. Just enough to get them to try it once. Enough to get them to pursue the conversation, or read the Journal, or skim the FAQ on your site.

I've been searching for a good 'elevator pitch' for two years, and finally found one I really like, on an Ontario CrossFit affiliate's page. After the Ontario Sectional in 2010, I scanned every Affiiate's blog for days. Consequently, I can't find the exact post again, though I've tried. If this is yours, email me and I'll give credit where it's due (and a free t-shirt!)

So....what's CrossFit?

CrossFit combines the best parts of weightlifting, sprinting, calisthenics, and kettlebells. Plus, we do a little bit of basic gymnastics. By sticking to the most effective exercises from each, we can do these really efficient workouts in about 30 minutes. They're hard, but they have to be. It takes a couple of years to be really great at CrossFit, but you can be good in a few months. Wanna try it?

Without being too technical, here are the parts that I like:

⚔ Lots of 'colour' - people associate different feelings with words like "sprinting" and "gymnastics"

⚔ Plain English, no jargon

⚔ Seems unscripted

⚔ Addresses scalability without saying the word

⚔ You don't have to write down any web addresses

⚔ Triggers a lot of follow-up questions

⚔ Defines CrossFit as a discipline (like karate or dance) instead of a 'workout craze'

⚔ Ends with a question

In Canada, we have a very popular show called, *"Dragon's Den"* (it's starting to catch on in the States, too, where it runs under the name *"Shark Tank"* and now features Mark Cuban.) In a country where 19.8% of the population reports itself as *"entrepreneurial,"* people seem to love to armchair-CEO along with the Dragons, who are venture capitalists.

In a nutshell: you've got a business idea. You need funds to expand your Box, or just get rolling. The banks won't lend to you. You can't scrape up 20k to get started in the facility YOU want. Where do you turn?

One of the toughest things about selling CrossFit is that it's tough to do an Elevator Pitch. While you're more likely to have to deliver that short summation on the street, to a potential client, it's also critical that you can get your idea across quickly IF you're trying to borrow money.

On Thursday, I spent 5 hours in sessions with IP lawyers, Patent specialists, and another colourful character - Sean Wise, the host of Dragon's Den. I did my Ignite! exercises first, so that I could retain as much information as possible. I turned by brain into a sponge. When it was over, I wanted a nap. Only now, two days later, am I starting to slowly turn that sponge over in my hands and mull over what I learned.

Wise knows of which he speaks, because he's a Venture Capitalist himself. His message is aimed at the Box owner who's trying to raise funds through an investor, but your REAL investors are your clients (and future clients.) You still need to sell them, too...

His four keys to a good elevator pitch:

> 1.Pain statement - what's the problem you're trying to solve? (*Hey, isn't it so boring to work out on machines all the time, doing 3 sets of 8?*)

> 2.Easy to understand (*Our workouts change every single day. You rarely do the same things twice.*)

> 3.Irrefutable - this is the challenging part in our industry. In this case, you're better to use social evidence (*I know a guy whose deadlift went from 150 to 350lbs!*) than to try and invoke The Hand Of Science.

> 4.Greed-inducing. (*It can get YOU there, too! I never thought I'd run 5k in my life, but now I'm doing a marathon in July.....*)

SELL IT SIMPLE

"You can't sell complicated to someone who came to you to buy simple." A great quote from a great post by Seth Godin.

The new-to-CrossFit crowd is gearing up. They're looking for trials and deals. They see CrossFit on television, read articles about it...they're going to ask, *"What's CrossFit?"*

In the search for the perfect Elevator Pitch, we're all getting better at describing CrossFit in fewer and fewer words. It's rare that I don't spend a part of my day cruising other Affiliate sites, looking for a better paragraph on who we are and what we do. Here's what I've found:

1) You don't have to tell anyone everything right off the bat.

2) There's no 'wrong answer.' People think CrossFit is either Boot Camp or Circuit Training. Both are false. Both are also true. There, I've contradicted myself: the only 'wrong answer' is *"no, that's not CrossFit."*

3) You're better to address their real reason for exercising than to try to change their view. *"You'll get really fit, really fast"* isn't perfectly parallel with *"I need to lose 30lbs."*

4) They'll learn the great stuff - that there's no ceiling, that it's great to be coached, that CrossFit is really about the Community - on their own. Let them discover those things on their own, as we all did, and they'll love it MORE.

5) Employ Gap Theory early. Show people that even the most elite are still striving upward, just like those in OnRamp.

I'm sure there's a lot more, and to discover some, I've just purchased *"ReWork"* by Jason Fried. His premise: that the company who can simplify the most will eventually win. That means a simpler message, simpler delivery, and simpler staff processes.

HOW TO PRY A BRAIN

"Mrs. Appleton! Mrs. Appleton! Misty says there are chicks in the daycare...and one is driving a TANK!!!"

This was the nine o'clock news yesterday morning at my daughter's school. The pageboy was a six-year-old with a cowlick, and the source of his excitement was a modified fish tank with a heat lamp. Down the hall in the daycare centre, chicks were hatching every day, and the younger grades were being trooped down long lines to see the miracle of new life. News travels fast in the hallowed halls of Elementary School...but maybe not perfectly accurately.

Our brains don't put information together in a linear fashion. They're associative and contextual, which means that data doesn't stick around for long unless it's perceived as relevant to other data. If there isn't an emotional connection, or if there's no contextual 'box' into which to place new little bits, they're quickly discarded.

This is bad news for the 'read-and-memorize' method of our education system. It's good news for your CrossFit box.

While the *worst* way to learn something new seems to be rote memorization, the *best* way is to put it in a story or joke. Create a picture, draw a scene, and it's sticky. And permanent. While the precise wording may not carry from one teller to the next, the story won't change. This is research derived from storytelling traditions of other cultures, and well laid out in "*Moonwalking With Einstein,*" by Josh Foer.

One example: the Pythagorean Theorem of Triangles. I learned it in the tenth grade, I believe, and promptly flushed it down the brain stem. Years later, when Homer Simpson has a flash of rare insight inside the nuclear facility where he works, he touches his head and blurts, *"Thesquareofthehypoteneuseisequaltothesumofthes quaresoftheothertwosides!"* Now, I remember the equation perfectly, because it was placed in a memorable context.

The best part for CrossFit boxes: the more lewd, randy, dirty, or disgusting the story, the better it sticks.

In our world, then, news is best shared as a story. A note at the bottom of your WOD page that says, *"Congratulations Mrs. Appleton on a 325lbs deadlift PR yesterday!"* would be better replaced with a paragraph about Mrs. Appleton's previous back problems; her struggles with motivation before she found her deadlift Bright Spot; her previous best; her skinned shins and chalky hands; the shakiness in her hamstrings as she pulled the big weight.

For more on the role of memory and spreading news, check into the Ignite blog (www.ignitegym.com) later for a post on *"Memory Palaces."* This is big stuff.

THE GFPs

Chances are, your Box has its own lexicon: a mini-language of slang, acronym, and inside jokes. Good for you.

There's a good chance that your staff does, too. In the insurance world, clients are usually identified during conversation by their initials only, and every single form has its OWN title that sounds like a random Captcha password. *"Did you do the OCF-18 for MP yet?"* Means something to me...but may not to you, if you haven't used HCAI before.

The beauty of slang is that it doesn't have to mean the same thing - or even anything - to anyone outside its intended audience.

We've been studying the effect of perception and PRE-ception for the past month. When we're doing Ignite!, it's important that we 'set the stage' beforehand. When you hear, from a friend, that Jim is a terrific guy; salt of the earth, really; well, you're willing to give Jim the benefit of the doubt.

This is another reason why advertising doesn't work: there's no context. A brain can't remember an ad for long, because there's no story anchoring the *"Big!BIG!BIIIIIG! SALE"* to the reader's memory.

How do you refer to the 'members' at your Box? I call ours 'The Family;' 'The Tribe;' 'members;' 'clients;' - almost interchangeably. Outsiders sometimes call us 'The Cult;' 'Followers;' etc. But 'member' and 'client' aren't words that carry a charge.

What if we all started calling our "members" GFPs? It would certainly change the conversation.

"Hey Chris - this member says there's something messed up with her account."

"Coop - I have a GFP here who needs your help...." - a bit different.

"Chris - can you print me off a new-client enrolment form?"

"Chris - we've got a new GFP in the house!"

Even if the GFP is angry, or posting sarcasm on facebook, or refuses to give you a reference on LinkedIn, you're still dealing with a GFP. And that simple trick of context changes everything about your relationship with that person.

Annoying clients .....well, aren't. Not anymore. How could a GFP be annoying? If a GFP has a beef, it must be legitimate, because they're a GFP!

Wolfgang Puck says we should treat each interaction as if it were our first and only chance to make an impression. The concept: *"Every Night Is Opening Night."* It's a common speaker's trick to imagine that you know everyone in the crowd, and everyone in the crowd is a GFP. When you know that everyone in the room is a GFP, conversation is easy. You're all friends.

You can deal with clients, or you can spend your days talking to GFPs. I prefer the latter.

***okay, you haven't solved it yet. GFP = Great F* People.

PEPSODENT AND COLORED BUMPERS

If you own a CrossFit Box or garage gym, you own bumper plates. They're a necessity. Aren't they?

For decades, folks have been doing OLY lifts with steel plates. They catch the clean, and then lower the weight with a little 'clink!' instead of dropping the bar. If they miss, they miss...but they don't drop the bar. You can make a case for bumper plates being safer, but is that the real reason we use them?

Bumper plates save bars, too. That's why gym owners like them. But do your members really care about your bars? After all, you're a millionaire business owner...why can't you take the value of one monthly membership and just buy a new bar? Sarcasm, of course...but many of your members don't know the answer.

The best feature of bumper plates is that they give clients a reward: after 21 thrusters, they can drop the bar. It looks great, adds excitement, and allows your clients to act out a dramatic sport ideal. Volleyball players get to spike the ball; baseball players can throw the ball into the crowd. We get to bail out of snatches.

This is important, because this REWARD is a critical part of the habit-building process. While bumper plates aren't 100% necessary for CrossFit, they do provide an opportunity for a benefit that ONLY they can provide.

Consider these:

A minty, "clean" feeling in your mouth has nothing to do with how toothpaste works (it would work even without the mint extracts and foamers. Both are actually aggravating your gums; that's what gives you the 'cool' sensation.) However, after you've established a tooth-brushing habit as a child, you won't feel finished until you receive that 'reward' sensation of cool mint.

Before toothpaste was popular, PepsoDent went from a near-bankrupt also-ran to dominating over 90% of the tooth-cleaning market by focusing on the reward rather than the benefits. Heck, less than half of the population brushed their teeth *at all* before PepsoDent helped build the habit.

Shampoo and dishwashing soap are the same, chemically-speaking. The difference is the perfume, colour, and frothing agents. The suds are the reward. Some shampoos (mostly anti-dandruff) employ different skin irritants like mint to give you the 'scrubbed' feeling, and most of us don't feel clean until after we've rinsed away a good lathering.

Most dry dog food is extremely similar to cereal. Missing are the human-friendly flavourings (though some now add artificial flavours like meat and fish.) What's stopping humans from eating them? The bone shape, the brand name, the dog pictures. In one famous study on conditioning, a professor handed out a bowl full of snacks (from which he also ate) for the length of one lecture. Students ate them without a hitch. Afterwards, he revealed they were dog treats. Some students vomited. This is the same effect applied in the opposite direction: a cognitive 'penalty' instead of a reward.

For more on these, read *"The Power of Habit"* by Charles Duhigg.

For this reason, I prefer coloured bumper plates. Black bumpers are great, and provide many fantastic 'reward' responses to help build habits in your members. Coloured plates make people feel like they're Pyrros Dimas.

THE LEARNING CURVE: YOUR GOLDEN TICKET

We now have NINE women in our Box who can deadlift over 300lbs. For most, it's taken at least a year of hard training. For one, though, deadlifting is as natural as walking. It's a movement she knows intrinsically....and she can do it with 350lbs on the bar.

She didn't KNOW, of course, that she'd be a great deadlifter. No guidance counsellor foretold her studly future in high school; no previous Personal Trainer found her biggest Bright Spot. Luckily, CrossFit did.

One small problem: she expects her rapid progress (1 year on May 20th!) to continue indefinitely. Four hundred pounds by September, she plans, and we offer her a nervous high-five.

What is the number one reason people continue to show up at your box? The learning curve. Most 'fitness facilities' and 'spas' fail to grasp that the greatest Sin, the Deadliest of the Seven Deadlies, is boredom. People stop coming when they've learned all they can from the Cybex machine.

In 2011, we were approached to offer our first Ignite Certification weekend. We'd been working toward this goal for nine months, but had never focused on the Certification course exclusively because the program ITSELF has been so successful. We realized we needed to write a textbook....but who had time to write with all the DOING we were DOING? We'd been gaining new clients, earning the trust and referrals of other therapists, talking about Ignite!, trying new things in the program, reaping the rewards....but never actually formalizing our methodology into something cohesive and replicable.

Enter Ignite Affiliate #1.

"We'd like to host a Certification," they told us. *"How's early June sound?"* We agreed, because...well, who needs sleep?

"We'd like to be an Affiliate," they said. *"What's your*

program like?" We told them. And then we started building the infrastructure.

At 4am, we wrote the textbook. At 7am, we coached CrossFit. At 9am, we talked to our Trademark lawyers. At 10, we edited. At 11, we sent out a plea to other Ontario Affiliates about what THEY would do with regard to territories and licensing....

...and I wonder, if the learning curve weren't so steep, would I keep coming back to the bar? Now that it's no longer hunger waking me up at 4am.....what is it? It's the Golden Ticket, that's what, and it's why all my GFPs show up in the morning. Lest we forget.

TRICKLE-DOWN RECRUITMENT

Nothing draws a crowd like a crowd. You've read that in Part 1.

Maybe you're no PT Barnum, but you can still get massive promotional benefit from a golden belt and a baseball cap.

In 2007, 70 people turned up for the CrossFit games. It was open to anyone, and they couldn't fill 100 spots.

In 2008, 200 people registered so quickly that the organizers (Castro and company) had to open up another 100 spots, and require prequalification. They also started tracking some of the top contenders, and the documentary *"Every Second Counts"* was birthed from the preceding months.

In 2009, the world was divided up by Affiliate density, and over a dozen Qualifiers were organized by Affiliates favoured by HQ. Qualifiers weren't standardized, but the CrossFit world watched the wicked WODs with glee.

In 2010, you had to qualify at "Sectionals," and then "Regionals" to make it to the Games. Canada had one Regional event. Couldn't make it? Oh well.

In 2011, when the Open launched, it was possible for 26,000 to participate in the first round of qualifying.

In 2012, there were more than 70,000 in the Open, and the Home Depot Centre sold out for spectators. ESPN3 was there, letting CrossFit Media staff practice producing the show for the 'real' mainstream to come in the years ahead. Reebok still has 8 years of sponsorship left.

Now, name another gym, fitness facility, workout paradigm, sport...even athletic event that's grown at the same rate in the last 50 years. There are none. No one's making movies about the road to the World Monster Truck Championships. No one's putting their homemade bull-riding movies on the Internet. No one's logging their archery results into online tracking software (of which there was exactly ONE choice two years ago. Now there are dozens.)

The spectacle rules. When we first ran the Catalyst Games in 2008, we anticipated lots of competition. We DIDN'T anticipate dozens of people with cameras. My favourite memory: a 510lbs deadlift, looking out through out transport door to flashbulbs exploding. Awesome. No other sport has ever given me that. And even better: we gave it to 20 members.

For the next 48 hours, hundreds of pictures surfaced on facebook, flickr, myspace, and me.com. We couldn't keep a handle on the content; we couldn't control the message; we didn't plan a media roll-out kit. We couldn't respond to every facebook album.

Instead, we offered a prize for Best Picture. Entries due by noon Monday, thank you, and the winner takes a baseball cap for their trouble. We got 300 entries on Sunday alone, put up our favourite five, and let members vote through a Vizu poll.

What was the prize - our gym's cost for all this publicity? A golden belt. Made by Champion Boxing. Under 100 bucks.

To recap: we put the event together. We told people about it. They brought spouses and friends. Each took pictures, added them to their OWN social networking site of choice, seen by 100-300 people each. They answered questions on each and every picture in an excited tone. *"You've gotta come and try this!" "Next year, I'm doing it for SURE!" "Wow, good for you! You look awesome!"* Then they visited the website (where we kept the hype alive for a week following,) took a survey that gave us very valuable data on potential clients, and checked back to see if their pick was a winner. Thousands of unique website visitors over 5 days. Bonus: the winner wore her belt to a football game that night, landing her a spot in the paper. Cost: $103 (including the hat.)

Do something remarkable, and people will remark.

By the way, this won best picture:

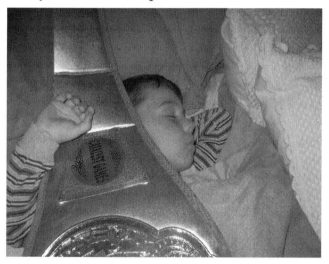

COMMUNITY, EVEN AROUND A COMMODITY

In the middle of Illinois cornfield, there's a tiny town named Ladd. Don't try to find it in your road atlas. On the outskirts of Ladd is Rip's Chicken.

This is the tiny dining area. Through the wall in the back, you'll see the start of the famous lineup.

Rip's is only open three days per week. You'll have to stand in line for over an hour before you're seated. The 'waiting' area is twice as large as the 'eating' area. There are two things on the menu: light meat, and dark meat; both served on top of a slice of Wonder bread, too hot to eat, with a side of pickles and a plate of crispies. We'll get to them in a minute.

Rip's has been serving the same thing since 1936. The chicken is good, but not different from a thousand other more convenient fried chicken diners in the Corn Belt. Same chicken, same fryers, same ol' Wonder Bread. A world of difference.

If you come on Wednesday night, you may only have to wait an hour to get a seat. You may not even have to stand outside, on the sidewalk. You'll cram into the 'entranceway' with dozens of others in a loose line. One of your friends will head to the bar - you can drink in line, of course; and the bar runs, conveniently, almost the full length of the waiting area. It's not hard to get a cold beer while you wait. Or three. There's not much to look at in line, just a couple of Rip's T-shirts. Very little to distract you from conversation. No real place to sit down.

When you finally reach the front of the line, a waiter - is he the owner? Is this Rip? - with a pen behind one ear will ask, *"How many light and how many dark?"* He's asking how many are in your party, and who prefers which meat. That's it. As for a seat, well....he'll get back to you.

The 'dining room' is small. The kitchen is in full view. You can see and hear chickens as they're lowered into the fryer. You can watch the boy peeling potatoes. You can watch Mr. Rip giving your order to the cook. You can see waitresses piling up plates of chicken, pickles, and fries in their arms: grease crackling, a dozen stacked plates

teetering precariously, and hope they're headed your way.

The chicken is seared up so tightly that it's much too hot to eat. There are no utensils immediately obvious, so you'll poke holes in the deep-fried batter to let some heat escape. The bread isn't to eat; it's for soaking up grease. In the meantime, there are pickles. And Crispies.

Crispies. Not kidding.

Crispies are little flakes of broken-off fried batter. They're smaller than Corn Flakes, but look the same. You take a pinch of them, roll them up in a slice of pickle, and eat them that way. You can actually feel your arteries harden as you eat them. Not exactly Paleo-friendly.

Thirty minutes later, you'll be stuffed with a sort of post-binge fulfilment that borders on post-coital. You'll throw a twenty on your greasy bill, check your shirt for stray ketchup, and head out to your bad parking spot a few blocks away. You'll walk, guiltily, past a line that's even longer than when you arrived.

Rip's doesn't advertise. Their website is bad. What's their secret?

1. First, nothing looks bad if it appears to be done on purpose. Horrific hairdos, odd clothing, bizarre art, inconvenient home design....if it looks like it was done on purpose, it passes. Voila: Crispies.

2. They have a line BECAUSE they have a line. It would be pretty easy to put tables and chairs in half the waiting area, right? But then there would be no waiting. There would be no anticipation. There would be no beer sales. You'd just have a restaurant.

3. They know what they're good at: light meat, and dark meat. And they'll stick to that, thanks. No "International Night," no sushi.

4. They let anticipation build. Sometimes, it's so busy that you KNOW you're not in the running for the batch that's just come out of the deep fryer. You're watching the kid peeling potatoes, thinking, "I hope that one's mine."

5. The novelty factor. The first time I ever took my girlfriend (now wife) to Illinois, I drove an hour out of my way to take her to Rip's. Just to show her.

6. Simplicity. No one at Rip's is bugging you to buy a 12-

punch visit card, or sign up for their Kids' Club. No one's pushing t-shirts. The waitress isn't telling you the specials. You're not distracted by moose heads with sunglasses on the walls.

Rip's could maybe do better. Or maybe doing 'better' would mean not doing quite as well.

PLANTING SEEDS VS. SELLING PUMPKINS

When you create relevant content for your blog, it's there forever. Your goal, when writing, is to answer a question that most haven't yet asked. What problem is your post solving? What gap is it filling?

For instance, in 2009, we wrote an article comparing CrossFit with P90X. We were as fair and objective as we could be. Turns out we were one of the few who made the comparison, and we STILL get website traffic from a huge spectrum of interested peepers.

We also put a piece together to answer the question, "Is CrossFit for Runners?" in the same year. We wrote it for a local audience, but since no one else has answered that specific question, and people search for that particular phrase, it's become a hugely popular article. So popular, in fact, that I pitched it to RunnersWorld.com. No response. They likely get a thousand pitches per day, after all, and ours was unsolicited. Spam!

Instead, on the RunnersWorld.com forums, a CrossFit advocate linked to our article comparing CrossFit to P90X as a resource. Others sent the link to their friends. When I noticed all the hits coming from RunnersWorld.com, I got myself a username and posted a link to our "Is CrossFit For Runners?" article.

No, we're not published in RunnersWorld. But we're hitting their core audience in a non-scripted way. We didn't start the conversation. But we're helping others make their point.

When we first lay out our wares for RunnersWorld - big, bright pumpkins - they saw only another oversized gourd in the patch. We thought we had the Great Pumpkin, Charlie Brown, and they thought we had pie filling. However, we managed to stick around long enough to sell some seeds. And when you buy seeds, you typically ask the seller how best to make them grow.

The take-home, for us:

1. Put out lots of relevant content that seeks to answer questions.

2. Opinion pieces are interesting, but no one searches for your opinion. Ever.

3. We're culturally programmed to share stories, not data.

4. A resource is better than an ad.

5. We're better to find discussions and help the process than play 'show and tell.'

Instead of advertising, find discussions and help. Avoid picking sides. Be a resource and a tour guide. Sell seeds.

TWO WAYS TO GROW

1. Poach customers away from the competition.

2. Expand the market.

Up until this point, CrossFit has done extremely well at #1. There existed (and still does) a crowd of folks who aren't content with just doing 3 sets of 8-12 on the Pec Deck. They had gym memberships at Bally's because that's all there was. Some grew complacent; some grew too competent at the Pec Deck to risk their reputation on something new. Some quickly jumped to CrossFit.

That group is dwindling, though. Eventually, that well will run dry.

If we continue to let McFit harvest all the newbies - that is, be their point of entry into the fitness world - we're going to be left with the minority: those who have the courage, sense, and malcontent necessary to seek the 'beyond.'

I don't know the ladies in the picture on the right. But I can tell the story verbatim: new client signs up for a 30-day trail. She's new; doesn't even own a proper 'exercise outfit.' Checks her hair on the way to meet her 'personal trainer,' who wears nonthreatening, frumpy clothing. Trainer explains that aerobic exercise is the way to burn fat, that Ms. Newsome would be best to start each workout with 25 minutes on the MagnetoBore Bike, followed by 20 minutes of slow, easy stretching; then should think about incorporating a little resistance training with very light weights. A circuit of 20 repetitions on each machine should do it. Any fewer reps, and Ms. Newsome may 'bulk up.' Machines are set up like this. Lift your legs like this. Feel the burn? Now cool down with 20 more minutes on the bike. Vary your 'cardio' by adding in that exciting new Elliptical Trainer. They're good for burning fat.

You've got to unlearn - unteach - all of this, the first time you meet Ms. Newsome. What if you meet her at a cocktail party, or in an elevator? How much time is it going to take to re-educate her? If you want to be the best teacher, it's usually better to be the first teacher.

It's up to us to make fitness accessible to the masses. When you post your WOD today, whose picture will you add? When you do your monthly challenge, whose profile will you highlight? Are your OnRamp classes trumpeted ahead of Nico's big 250lbs clean? Do you emphasize to the world that CrossFit will improve a person's skill set, and thereby performance at everything .....even step aerobics classes? Do you let people get away with calling your OnRamp class *"bootcamp?"*

This is more than marketing. It's a moral imperative that we become the first fitness professionals that people meet. We need to be their entry point, not just the signal fire, high on an unreachable hill. Imagine Ms. Newsome - the one on the bike - asking Coach Frumpstein about that new CrossFit thing she's heard about; what the likely response?

Also, this picture is used as a promotion. They're *trumpeting* this process. Think about it.

CAMPFIRING: SHARING STORIES

There are a thousand ways to do this, but the most important parts are:

1. Keep them excited

2. Give them a story to tell and a reason to tell it.

CrossFit does a lot to handle #1 for you. The program is exciting, and if you work hard to keep your Box exciting with great coaching, good music, a competitive atmosphere, and a general atmosphere of triumph, #1 will almost fall into your lap.

#2 takes work. They'll write their own stories if you give them opportunities. In a world that's quickly running out of sunsets into which to ride off on horseback, you have to give them chances at being heroes. Pairs workouts, special events, points systems, quadriceps pain, PR boards, online tracking....we cover that stuff at length on 321GoProject.com. If you're doing CrossFit, you have a story to tell.

The trick is getting them to tell it. People are shy and humble at all the wrong times. You have to give them question-starters.

"Where'd you get that cool shirt?"

"What's the trophy for?"

"Why is that red card tacked to your wall? Catalyst Games? What's that?"

"Why are you walking that way?"

"What are you guys talking about? CrossFit? Is that like P90X?"

"What did you have to do to get that hat?"

"Why are your shins all scraped up?"

"Where do you go on your lunch hour?"

"Who sent you this birthday card?"

"What's this newsletter about?"

"So....what did you do this weekend?"

Give a person a campfire, and they'll start telling stories.

These tales – shared context – are so important, you should consider a section on your website devoted to clients' stories.

People love to tell their own history. Everyone possesses a bit of drama that's special - if only to them. While promoting our Catalyst Games website, I send every single participant an "Athlete Profile" questionnaire. My goal is to both highlight the athleticism to be displayed, and also to make the point that *"anyone - even YOU - can DO this!"* So every athlete has their "Athlete Profile" posted: a huge spectrum of talent, experience, and aesthetic.

Last year, we hosted a *"What's Your Catalyst?"* contest on facebook. Folks were asked to telll us the WHY behind their WODs. We received lengthy histories, punchy drama, and a few that choked us up a little. We hung on every single word.

If a prospective CrossFitter is reading your site, they'll be intrigued by a link called "Client Stories." Every gym now has a "Testimonials" section, full of vanilla-flavoured predictability, usually a sentence or two about how positive, cheerful, and motivating Sally Mae was while they walked on the treadmill. Folks are largely immune to Testimonials.

But stories? No one's immune. Give me 1000 words on providing an inspiration to your kids, or battling cancer to the end, or just becoming the athlete you were never allowed to be....I'm captivated. Give me a couple of quality photos of you hammering through "Grace," and I'm in love with you.

If your story is on my website, it goes without saying that you endorse my Gym. And now, the new client can recognize faces, feels the sense of community, and can easily break the ice with a group in an intimidating environment. Win-win. Plus, CrossFitters like seeing themselves in print as much as anyone else.

As CrossFit Affiliate owners, we've got it easy.

Read this email I received over the weekend:

Hi Chris, my name is ███████████, *I am a crossfitter and go to crossfitmississauga. Tonight I was chatting with an old friend who lives in the Sault and we got onto the subject of fitness. She talked about how much her trainer costs and all that Globo Gym garbage so I told her about Crossfit and then googled you guys and told her. Ok, so I have talked up crossfit like crazy to her and I need you guys to share it with her.* ▮▮▮▮ *is her name and she will be calling soon. I think that she may be a beast.... From one crossfitter to another thank you, and please help my friend discover how amazing CF is, thanks Chris!* ▮

You think anyone's writing an email like this to the owner of Bally's, 24-Hour Fitness, Gold's, or GoodLife?

BUYING IT – MY (BRIEF) LIFE IN FITNESS SALES
In 2000, I landed my 'dream job': managing a fitness equipment store. After years of working from 6am-10pm, driving through all weather conditions, shuttling members of the 'Ski Team' around like a parent, here was my chance. I could be IN the fitness industry from 9-5, making an actual salary, and still helping people. All I had to do was learn to sell stuff. How hard could THAT be?

I found out quickly. No matter how many books I read, or speakers I attended, I never once made my sales quota for the month. Two years in, I could vomit data about treadmills to anyone who came into the store...but I couldn't tell a story, and so couldn't convince anyone to buy. This is because I don't know any stories about elliptical trainers. Somewhere, I'm sure there IS a good story or two that doesn't involve a hilarious mishap...but I've never heard it.

The irony didn't strike me for years afterwards: at 9am, I'd dutifully dust off the machines, and spend the next eight hours extolling their virtues to anyone who came through the door. I'd tell them that a treadmill that cost $3000 was 'better value' because it would outlast all the miles they'd be sure to put on it. I'd push the $4000 home gym because it had more workout options...just follow the chart printed on the weight stack over here, see? Mindless. Simple. You can't help but exercise on this baby! This exercise bike will even track the miniscule amount of calories you'll burn on it!

At 5pm, though, I'd head through the back doors to the parking lot. There, an athlete would wait for his personal training session. We'd push sleds, sprint, swing plates, carry heavy stuff...but not use any of the equipment from the store. Not once. Not even a little pair of spring collars.

It's probably obvious by now: I couldn't sell the other stuff because I didn't believe in it.

Jerry Seinfeld: I have to go take this stupid lie detector test. How do I beat it?

George Costanza: You're asking me how to lie better? That's like saying to Picasso, "Teach me to paint like you can."

Jerry Seinfeld (rolling eyes): Well, whatever. I gotta go.

Costanza: Remember, Jerry: it's not a lie if you believe it.

The best religious leaders, salesmen, politicians....they don't have to 'sell' anything, because they believe their own message. If you don't, people will know. Can't produce your PR time for "Murph" when a new client asks? They won't stick around. Immerse yourself, or risk being exposed.

On the other hand, if people know your best times; SEE you doing CrossFit; HEAR you raving about Paleo........

SHARED SOUVENIRS

Twenty-five years ago, kids in Ontario had to complete a standardized fitness testing program called*"ParticipACTION."* It was mandated by the provincial government, and was nothing more than a series of physical tests like pushups, pullups, situps, a 400m run.... Every kid who completed the course received a 'Participant' ribbon. But you could also earn a Bronze, Silver, Gold... or an "Award Of Excellence" if you completed a task in the top 5th percentile in the Province. Since most of my ribbons didn't warrant saving (somewhere in a garbage dump are a half-dozen "Participant" ribbons) I didn't.

Last month, at my daughter's gymnastics class for kids, another parent approached me and asked if I remembered the medals. She'd won two "Awards of Excellence" and was sure she still had them somewhere.

Over the past six weeks, I've been coaching a ragtag group of 9-year-old hockey players. Their skills vary widely. Their physical development is wildly scattered. Some are already muscled; some can't coordinate a running motion; none had ever done any off-ice training before.

Each week, I'd hold a little challenge at the end of the session. Most of the parents would be there to pick up their kids, and I wanted them to see a high note: kids tired but cheering, yelling, grinning and fighting. The first week, we had all seven kids doing a flexed-arm hang (paused pullup) on the pullup bars at once. Kids were yelling, parents were cheering; a great experience. I was hoarse after the first 30 seconds, and I yell. A LOT.

When it was over, one kid said, *"Is there a prize?"* I had to think of something quickly. So I made up little postcards that were like *"Get Out Of Jail Free"* cards (below.) The winner of the flexed-arm hang this week could redeem his card next week for 10 free reps on any exercise. They could use it to win a challenge, or just take a rest. Whatever.

In the sixth and final week, we did a miniature version of "Kelly." Three boys were tied until the very last minute. I reminded them that they could use their postcards to get ahead. One boy stopped doing box jumps and asked, *"Do we get the cards back?"* *"No,"* I said. *"I keep them."*

Not a single kid turned their card in. The next day, three parents signed up for the OnRamp program. One dad: *"Neat trick, getting my kid to put your logo and website on our fridge for six weeks."* It wasn't supposed to be marketing, but it sure turned out that way.

To us, it's a postcard. Eleven cents of production, eight seconds of sloppy handwriting. To them, it's an Award of Excellence.

GAP THEORY, EXPLAINED (FINALLY!)

Lowenstein's research on the Gap Theory of curiosity has direct bearing on your business.

As discussed in *"Made To Stick: Why Some Ideas Die and Others Thrive,"* Lowenstein wanted to know the reason people would stay to the end of a bad movie; why they'd watch a football game to the bitter end, even if they weren't fans of either team; why they'd read a mystery novel even after they'd figured out the identity of the killer.

What he discovered was that people built themselves a

'knowledge gap' and had to fill it in. To not fill it in was painful. They'd create a framework using known criteria, and then do whatever necessary to fill in the missing piece. For instance, in the case of a murder mystery, they'd paint themselves a picture using the information a clues given: the history of each character, the fingerprints found, the bloody shoe... But if there were one thing missing (the killer's identity,) they'd go to great ends to find out. To complete the picture. To fill the Gap.

This is a totally natural instinct, and it applies directly to your CrossFit Affiliate. Where common gym 'programs' - bodybuilding set and rep paradigms - and plans like P90X fall apart is this: there's a ceiling. After 3 months, you've seen it all. The gaps are filled. Yes, you can increase weight or repetitions, but there's no longer anything to be curious about. The knowledge part of the equation has been satisfied.

It should be obvious that CrossFit creates as many knowledge gaps as it fills. Every time you improve one aspect, you'll spot a weakness in another. For instance, your "Michael" time is terrific; your "Grace" is abysmal. So you take a month and do some extra work on your Clean and Jerk. Meanwhile, your CrossFit Total is lagging behind the best in your Box.....

Your job as Affiliate owner is to define the gaps. To paraphrase a famous line by George Bush: *"There are known knowns. Those are the things we know. There are known unknowns. Those are the things we know that we don't know. Then there are the unknown unknowns: the things we don't know that we don't know yet."* If you followed that, then you'll understand that new CrossFitters aren't savvy enough to yet know what they don't know. Tell them.

"Hey, your Clean and Jerk should start this way....."

"Your kipping could improve a little, and you'd be faster at Angie...."

"Sometime, let's get together and practice your bench press technique...."

"Your stride could be a bit more efficient. Want to try POSE? It will hurt less than what you're doing now....."

This also underscores the necessity of teaching new exercises with every group before you start the WOD: to show people how much they don't know. As long as you keep opening gaps, they'll keep striving to fill them.

CREATIVE COACHING: SHEPHERDS AND COWBOYS

Coaches differ in personality, but that doesn't mean that one style is better than another. Different styles attract (and keep) different clients.

Consider two styles of animal control, the Cowboy and the Shepherd:

The Cowboy:

> ⋏ Guides the animals by herding from the rear, or the middle, of the group

⁁ Is loud

⁁ Slaps leather fearlessly

⁁ Throws himself in the way of the charging animal

⁁ Prefers confrontation to provoke immediate action

⁁ Uses the tools available, including voice, but also whip and heel;

⁁ 'Breaks' animals, and then builds them back up better

⁁ Uses a one-on-one approach most often

The Shepherd:

⁁ Changes a stubborn animal's direction a little at a time, not head-on

⁁ Leads from the front, usually with bait, or a promise

⁁ Avoids direct confrontation, because blocking a sheep from grain will only create more desire

⅄ Creates safety in numbers

⅄ 'Teaches' the animals with the carrot instead of the stick

⅄ Uses the group dynamic most often

Both:

⅄ Love the animals

⅄ Can coexist in the same barnyard

⅄ Use the same tools (hay, water, pasture)

Of note: though the 'cowboy' figure is more romanticized, it's no coincidence that the largest grassroots-driven movement of all time refers to its Messiah as *"The Good Shepherd."* If people can relate to you as one of them, part of The Resistance, a leader in name and action, they're more likely to follow. It's sometimes easier to convince the flock to move in a single direction than one single wild stallion. So says me, but hey - I come from generations of shepherds.

Now in my fifteenth year as a Personal Trainer, I know there's no formula for guaranteed success. There are Trainers all over the social skills / education graph. Sometimes, a terrific personality like Richard Simmons can get by on exuberance and a great haircut. Sometimes, though, a genius like Mel Siff isn't heard - or can't capitalize on his life's work - because he's not *out there* enough.

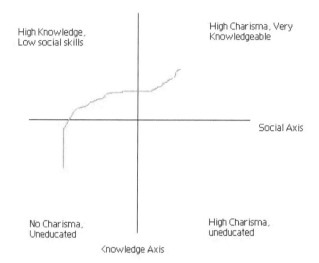

There should be a third dimension, of course: coaching skills. Knowledge and charisma are both important, but if you can't translate your knowledge into action on the part of your client, it's useless. If all that charm - practised or natural - can't motivate a bar off the floor, it's not enough.

When I started, I'd argue on discussion forums and in chat rooms that education trumped experience, because I had a lot of one and very little of the other. *"But you could be teaching the wrong stuff for years!"* I'd argue. That was 1996. Now I recognize the necessity of both.

The curve above represents my path, I believe, toward my current position: owner of a large facility, with an expanding client base and a valuable brand asset. Two others make a great living here, as well as gym staff and interns. As far as I've figured it, here's my mental checklist for every client appointment:

    1.A great greeting.

2.Banter during the warmup to include a personal detail mentioned at the last meeting (*hey, how was your daughter's play?*) Let the client know that you care about what happens in their life.

3.Ask how the homework assigned at the last meeting played out.

4.Brief outline of the goals of the workout.

5.Skills and reinforcement. Keep it positive and corrective. This is where you want 100% perfection on technique. I also try to keep the client smiling during this portion - this is the frustrating part, where people can get down on themselves.

6.Break out at least one scientific explanation, but keep it short. This isn't just good salesmanship (*"look what I know!"*) it's also building a more knowledgeable clientele.

7.Outline the 'challenge' portion of the workout (or the WOD)

8.Outline the goals of the WOD – i.e. anaerobic capacity - and your rationale for the weight chosen (*"I know you can do more, but I'm concerned that grip strength will limit your performance, instead of work capacity. I want you to keep moving, so I've chosen a lighter weight."*)

9.*3-2-1 go!* Voice and inflection change, posture changes. Shorter sentences, exclamation points, no more technical instructions. Commanding tone.

10.Collapse. Sharing of water. Now's the time to tell a story. *"Last year, we had this tournament called 'FranFest.' One lady lost a tooth. She kept going anyway. Hahaha...."*

11.Stretch and review homework challenges for the week. Encourage contact by phone or logging workout results.

12. Any questions?

13. Book the next appointment, if not already scheduled.

14. Mention something coming up in the client's life *("Enjoy painting that fence this weekend!")*

The very fact that it's a checklist makes it imperfect. You have to be able to touch on all of these without seeming to refer to a spreadsheet-in-the-sky. If you can't do anything else:

1) make them laugh

2) remember things that are important to the client

2) impress upon them your technical knowledge in a non-academic way. One more example: after I explain rotational torque, in 30 seconds or less, with a chalk stick-man on the gym floor, I usually say something self-demeaning, like, *"...or maybe I'm just making this all up."* They usually laugh. They won't remember any of the content, but they will remember that I know, and that's enough.

PRAISING EFFORT, NOT SKILL

In Bradenton, Florida, Nick Bollettieri coaches tennis. In his 80s, Bollettieri has been coaching at the Academy that bears his name since the 1970s. Many of the top players in the world have passed through his doors.

As Mathew Syed wrote in *"Bounce"*, Bollettieri Academy appears a lot like any other first-tier Tennis school: rows and rows of courts; pros in white, sporting the Bollettieri logo; dozens of young athletes working on their two-handed backhand. The difference isn't obvious until you look at the faces: grim, determined. Sweaty. Jaw muscles flexed, they're clearly focused on doing better, and working hard to get there. This is NOT the case at other Tennis centres.

Does Bollettieri somehow sift out the hardest workers? Is he so tough that the top contenders self-select?

No. Bollettieri does a lot of the things common to great coaches: he keeps messages simple. *"Move to the left earlier,"* he'll say. He only tries to correct one thing at a time. And one other trick:

He praises effort, NOT talent. *"Good. You're working hard." "That's okay,"* he says, when a student hits a forehand long. *"It's not the outcome, it's how you respond to the challenges."* And kids DO respond: they work harder for Bollettieri than anyone else.

This is the main theory behind Carol Dweck's Praise Experiments. Essentially, kids react positively to praise for their performance...at first. Long-term, though, it can hamstring them.

Dweck's experiments showed that kids who were showered with praise for their OUTCOMES were less likely to challenge themselves in the future (risking self-esteem,) less likely to progress much past their comfort level, and less likely to achieve a high level of accomplishment AT ALL. Praise a kid for scoring an 'A' on a test? They'll learn to avoid things at which they don't naturally excel. Praise a kid's amazing box jump skills? They're LESS likely to try higher boxes next time. After all, we all like being praised...why risk it?

The key is not to forgo praise, but to praise the RIGHT thing. And the RIGHT thing, says Bollettieri, possibly the most successful Tennis coach in the world, is EFFORT.

EFFORT is a constant. You're either trying hard, or not. Trying hard leads to purposeful practice. Conscientious effort is the delivery service for champions. Encourage hard work. Acknowledge talent, but don't make it the frame for your praise.

PURPOSEFUL PRACTICE

Many Affiliates write their own WODs. Many coaches prefer longer-term progression, with planned periods of strength bias or endurance focus, written right into the WOD. We believe in an open road with lots of off-ramps and on-ramps.

Our CrossFit groups, by and large, follow the main site with some additional strength work. We do other groups - Barbell Bettys, Frat Barbell, Enduro, the Nutri-Ninjas - with different focuses, but all using a CrossFit model. In each of those other groups, folks can emphasize something specific, but always with the intent to return to the 'main' group.

The point of such digression is to provide purposeful practice. General fitness can be greatly enhanced through the short-term specialization of one trait at a time, we think.

The important part here is to be clearly delivering workouts with purpose beyond killing people. As the 'boot camp' rave dies a well-earned death, the notion of kettlebellocide is going to lose its vogue. We need to be ready with science.

Does every participant in your 6am CrossFit group know the training value of 1-1-1-1-1-1? Can the guy who finished last in your noon group tell his friends why he was doing ring dips, and why it was worth those burns on his upper arms? Does the first-time visitor to your site, curiously checking the workout *"just to see what this is all about...."* understand WHY a 21-15-9 has metabolic value?

You don't have to write the same paragraph every time. You don't need to quote studies. All you need is a paragraph:

"We do max lifts because we want our progress to be measurable. Our Central Nervous System needs to learn to be more efficient, and recruit more force in less time."

"Today's an aerobic emphasis. We don't do this often. We believe that low-level "cardio" is boring, unnecessary, and high-risk for your joints. But we like to measure our progress. And we like going fast."

"This may look like an ordinary circuit; it's not. There's no chime to change stations, nowhere to jog on the spot, and no hand towels. We're trying to use the Valsalva manoeuvre repetitively to artificially raise your heart rate, creating a metabolic hole big enough to kill off the dinosaurs."

If it spurs discussion in the 'responses' section of our blog, even better.

SINGULARITY

This is Alexei Sidorovitch Medveyev.

He's one of the greatest weightlifting coaches of all time, pioneering huge advances in periodization, biomechanics, and force development. His USSR teams dominated weightlifting from 1970-1974.

A totalitarian approach to managing athletes has its obvious drawbacks. It can also teach us much, even 40 years later. Medveyev could control when his athletes slept, and for how long; when they ate, and what; what they lifted, and when. Under his guidance, the Soviet Weightlifting program experimented with color; sound; and even smell, marching their athletes through different types of forest after their workouts and measuring relative recovery to the 10th power (spoiler alert: Siberian Fir is best.)

You can read more about these 'best practices' in Managing The Training of Weightlifters (pictured below.) Worth the cover price just for the short paragraph on steroid usage recommendations for women.

Medveyev also experimented with coaching methods. Concerned with far more than just load, bar speed, and reps, Medveyev measured the effects of voice quality; instruction quantity; and total practice time. Prilepin's Table was developed during this period. Other ideas were tried, measured, and discarded.

One of Medveyev's guiding principles: never give an athlete more than one instruction or correction in a training session. Yes, they may need to raise their chin; they may need to stand taller; they may need to lift their hips more. All of those may be true, but only one may be corrected at a time. One instruction was useful; two instructions handicapped the athlete, splitting their attention.

When a cue was mastered, the next was given. Information would be prioritized based on relevance, or timing. Do the same with your new contacts: on their first visit, they need to hear that CrossFit is novel, or different, or challenging, or fun, or Sport.

As teachers, Coaches, and experts trying to deliver their message, we should remember this: one point at a time.

- Chin up.
- CrossFit is fun.
- Gluten causes gut problems.
- Widen your grip.
- Novelty helps you stick with it.
- Hips up a bit.
- Bring your friends.
- Greg Glassman.
- Babies are great squatters.
- Poke your chin through.
- No mirrors.
- Pull your shoulders down and back.
- Protein supplements usually have a lot of sugar.
- CrossFit is like Personal Training.

One point, one message, per contact. That's it.

THE TRIBE – SHIBBOLETH

If you're browsing through the book of *Judges* in the Bible, you'll stumble across this short passage (or one of its paraphrasings):

> *Gilead then cut Ephraim off from the fords of*

the Jordan, and whenever Ephraimite fugitives said, 'Let me cross,' the men of Gilead would ask, 'Are you an Ephraimite?' If he said, 'No,' they then said, 'Very well, say "Shibboleth" (שבלת).' If anyone said, "Sibboleth" (סבלת), because he could not pronounce it, then they would seize him and kill him by the fords of the Jordan. Forty-two thousand Ephraimites fell on this occasion.

Here's what happened: the Gileadites defeated the Ephraimites for control of the Jordan River. The Emphraim refugees tried to return to their homeland - through the Gilead army's ranks, and across the river. The Ephraimites would claim to be Gileadites to get through the ranks, and to test the validity of their claim, the Gilead guardsmen would ask them to repeat the word, "*Shibboleth.*"

See, the Ephraim tongue had no occurrences of the "sh" sound. Therefore, when trying to pronounce the word, the Ephraimites would say, "*Sibboleth*" (the 's' sound, not the 'sh' sound.) Then the Gilead men would kill them.

In CrossFit, we have our own "*shibboleths*" - words like 'AMRAP' and 'WOD' that quickly identify a CrossFitter. When you're on a cruise ship, and the gal beside you at the nickel slots talks about "*hitting a quick Fran*" before coming down to deck level....odds are, she's in your Tribe (and even if she's not, the conversation is going to be worth having.)

A shibboleth is terrific as a unifying factor: it creates a sense of belonging, of similarity, and sharing something unique. However, if can ALSO act as a sentry, and deter wannabe Gileadites who are trying to cross the Jordan. If, during an introductory class, the Coaches carelessly throw around the CrossFit Insider Lexicon, they're sending a signal that they belong to a group and that the new recruits do NOT. They are projecting elitism, and they'll ostracize the newcomers if do it too often.

It's part of our genetic heritage to seek people who are "like us" and avoid people who speak a different language. Perhaps it's worth mentioning some of the odd-sounding CrossFitisms in your OnRamp group, Personal Training sessions, or introductory classes?

The original radio show about 'Shibboleth' was from *The Age of Persuasion*, and it's a great one to download. You can do so through the iTunes store (it's changed its name to *'Under The Influence,'* but the older episodes are still available.)

Feel bad for the Ephraimites? Well, "*Shibboleth*" originally referred to the part of the stalk that held the grain. Over the centuries, the agrarian habits of the Gileadites - wherever they are now - are probably giving them diabetes. It's something.

BUILDING THE APOLLO

On November 21, 1934, a young girl - 17 years old - paced

nervously backstage. She was at the Apollo to dance in an Amateur Night contest. First prize: twenty-five dollars. Big money for a teenaged black girl in Harlem in the 1930s.

As she watched, the Edwards Sisters - an amazing duo of teenaged dancers - knocked the crowd off its feet with an unbeatable routine. The young girl was intimidated. She'd come all this way; she NEEDED the money; she was shaking with nerves; and she knew she couldn't beat the Edwards Sisters.

So she sang. She sang *"Judy,"* by Hoagy Carmichael, a song she loved to sing for herself but had never performed. Then she sang *"The Object of My Affection"* by the Boswell Sisters. She wasn't perfect, but she won $25.00.

That was Ella Fitzgerald, and she was the beneficiary of remarkable opportunity: a theatre in New York who allowed "coloured" people to sit with - and compete with - whites; a backstage area littered with enormous talent, including James Brown (booed offstage several times) and a laundry list of other huge talent. She practised with them; sang with them; collaborated and competed with them.

Just like Bill Gates, whose high school had one of the first 4 publicly-accessible mainframes in the USA. Just like Mozart, whose father was a composer. Just like Keith Richards, who met Mick Jagger on a train station platform on his way to elementary school. Just like Nicole Carroll, and Dave Castro, and Annie Sakamoto, and the others who walked into Greg Glassman's world...and now form the regime at the top of this little game we call CrossFit.

Regardless of where they wound up, the convergence of opportunity to practice; access to feedback; and an abundance of similar starving artists is what built the individual. Differentiation and sameness occurred, and they all launched to greatness in their own right.

It may be that the woman in your 7pm group isn't very good at front squats. On the other hand, she may row a 1:40 500m in the last round of the WOD tonight. She may anchor herself to that Bright Spot until she finds another...like double-unders, maybe. And then, handstands against the wall. And, someday, when she's practising front squats, another member will say, "*Hey, it goes like this.....*" and that cue will make all the difference.

It could be that the overweight guy who's wearing beach khakis to the 6am group has bad knees. On the other hand, he has remarkable grip, and soaks up your praise on high-rep hang cleans. Others are jealous, and they tell him so. He puts those compliments in his chest pocket. Soon, he finds another Bright Spot: he can buy real gym shorts off the rack. Six months later, he's the heaviest guy at the Level I Cert...but he's come a long way, baby, and he can tell you more about weight loss than anyone in the room. By 2012, he'll have ten clients who would never have come to your Box without him.

Are you building the Apollo?

DELIVERING PRIDE

Last spring, a large part of the Catalyst Family attended a local 5k/10k.

This is not a course on which records are set: on almost 80% of the run, you're either climbing or descending. Climbs are steep; rocks are plentiful. The scenery, though, is gorgeous; the company can't be beat; and the kids' race is a stroke of genius.

Warming up at home, we had a 'family stretch' after breakfast: me, on the floor with my six-year-old, my three-year-old, and my wife. I was preparing for my first 10k race; my daughter, for all the cookies she'd encounter at the finish line. My son - three - wondered why HE didn't get to run in *"the big race."*

Perhaps tempted by all the cookie talk, he maintained that he wanted to participate all the way to the event. The $5 entry fee got him a backpack, granola bar, water bottle, vitamins....but the REAL payoff was the pride.

Finishing the 10k in fifty minutes, I barely had time to recover before the start of the Kids' event. The under-5 class ran 500m; halfway, my son asked for a ride on my shoulders. I reminded him of his Bright Spots (he'd already run halfway,) showed him how close he was to finishing *("after this corner, you'll see the big clock!")* and then let him make the decision. He chose cookies. Let go of my hand. Sprinted. Crossed to dozens of cheering grown-ups. I choked up.

My daughter, during her 800m run: *"It's easy. Do I sprint now? Now? Now?"* - when it was finally time to sprint for the finish, she tripped over a hole in the ground at full speed. For a very brief moment, doubt crossed her face; but she jumped up and ran her fastest to finish. It was exhausting for dad, but liberating for her, and she went straight to the cookie tent, wearing a new medal in Catalyst green.

We had over a dozen first-time "racers" from the gym with us that day. Some had never done 5k before. Some had done a 'time trial' with our Beginner Running Group. Those people all had a Personal Best - a first-time finish, or a fastest time. A few of the bravest ran their first 10k on that rock-hard course. Returnees - including many who were first-time racers LAST year - had personal bests. Our fastest (10k over hills in 38 minutes) was two minutes faster. And then we all went for fish and beer.

FOSTERING THE JONES

Last week, we went for a row.

Our skill work in the 7pm group consisted of some stroke practice on the Concept2: two minutes of rowing without any arm pull, followed by two minutes of hard pulls with a low stroke rate (under 23 spm.)

While James rowed, I repeated: *"Legs. Back. Arms. Arms. Back. Legs."* Most coaches can visualize the progression of the stroke through that short series of cues.

"Hey!" said James, *"Those are the same cues we used last week on that deadlift high-pull!"* He was right. I had used the same cues for both exercises, and though I hadn't overtly made the connection between SDHP and rowing, HE had the epiphany himself. All around him, the room lit up as light bulbs went off above the heads of the other rowers.

Your brain loves to make connections. As David Rock points out in, *"Your Brain At Work,"* creating a new synapse - a connection between little bits of information - triggers the release of dopamine, a chemical which makes you happy. Cocaine works the same way. Dopamine is addictive; it's a reward mechanism for learning new information; and it's healthy, because it helps you store engrams more efficiently.

Hearing new information, though, doesn't trigger the same response. If I had just told James that a SDHP involves a pull action that's very similar to that of a row, he wouldn't have had the dopamine release, and the new connection wouldn't have been as satisfying. The JOY - the reward - came because he closed the gap between bits of data himself.

How do you trigger the dopamine release in a client?

First, establish Bright Spots. What does the client already know *(ie, what are they already doing right?)*

Next, establish Future Bright Spots *(how will they know they're progressing? What's the first sign they'll have?)*

Illustrate the gap in knowledge (see *Lowenstein's Gap*

Theory.)

Give them a 20% bonus (start them on the path.)

If necessary, keep prodding them toward the revelation. However, the bigger the jump in knowledge, the more rewarding the dopamine release will be when they DO make the connection.

It's difficult to know how much to lead a client toward new knowledge: too much, and they won't make any new connection themselves; too little, and they may not make the connection at all. Some practice will be required of the Coach. The reward, though, is better than cocaine....

IDENTIFYING BRIGHT SPOTS

When we started using CAT Testing as our intake vehicle for Personal Training clients, we told the newbies that we were trying to find both their weakest link AND something at which they were already good.

Intuitively (for once!) we realized that giving someone a bonus - a touchstone exercise at which they excelled - would keep them coming in more regularly. Teach a woman to do double-unders? She'll show up for every workout where you incorporate skipping techniques, because she's already good at it. Got a tall guy in OnRamp? Let him pull a decent weight before he starts CrossFit. Whenever a deadlift comes up, he'll show, because that's *"his thing."*

Sounds like we were onto something. Two studies quoted in Switch talk about the benefit of giving people a 'head start' - or making them aware that they're "gifted" before they get rolling.

In one, researchers quizzed hotel room cleaners about their daily exercise levels. Despite their high work output daily - they're moving quickly through hotel rooms, with a time limit, for 8 hours per day, with gear - most described themselves as a "non-exerciser" because they weren't members of a gym. Their work output, though, was quadruple the typical half-hour on a treadmill. CrossFit? No, but much tougher than the workout of most gym-goers. Here's the beautiful part: when researchers made the results known to the cleaners, they dropped an average of 1.8lbs in the next month, without changing anything else. They didn't join gyms; they didn't eat better; but they worked harder, because they were exercising. 1.8lbs doesn't sound like much, but in a huge sample, it's significant, especially when food and other variables are controlled.

In the second, patrons of a car wash were given a new punch-card to earn free cleanings. One group was given a 8-punch card; after they'd accumulated 8 punches, they got a free wash. The other group was given a 10-punch card, with two punches already tallied. They, too, had to earn 8 more punches before they could get a free wash.

After three months, the second group was twice as likely - 36% to 18% - to have filled their cards. There were no other differences between the groups, other than the 20% bonus.

If you're trying to keep someone at your Box longer, why not exploit their strengths? Even better, brag 'em up in public! We use a 'like' board at our Affiliate to trumpet achievements by members, but pulling them into the middle of the circle during skill work is also great......

GOAL-SETTING FOR STAFF AND MEMBERS

In the first section of this book, I talked about Bright Spots, measurement and goal-setting. Essentially, using Bright Spots to ignite change in your members works like this:

1. What are you already doing right? That's your first Bright Spot.

2. How can we duplicate those behaviours, so that you're doing them more often?

3. How will we first know it's working? How will we

recognize the first signs of success? That's your future Bright Spot.

4. Where will we go from there? What's the NEXT Bright Spot?

I'll use an example from our own experience. We were in the process of hiring a full-time staff person to really ramp up our kids' programs, and add several new programs into the mix. The staffer was a national-level gymnast; a national Champion wrestler; an Olympic lifter; a teacher with a year's experience; a coach for kids' programs. Even without this dream candidate, you can steer your program toward success if you clearly lay out measurement goals in advance.

1. Essence Of The Job Goals: Create a kids' program for CrossFit. Create a kids' Jiu-Jitsu and tumbling/mat gymnastics program. Create a Workout of The Day for MMA fighters (mmawod.com, karatewod.com, jiujitsuwod.com, fightwod.com.) Use these classes to help further develop our Ignite! brain development program with the Education Coordinator.

2. Project Goals: In a twelve-month period, develop revenues through combination of the above that will warrant hire as a full-time coach and coordinator. (We've set this number in stone. You should be as clear as possible, using timelines if you can.)

3. Professional Development Goals: Become CrossFit Kids certified. Become the first Certified practitioner of our Ignite brain enrichment program.

4. Performance Goals: schedule, attire, code of conduct. We have a staff manual for this purpose, but touching on key points is certainly worth an hour of your time. We also do an hour of training on the MBO system, and then address more advanced issues as they arise.

As with other business processes, it's useful to timeline

these goals as well to keep everyone away from procrastination.

RULES

What seems like common sense to you...may not be all that common.

To me, it's an obvious foul to drop an empty bar on the floor. To that new guy, who walked into his first CrossFit group on the weekend without any idea what a Snatch is? Not as obvious.

To you, it's probably clear that you don't want wet, salty feet in your change room. To her...well, she's nervous enough about wearing gym clothes and working out in front of people for the first time EVER. Worried about her hair afterwards, and not embarrassing herself. No, she wouldn't do it in her house, but here, she's trying to remember enough details that 'little' things slip her mind.

After a few years, you get tired of telling people that your 'open gym' hours end precisely at 7pm, when CrossFit groups take over again. But if you DON'T tell them, don't expect them to know.

Every so often, it helps to review the rules. Do it in a light way (make it funny, if possible.)Usually, 10% are causing 90% of the little issues faced. Most of the 10% will be embarrassed when confronted; some will question the rules; but most simply won't know them. Are you projecting what YOU know onto everyone else, and mistaking it for common sense? I certainly was.

THE REEBOK ERA

SHIFTING COWS

Eight years ago, I was standing in a transition zone for a local triathlon when I had my first exposure to CrossFit.

Although I was a powerlifter by then, I still loved cycling, and had remained friends with a lot of local endurance athletes. The job was easy, and most of my day was spent talking to people.

One kid - a soon-to-be soldier - had been peppering me with questions about training for almost a year. He'd been interested in sport science throughout high school, and would frequently stop by the shop where I spent my daytime hours selling treadmills to talk about periodization, squatting, and high-rep workouts. He was just a kid, and so when he asked if I'd tried CrossFit, I didn't take him seriously. I feigned interest - it sounded too military to appeal to any non-Joe - and passed it off as an early-internet fad.

I should have appreciated that the appeal of CrossFit, to this kid, was the military component; that's what got him stirred up, and so those were the points he emphasized. Rope climbs and weighted runs didn't have much appeal to me then. Had I looked, I would have seen deadlifts and back squats, because those were the points I'D find most relevant. My loss.

In 2005, this kid had the purple cow: he was doing CrossFit.

By 2008, he wasn't alone. There were thousands of people worldwide doing CrossFit. Most of the 'gurus' had heard of CrossFit, at least - Dan John and Mark Twight were talking about it, and making names for themselves at the same time; '300' was apparently the result of CrossFit and not retouching....but there were few Affiliates.

We signed up as part of the 'second wave' - if our annual Affiliate Fee is any indication - and, for a time, were the only CrossFit Affilate around. The purple cow was in OUR pasture.

Imagine the scale of change in the years since: from answering the question, *"What IS CrossFit?"* to our clients and to ourselves; talking about the program; defending it, primarily, against the 'fad' label. These days, we're lazily linking professionally-shot videos, talking about top athletes as if they were NBA superstars, talking about 'the season' and 'the Open' as if we'd been doing it all our lives. Reebok's driving trucks around, flying helicopters, making shoes. Three thousand OTHER Affiliates means that our purple cow now has a lot of friends....

What's next? Consider that, with the further saturation of the market, potential new clients aren't just going to 'try CrossFit.' They're going to look for the CrossFit:

- that's most convenient

-that's cheapest

-that's friendliest

- that's cleanest

- with the best coaches

- that's most complementary for "their" sport

- that's most competitive

- that's least competitive

- that has the most women

- that has the most men

- with the hardest programming

- with the easiest programming

- where their friends already go.

Which one are you?

CrossFit HQ gave birth to the *first* purple cow: the program, for free, on an internet blog. They handed you a clear process to achieve the *second* purple cow: *"Here's how to own a CrossFit gym. Here's how to coach the way we do."* The next purple cow is up to you.

Be prepared to find a way to be different in a field full of the same cow.

CHANGING YOUR BUSINESS: BULLETS, THEN CANNONBALLS

In naval warfare during the 1800s, ships doing battle didn't have unlimited resources. They didn't have lifeboats; they didn't have much ammunition. A missed shot could mean a big missed opportunity, and sighting in a cannon (especially the early barrels without rifling) was very complicated.

To this end, smarter captains would first fire their muskets...not in the hopes of doing much damage, but just to sight in the target. If they could get close enough to strike the enemy with a musket ball (cheap, plentiful) they could rely on the BIG cannonball (scarce, expensive) to make a larger impact.

Jim Collins is featured a lot in this book, and it's because his first book, *"Good to Great"* is a classic must-read for business owners, right after *"The E-Myth"* by Michael Gerber. His newest book, *"Great By Choice,"* has been paraphrased in here several times, too.

One of the key concepts in the latter book is to fire bullets, THEN cannonballs. In a nutshell, it's less wise to make huge changes in your offerings without first attempting smaller trial groups.

For example, if you were starting an Ignite! program in your box, you'd first try the idea out on a few parents: *"Hey, would you like your kid to get homework help while you're doing CrossFit?'* You could also try to sell a school on the concept: *"We can show you exercises to do in the classroom for about five minutes that will enhance learning and focus in your students."*

Perhaps an even smaller bullet: adding math challenges into your CrossFit Kids groups. See how they go. Collect feedback. Then, fire the Cannonball: Affiliate with Ignite.

In our own case, we took the tentative steps toward CrossFit Affiliation by first firing several bullets: we ran a study on adherence (since published in CFJ.) Then one of our coaches took a stab at CrossFit and chronicled his experiences. When we noticed people reading his blog, we opened an invitation for 12 people to train with us, following the CrossFit.com main site, for 1 month. Every spot was taken.

Next, I joined them, and we built the group up to 20 people...with NO coaching, just empty space within our Personal Training facility. Finally, we Affiliated, after six months of just trying the program ourselves, or offering a non-coached version for free. We opened up a noon group; we ran a 6am group, and a 7pm group in a space above a womens' clothing store. Hardly hardcore. After another year, we signed a lease to a concrete block. We opened a commercial gym with open time and CrossFit groups 3x per day. We ran weekend *"intro to crossfit classes"* that lasted three hours, paralyzed everyone, and rarely got us clients as converts. We read Nicki Violetti's OnRamp program, and started keeping people around more. Three years later, we're still firing bullets: our *Enduro* Program was a trial.

Ignite, too, used some bullets before the Big Cannonball: we fired at schools, attracted the interest of the autism community, and THEN Ty quit his teaching job and started doing this full time. Now there are dozens of NeuroMotive Coaches...but we didn't fire the cannonball first.

After all, you only have so many, and it's better to sight your target and test the range with bullets first. Rolling out a new program? Great. It's exciting. But test it, first: grab a few trusted clients, and give them a little piece of mango. *"Hey, we're thinking about trying a Mobility class on Sundays. A few of us are going to get together this week and play with it a bit; want to come?"* We've involved the talents of some very talented clients this way who will show up to our events as volunteers, just because they're so interested.

THE CROSSFIT LEVEL 1 CERTIFICATION

Once upon a time, I did a Level I CrossFit Certification. It was fun.

Next, I lived happily ever after.

Possibly the #1 reason that people stick with CrossFit for longer than any other fitness endeavour? The learning curve is steep. Even the first ascenders - Amundsen and Co. - set a solid example by seeking coaching often.

One of the top 3 reasons to open a CrossFit box? The learning curve. Most people list 'boredom' as their main rationale for opening a small business, ahead of 'making more money' or 'self-satisfaction.' They want the challenge.

One of the hottest topics on the Affiliate discussion board is the requirement for Coaches to recertify after 5 years, at a cost of $500. Some Level 1-Certified Coaches hadn't initially anticipated this requirement, and their responses ranged from, *"I don't like it, but it's worth it anyway"* to *"I'm calling my lawyer!"*

Why recertify? The answer should be obvious: demonstrate that you still know the bare minimum. Should a Coach be qualified indefinitely, forever and ever, amen! after they've completed a weekend course, even if they NEVER practice their Coaching skills? Of course not.

Why retest? It's the only way to find out.

Why every 5 years? Because things change, baby. Let's consider the landscape five years ago, in 2006:

> ⚔ CrossFit Kids didn't yet exist online (August, 2006 was their first posted WOD.)

> ⚔ CrossFit Endurance, CrossFit Football, MobilityWOD, Powerlifting with Louie Simmons,

POSE running, Paleo...these things weren't around yet in 2006.

⚏ The CrossFit Games hadn't yet been invented.

⚏ Nicole Carroll still performed most of the Certification weekends herself, as I understand.

⚏ There were less than a QUARTER of the current number of CrossFit Affiliates.

⚏ Facebook was around....but you weren't using it.

⚏ Twitter, LinkedIn, the iPhone...none of these were around yet.

With all the things we've learned from these, I'm confident that we'll have some new material by 2016.

If for no other reason, mandatory recertification will cull the herd. That girl who opened up down the block, after only a weekend course, who doesn't know anything about anything? Well, if it's true, then she won't recertify in 2016.

TWO ON EVERY BLOCK

There's one place where CrossFit Boxes compete against each other: the Games. That's it.

Before you think I'm being naive, consider this: the most likely business you'll find next to a car dealership is another car dealership. Auto sales across brand lines benefit when the showrooms are neighbours. They build beside one another for a reason.

Cafes, too, benefit when several are grouped together (what's the French word for 'group' again?) If you're headed downtown for lunch, and Cafe Camille is jammed, you simply walk next door to Cafe Michelle. Their businesses thrive on the 'Cafe Block' model.

There's a fear among veteran Affiliates that the 'new kids' will undercut their price; will tempt with novelty; will have nicer bathrooms and startup funding that we didn't have. They'll have sponsorships and painted walls and an appetite for cannibalism. They'll "dilute the brand," whatever that means.

Here's a story. I'm sharing it not to beat my own drum, but to share what's more likely to happen in the long term:

At the start of June 2012, a Personal Training studio closed its doors across town. Its owner opened a new "urban gym" about a block from us. We paid little notice until Friday, when two of their members called to inquire about packages. Then, at 7pm, one of their coaches signed up for a CrossFit membership.

None of our members have gone over. Without trying, we're +3 and ecstatic about it. I wish the 'urban gym' the best of luck - owning a gym ain't easy - and hope they'll stay friendly.

A final note: if you're thinking of starting a CrossFit gym, good. If you're building your business model around taking current CrossFitters from other CrossFit gyms, we need to talk. Lower prices and snappy graffiti won't trump a good social contract.

A year ago, I posted on a book I'd been reading called, *"Blue Ocean Strategy."* I compared CrossFit boxes to McFits everywhere: the drive-thru, elliptical-and-pec-deck "fitness" sold by most chain gyms.

What I didn't compare - because I didn't yet have the experience - was differentiation between CrossFit boxes in the same locale.

I'm always excited to get emails from readers of this blog - frankly, I'm always surprised to see just how MANY come through here daily - and the most common theme goes like this: *"I run a great program here at CrossFit Pluto. This other guy, at CrossFit Uranus, doesn't. You wouldn't BELIEVE the stuff this guy pulls!"*

The greatest insight I got at the CrossFit Level 1 Certification was via Jon Gilson, on the muscle-up: *"Okay, so you've been coaching this woman for three months. She can do a chest-to-bar pullup on the rings. She can do a deep ring dip. She just can't transition. She watches videos; she listens to you; she just can't do it. One day, a visiting coach walks into your box, walks up to her at the rings, and says, "look down earlier." Instant muscle-up. Does that mean you're a bad coach? Nope. Different things have different meanings to different people."*

Rather than arguing over the technical proficiency of your triple extension, or your gymnastics prowess, or the brand of bars you use....why not do something slightly different?

Any disagreement based around a fine technical point will be lost on the community: *"We use an Ivanko Super Slick Billion-Bearing Wax-Packed Gold Medal Bar for all our lifts. They use the inferior Ivanko Super Semislick Billion-Bearing Wax-Packed Gold Medal Bar. They obviously don't care very much about your progress!"*

Worse, no one wants to attend an argumentative Affiliate. What's the best way to win a fight online? Don't get into a fight online. Move in a different direction.

Adult program options:

   ⚔ Martial Arts

   ⚔ Gymnastics

   ⚔ Competitive (competitive training group - 'Team' - or an annual points series, OR league play)

   ⚔ Sex-specific (Barbell Bettys)

   ⚔ Endurance

   ⚔ Powerlifting or OLY Lifting

   ⚔ Beginner

⋏ Intertwined personal training and CrossFit as a package

⋏ Rehabilitative

⋏ 'BootCamp' option - travelling CrossFit roadshow at hours around the "office" schedule

⋏ VERY short workouts - "CrossFit Recess!" for local businesses

Youth program options:

⋏ CrossFit Kids (possibly the best expansion you could offer.)

⋏ High school leagues

⋏ Martial Arts

⋏ Sport-specific

⋏ Cognitive training and rehabilitation (IgniteGym.com)

There are more, I'm sure. Specialization in one area doesn't preclude another. There's a good chance that your neighbourhood Boxes aren't doing all of these things, and may not even have an interest in doing them. That's fine.

Even if you're the only kid on the block, program expansion means more revenue from people who you already care about. It means a better offering to your GFPs; more excitement around your Box; and easier usage from current clients (*"I can bring my kids to CrossFit and they'll do their own program while I do mine? Awesome!!!"*)

Part of your mandate is to increase the number of people in the world who can look after themselves. Build that number instead of fighting for every Karen Kantchoose. There are enough popsicles for everyone.

*Look: if there really is a CrossFit Pluto, I owe someone an apology. And I want to buy one of your t-shirts, too.

TRIPLE?

If CrossFit continues its current rate of new Affiliate growth - which IS possible - its numbers could triple between 2010 and 2013, from 2000 to 6000 worldwide Affiliates.

Why is it possible, when even Gold's Gym, 24 Hour Fitness, and Bally's haven't reached that mark? Simple: the world is different.

In the franchise model, every gym is the same. This creates consistency in the mind of the consumer, which is great in the short term...but not in the long.

"I went to Gold's last summer while I was visiting my cousin in Utah. I didn't really like it....so I won't join here."

When the CrossFit message was new, the same stereotype (if you've been to one, you've been to all) pervaded. Now, though, different CrossFit boxes are perceived differently by consumers. Some will feel more 'at home' in an Affiliate who puts a higher value on competition; some will feel alienated. Some distance runners will choose the CrossFit Box with more rowers and Endurance-based WODs; some powerlifters will make the switch to CrossFit because the Box has Atlas Stones and, man, I've always wanted to play with those....

Specialization is a bone of contention among Affiliates. Whether you perceive your specialization or not, though, your potential membership recognizes your accent. Yes, you're speaking English...but in a way that's different and charming.

Imagine the number of CrossFit Affiliates tripling in your city within the next two years. You're being pressured from the top (HQ) down (don't worry, it's a good pressure.) You're also being pressed by the consumer: how are you different than CrossFit ShakeWeight down the block? That's bottom-up pressure, from the grassroots.

Specializing doesn't mean embracing one aspect of CrossFit at the expense of all others. It just means moving a little off-centre.

"We do powerlifting, but our real speciality is our endurance program: we cycle indoors and outdoors, and we have weekly pool time."

"Well, we're similar to CrossFit MoshPit, but we really love to focus our energy around getting people stronger."

"We love CrossFit, and we put the community ahead of competition."

You may not want to specialize; consider, then, what sets you apart from the others. Those are your strengths. In the same way that you hope double-unders don't come up during the Open, you hope that your new prospect doesn't ask about Yoga and mobility classes. Those are your weaknesses. They will be exposed.

If you're currently planning for 2015 (and you should be,) consider where everyone ELSE will be by then...

IN-SCHOOL DELIVERY

Yesterday, we did our first visit of the new school year to a local high school. We've been in schools for months now, but hadn't made it around to this particular school yet.

We were there to talk about Ignite! - the ways to improve learning, focus and attention in students through exercise - but were startled to find that several classrooms had already added treadmills beside the desks.

I was shocked: a school Board spending money on treadmills to improve learning... without increasing access to exercise? Without coaching on solid fitness habits? Without realizing the resources already available to them?

But of course not. Change means purchase, in our culture. The 'fitness' paradigm pervades even the classroom. On a good-better-best scale, this is still a 'good': teachers recognizing the need to stimulate BDNF during learning times. At least we're part of the conversation, now; our mandate simply changes to educating teachers on the BEST implementation of exercise in the classroom. Big hurdle overcome.

If you're running a CrossFit Kids program, and want to start running groups in schools, you're not alone. We've been pursuing the in-school market for three years, and have made significant inroads (including two co-operative studies between our Affiliate and local school Boards.)

First, read *"Spark!"* by John Ratey. This is why it's our moral imperative to get exercise INTO the classroom in any way possible. (Want the BEST way? The Ignite *"Enrichment Through Exercise"* book is available on Amazon.com. As CrossFit coaches, you'll be immediately able to recognize ways that CrossFit and learning overlap.)

Next, find your State's white paper files on education delivery, philosophy...and curriculum. If you can match your service to the curriculum goals of the program, then you're working from inside the machine. If you can't find a clear correlation, then make sure to use the language of the Learning Strategy or curriculum guidelines, at least.

Third, if you can't make your program applicable to the curriculum guidelines, consider another angle. Here are three:

> 1.IgniteGym.com. I'm one of the developers of this program, and it has been HUGE. The opportunities for new markets with reliable income is great; the ability to HELP kids learn better, focus...or just plain care about education is tremendous.

> 2.Anti-Bullying. In Canada, at least, the anti-bullying movement has taken a massive priority for most extra-curricular funding. We have several MMA

fighters at our Box, and we visit schools to deliver a video featuring the fighters (or invite schools to bring kids in to talk to them.)

3.Anti-Aggression workshops. On the other end of the scale is the teacher training for dealing with aggression in the school setting. To be frank, it's poor. In an overly-aroused state, a student is unable to make clear choices - and is also unable to bring himself down to a calm level. After we did a presentation on Ignite! to 120 social workers last week, several approached us to provide an answer to the anti-aggression problem. We'll be putting together a course over the next few weeks that bridges the Ignite! curriculum and the anti-bullying workshop. You can build your own (or just ask politely, and I'll share ours.)

More than ever, it's critical that teachers, parents AND students hear the message of practical fitness and solid eating habits. It's not just a potential market anymore.

GROWING TOO FAST?

Disclaimer: I believe in being ready.

A few years ago, I was lucky enough to have *E-Myth Mastery* recommended to me. If you haven't read the book, it goes like this: you have to stop working IN your business, and start working ON your business. That's nearly a cliche by now, so here's the most important part:

You need systems. Automate wherever possible. Automate the hiring process (use the same process to groom coaches every time.) Automate the firing process, the check-in process, the Certification process. Write job descriptions for everyone, including yourself. Write a dress code. Write a telephone script. Write checklists for everything - opening the Box, closing the Box, choosing a radio station, CLEANING, writing blog posts...everything. Yes, it takes time, but once it's done, you have a business.

A business isn't the coaching, unfortunately. It's not about your prowess in the push press. A business is the body, made up of the systems, dependent on the cash flow. Sorry.

There.

Now: *come quick! Something marvellous has happened!*

It likely started before the CrossFit Games were on ESPN; before, even, Reebok came onto the scene. A wave had been building, and few of us saw it coming. We were used to the slow buildup; the long tail; the grassroots expansion of our CrossFit business. And then...on Tuesday, everyone showed up.

And they brought their kids. And dogs. And their ski poles, some of them.

They all brought their friends, their fears, their femoral problems...

Many Affiliates have sent emails asking how to handle the rampant growth without losing their current base or alienating the newcomer. Here's what we've done:

> 1.Two years ago, we created progression posters for 12 common CrossFit movements (you can download them from DontBuyAds.com, change the colour, and make them your own if you like.) When a group member arrives early, and isn't sure how to scale their pullups, they look at the chart...

> 2.Last year, we did the same thing with our warmups: standardized them. If they arrived early, CrossFitters could do some extra mobility work before the WOD.

> 3.We offer 'Express' groups - 30 minutes, including warmup, and you're out. METCON only, and the Express groups run a half-hour before the regular,

larger groups. No, they're not ideal; all burpees and no push press makes Jill a weakling. However, people don't do the Express workouts exclusively, but sub them in sometimes midweek when they have an early meeting. With the bootcamp crowd coming in from the parks soon, too...they're familiar with the format.

4.We paved a big ramp in front of our giant door. We spill out onto the sidewalk most days now.

5.We have a LOT of 'open gym' time. I know there are MANY business 'experts' in CrossFit who oppose this model. However, consider that 90% of our CrossFit group attendees pay a little bit more, every month, to have open gym access when they can't make a group, or want to practise skills on their own, or just want to 'play'....if you're nervous about launching 'open gym' time, you can offer it on any system you like.

6.We have a clear system of progression from member to Coach. Want to lead a group? First, you work the desk. Learn everyone's name; help people out during Open Gym; mop. Then you help out with the monster-sized groups. Then you get a little group of your own with little numbers; build that up, and you get more.

7.We lightened the hell up. On a Saturday when 34 people arrived for our partner WOD, we cleared off the chalkboard and build a NEW WOD that included box jumps on tires, 400m runs, log carries, and tuck jumps. Most of your CrossFitters aren't there to take a stab at *Fittest On Earth*; they'd rather die in the trenches with their brothers, and then share a Lucky Strike afterwards.

8.Some are there to take a stab at Fittest On Earth.

We run a 'Green Army Training Team' that gets coaching for competition, rather than the regular WOD. they come in at an off-time, as a team. They get 'homework.' They visit during Open Gym and train. Generally, these people realize - and are more than willing - to stand out from the rest, and make extra effort to accommodate the coach if the attention they receive is of an equal amount.

9.We don't require preregistration for groups. Preregistration is great, if you want to maintain control. Not great if you want to expand, provide an amazing experience, and make your program accessible.

CHANGING OUR TUNE

Stolen from a friend's facebook status:

"In the gym today for spin class. Walked past two girls. One was doing wall ball, and the other said, 'Hey, you look just like the girl in the commercial!'"

In one of the first sections in this book, we discussed "The Elevator Pitch." Two years ago, the the biggest problem facing the CrossFit Affiliate: how to answer the question,

"What's CrossFit?"

Now that everyone knows the answer (or has formed a perception, or their answer,) the question will change.

"Why can't I just do CrossFit at my current McFit?"

In other words, why do I need to come to YOUR gym to do CrossFit?

Ready with your answer?

MICROSPECIALIZATION

As the CrossFit pool spreads out in your area, your best option for excellence may be to deepen: to specialize in one area. I'm not suggesting that you stop pursuing virtuosity in gymnastics, for instance, in order to become better at deadlifting. I AM putting forth the idea that your local CrossFit community - and your own Box - can benefit by being the go-to resource in one area.

There are different levels of specialization: MACROspecialization means that you make the best breakfast; MICROspecialization means that you make the best espresso, and yours is the only franchise in town with a cinnamon shaker. Drilling down into an area of speciality to further your expertise, in my opinion, is the next level of customer service. Not differentiation - offering more services to expand your market - but specialization. CrossFit heresy? I think not.

Developing mastery in a wide range of physical pursuits requires short-term focus on weaker links, in order to bring up the whole. The highest-level Games competitors, for instance, don't rely on their OLY coach to teach them how to swim. Rather, they spend one day per week with each, and another day with a POSE coach, a weekend with a gymnastics coach...a week with Louie Simmons.... they seek to expand their expertise by focusing on each area individually, before folding it back into CrossFit.

Jim Collins talks a lot about his 'Hedgehog' concept: being really, really good at one thing, and using it at every available opportunity.

What if, in your City, I could purchase a citywide CrossFit membership, and attend CrossFit Eastside on Monday, CrossFit Southside on Tuesday, CrossFit North on Thursdays...... would we all benefit?

What if, in your Town, there existed a Fire Ring - a group of

CrossFit Affiliates who banded together to share knowledge, programming, throwdowns, guest speakers, All-Star teams.... and differentiated themselves accordingly? One, an expert source for powerlifting; one, the source for martial arts; another, for POSE running. What if I could purchase a membership, shared between all three, and attend class at any?

What if, as an Affiliate, I didn't HAVE to offer a 9am class, because CrossFit North does? What if I could offer Open Gym time to members of CrossFit East? What if my members could book personal training at CrossFit West on their lunch hour, and their husbands use the same Personal Training Package at my place after work?

What if, on Saturday mornings, some members from CrossFit Mike came to MY box to do the WOD while their kids did their CF Kids class, and some of MY members went to CrossFit Mike to AVOID the CFKids whirlwind?

What if, come Games time, one member of your Box really wanted to compete at Regionals, but missed the cut on your team....and CrossFit Bill, down the road, didn't have enough competitors to form HIS team (remember this one if you see me wearing the wrong t-shirt at Canada East this year, please.) Will this someday be acceptable?

It could be that you're the best in town at everything. Heck, we may as well call you CrossFit Google. Will you still be the best CrossFit box for gymnastics coaching when there are 6 Affiliates in your city? 12? 24?......

NICHES

In 2009, there wasn't a "Masters" division at the Games.

In 2010, they were a bit of an afterthought, away from the 'main show' in the arena across the street.

In 2011, the Masters area was JAMMED for nearly every event at every age category. Masters were given the same treatment from Reebok as everyone else, and Johnny Mac's crew ran an exciting, professional-level event.

In 2012, Masters-only events are cropping up in most Regions to keep mature athletes in a 'ready state' before the Games. Their numbers still don't necessitate a Regionals playoff, but we're getting closer.

Niche: CrossFit Masters specialization.

In 2010, there wasn't a "Youth" division at the Games.

In 2011, the CrossFit Kids event was well-planned, but never hyped, and attendance was disappointing (to me, at least, as I watched from the sidelines.)

In 2012, we had 14-year-olds in the Open. Still in its infancy as a sport, CrossFit doesn't yet attract the attention of parents who aren't themselves CrossFitters; that means travel for competitions hasn't yet flourished. Within three years, these competitions will feature athletes from all over the world, not just the Southeast.

Niche: CrossFit Kids Events.

The competitions are easy to set up: contact area high schools and middle schools, divide ages along the same calendar as high school sports, share expectations with coaches, and put up a prize. The novelty of CrossFit, for these young athletes, will require less creative programming: just have them climb ropes and carry logs, if you like. It's all new to them!

Have we used the Games to support our entire offering? Is every potential client served by a competitive outlet; a measuring device for worldwide comparison; an objective scale for progress? Not yet.

The Paralympics (and Special Olympics) are massive worldwide organizations with millions of followers, and thousands of athletes. Several projects in the CrossFit world are providing training and challenges for Adaptive Athletes, but there doesn't yet exist a comprehensive 'championship' for those who require WOD modification, or 'MODWOD.'

Niche: Adaptive Athletes.

 Likewise, in the early stages of CrossFit's move toward 'cognitive fitness,' there doesn't seem to be a Cognitive Games on the horizon....yet. By incorporating CrossFit into cognitive processing, rehabilitation, and in-school curriculum, we're making forward progress in this area with Ignite. We have daily "COGWODs" already. As our ranks swell, so will follow the brain trust.

Niche: Cognitive Fitness. Enrichment Through Exercise.

Though many of us don't miss our MobilityWOD broadcasts, few therapists are incorporating CrossFit INTO the rehabilitation process. The #1 obstacle in a rehab setting is adherence: boring leg extensions and stretchy tubing makes for patients who resent their therapies. It's equally understandable AND preventable: novelty alone makes rehabilitation much more enjoyable for the injured client.

Niche: Rehabilitation.

These are coming. Two years from now, you'll look back and remember when the CrossFit Games was small, took place on a single weekend, and was only televised on ESPN2. Get in front of the train.

WE ARE NOT THE COMPETITION

Astronomers predict that a comet, named 2011 AG5, could hit earth in 2040 and 2047.

It will have five chances to strike the Earth; if it misses on one pass, the gravitational pull could possibly push the comet into a 'keyhole' that leads straight back at us. Though the threat is small,and shouldn't cause any great panic, it IS real. Let's examine the multinational plans discussed so far:

1. uh...We have no plan.

We don't even have the first considerations for devising a plan: if the threat is real, who should be in charge - NASA? The military? Russia? China? Mark Zuckerburg? Who should develop the super beam technology, or the warheads, or....? Who should defend the technology? Who should *pay* for it?

When a real threat faces our species, we hope that our small feudal States can band together and face the the challenge collectively. However, territorial grudges and long-standing historical line-toeing will likely bind the hands of all with opposing thumbs. Old wars, though rendered irrelevant by the larger threat to all, will still likely hamstring our ability to get our acts together in time. Heck, it's almost too late NOW....if the threat is real. The danger is no longer the hurtling rock, but our ability to move forward to meet its advance as a comprehensive entity.

There's a tendency among CrossFit owners, old and new, to consider other CrossFit Boxes to be 'the competition.' When asked, *"how many others are in your area?"* they answer with the number of other Affiliates...not the number of GloboGyms, those orchards ripe with low-hanging fruit.

Meanwhile, the Globos are marshaling their own resources. They didn't get to the top by killing off all new fitness ideas, but by absorbing them. Rather than compete with climbing gyms, they add walls of brightly-coloured rock behind the treadmills. Rather than compete with Billy Blanks, they ran 'cardio kickboxing' classes on Saturday mornings. Rather than beat Muscle Beach,they adopted Arthur Jones' miraculous machines. They thrive by adopting the more extreme ideas, removing the sharp edges, and making them palatable to cardio Queens and pec-deck princes alike.

The best "expert predictions" of Goodlife Fitness - by Personal Trainers they've positioned as 'industry experts' -

for Hot Fitness Trends in 2012 included CrossFit . While they're trying to draw a straight line between TRX training and CrossFit - and clearly don't have their head around the counterculture element yet - it's obvious that CrossFit is on their radar screens. They're working on it. They can't say, "CrossFit"....but they've stopped decrying its "risks." When they stop berating you, it's because they're setting up shop next door. When they stop talking about your poisoned water, it's because they're building a bottling plant.

When owners of a CrossFit Affiliate were interviewed on a national news program in Canada, they spoke about the importance of rest and sleep. Immediately afterwards, a rep from GoodLife (our largest national chain of Globos) talks about 'giving their members what they want' and incorporating CrossFit-like "classes" in their gyms - for free to their members.

So far, these attempts have come off as half-baked....but *"The Biggest Loser"* is showing them how to incorporate CrossFit into their Planet Fitness world. I love watching Trainer Bob doing snatch pulls from boxes in the parking lot,and so do others. The audience determines the offering....what MayBell wants, MayBell gets. And soon, MayBell is going to want knee socks and board shorts.

BigGlobo is going to give her that opportunity. She may just be doing Body Pump with 5lbs foam-packed 'barbells' in the parking lot of McFitness....but she'll think she's doing CrossFit.

This is the next challenge. This is our Near-Earth Object. No longer the tooth-smashing 'us against them,' but the appearance of sameness. They're going to try to assimilate CrossFit into their model.

Time to decide what we're REALLY about. Time to change the focus from, *"We're Crazy"* to *"We're The Experts."* Time to work together, and build inter-box Community. Time to grow up, and form a Nation whose borders are distinguished by more than the tattooed guards.

PALEO BEHAVIOURISM AND VIRTUOSITY

As CrossFitters, many of us believe in a more simplistic diet: eat things without an Ingredients List. Stick to the perimeter of the grocery store. Eat meat, vegetables, fruit, nuts and seeds....

Our nutritional plans are the envy of every other sport. Why not expand that forethought and care into the rest of our lives? Some simple suggestions, from someone who's been observing the CrossFit community for a long time, and interacting with multiple Affiliate owners every day:

1. Get up early. Do the stuff you love first thing in the morning. Do something creative to prime your brain.

2. Don't defecate where you eat. Stay upriver from garbage. Don't poison your own food supply.

3. Marry outside the tribe to increase diversity. Learn things that don't come from CrossFit HQ. Read other sources of information, take what you can, and implement them in your CrossFit practice. Tell others. Don't ignore information like periodization just because 'no one else does it....'

4. Find a state of 'flow.' Our brain is primarily wired to be in a state of semi-alertness; we run on autopilot a lot of the time, always ready to react. We're not built to process every bit of information as if it's the first time we've encountered it. Do something that occupies your body, and your brain will catch up.

5. Be an example of empathy and good manners.

6.Constantly till the soil. Reevaluate your programming. Test people. Don't make excuses; make things grow.

7. Move around every few minutes. Don't just wait for one all-out burst at lunchtime or after dinner.

8. Find joy in doing things, not having things.

9. Lead or follow in an obvious way. If you're the Coach, demonstrate suffering (tell them YOUR Fran time.) If you're not the Coach, be the best student in the class.

10. Spend more time in the dark. Screens off, lights out.

Remember, the winner is the one who survives longest, NOT the one who eats the most.

Made in the USA
Columbia, SC
25 February 2019